MG MIDGET
& AUSTIN-HEALEY SPRITE

MG MIDGET
& AUSTIN-HEALEY SPRITE

RESTORATION / PREPARATION / MAINTENANCE

JIM TYLER

Published in 1993 by Osprey Publishing Ltd
Michelin House, 81 Fulham Road, London SW3 6RB

A catalogue record for this book is available on request from the British Library.

ISBN 1-85532-229-3

Page design by Geoffrey Wadsley
Edited by Shaun Barrington
Phototypeset by Tradespools Ltd., Frome, Somerset
Printed in Great Britain by BAS Printers Limited, Over Wallop, Hampshire

PAGE ONE *An Austin Healey Sprite (with good body condition) awaits professional restoration to original specification in South London. In the background, a late model MG Midget emerges after remedial treatment. (Photo: Dennis Baldry)*

TITLE PAGE *Do you prefer Midgets or Sprites? Most enthusiasts would prefer this Sprite (a rear view of the same car illustrated on page one), to regain its bumper as part of the restoration. (Photo: Dennis Baldry)*

CONTENTS

ACKNOWLEDGEMENTS

The author gratefully acknowledges the help and assistance given by many individuals and companies in the preparation of this book.

Special thanks to Graham, John and Bob (shop) and Trevor and John (workshop) of the Bromsgrove MG centre for all their help and advice over the years, and for allowing the author access to their workshops.

Graham Hickman and the staff of Rolling Road Auto-Tune Services (RATS) gave the benefit of their years of experience in performance preparation.

Adrian Wadley is an excellent welder who helped with the body restoration of the project car and who proved an invaluable source of help and advice on the subject of MiG welding. Alan Gosling of Central Garage, Martley, has always been willing to help and advise.

Even closer to home, the author acknowledges the patience and tolerance of his understanding neighbours, and the assistance of his wife Viv in cleaning old underseal from the project car.

Thanks too to the Osprey Automotive team of Publisher Nick Collins, ably assisted by Shaun Barrington and Aimee Blythe.

Grateful thanks to Autodata for allowing us to reproduce the illustrations taken from their workshop manual.

Finally, many of the author's friends have, over the years, contributed to his understanding of car maintenance, repair and restoration.

INTRODUCTION

The Austin Healey Sprite and MG Midget between them enjoyed a production run lasting from May of 1958 until November of 1979, during which time more than 350,000 of these diminutive and endearing sports cars were manufactured, making this one of the most successful small sports car families of all time. Although the distinctive and spartan Mk.1 'Frogeye' Sprite appears to have little in common with the relatively luxuriously appointed Mk.4 MG Midget, and both vary considerably from the models in-between, owners of all of the variants share the pleasure and privilege of belonging to the large and immensely happy clan of Spridget enthusiasts.

As this is written, some thirteen years after the Spridget line was discontinued, the cars remain a common sight on the roads of the UK and of many of the Spridget's export markets – and these survivors are by no means all cossetted classics which are used infrequently when the sun is shining (the fate of many classic cars), but are often still providing sterling service as everyday transport for their owners.

Few cars of any make or type have survived the years in such numbers, and for the Spridget to have done so speaks volumes for the quality of its Abingdon manufacture, but says even more for the dedication and enthusiasm of its owners. The Spridget owner usually derives so much pleasure from his or her car that it is comparatively rare for an example to have been consigned to the scrap heap or broken up for spares.

The fact that so many Spridgets remain on the road has now paid handsome dividends, because British Heritage have re-introduced complete body shells for most versions of the car, along with all repair panels, and because Heritage panels are pressed using the original tools, they are invariably a better fit and easier to work with than many of the 'pattern panels' which owners of other classic cars must contend with.

The Spridget is also well served for mechanical spares. Those which are not still in production by the original manufacturer or which are not being re-manufactured by a third-party are available fully reconditioned, and most items of trim and electric components are similarly available.

Not only are more spares readily available for Spridgets than for most other classic sports cars, but those spares are usually very attractively priced. Coupled with the car's relatively low fuel consumption and insurance premiums, this makes the Spridget probably the most economical of classic sports cars to own and use on a regular basis. The Spridget began life as an affordable sports car for the masses, and that is exactly what it remains today.

Despite the Spridgets general economy, buying the wrong car could land the new owner with potentially huge bills if mechanical repair and especially if major bodywork restoration proved necessary. This book is intended to help the aspiring Spridget owner to select the right car, to bring it – if necessary – to safe roadworthy condition and to keep it there. It is not a workshop manual, nor a general guide to the art of vehicle restoration; there are many excellent books which cover those specific areas. This book is intended as a companion to a workshop manual, and is written from the viewpoint of the person who has limited or no knowledge of mechanical matters or bodywork repair and who has limited facilities and tools.

The author has based the text largely around the complete restoration of a 1974 Midget which was in very poor condition (with a majority of seized or damaged components), replicating the conditions in which the average DIY enthusiast might operate. This has entailed working in cramped conditions, using the most common or basic tools wherever possible to overcome the many and varied obstacles to repair and restoration.

This approach has highlighted many of the problems which the restorer of an elderly car will encounter but which are rarely mentioned in workshop manuals – however good – because such manuals are invariably based on good, clean (if not new) examples of the car.

However enthusiastic the reader might be, there are certain tasks which are best left to professionals and a few which really demand the skills and facilities of the professional (such as welding a complete front or rear end onto a bodyshell). Other tasks such as stripping and reconditioning an engine or gearbox *can* be accomplished at home but it is recommended that the work is carried out professionally. This is because; A. it can prove less expensive to do so; B. because it would be heartbreaking to discover that

the DIY reconditioning is less than perfect *after* the car has been restored and is out on the road and C. specialist tools and equipment are needed. Although such tasks are described in this book, they are all prefixed with the advice that the work is best carried out by professionals.

Many of the components of the Spridget are referred to by different names in different countries, and even within a single country it is by no means unusual for a component to referred to by two or more names. The author has endeavoured, as far as possible, to use the terminology which would be used within factory literature. If you can obtain a copy, the factory parts catalogue will furnish you with the correct component numbers for your car, and this is especially useful for avoiding misunderstandings when ordering spares by mail order.

In addition to the part number you require, always quote the engine number, year of manufacture and original market when ordering spares through the mail. Mistakes do happen, and often you will only discover that you have the wrong component when you come to fit it.

The famous 'Frogeye' grin that has captivated the hearts of motoring enthusiasts for over thirty years. These are the most coveted of all Spridgets.

1 · A SHORT HISTORY

The Mark 1 'Frogeye' Sprite is one of the most important sports cars ever produced because it spawned a whole new generation of small, affordable, monocoque-bodied sports cars. Perhaps more to the point, it was the first truly mass produced small sports car, and as such it brought low cost sports car motoring within the reach of everyone. At the time of the launch of the Frogeye Sprite, however, the concept of the small two seater sports car was far from new.

The first car to be named the 'MG Midget' appeared way back in 1928, and it was a small two seater sports car featuring a then very advanced overhead camshaft engine. The Midget of 1928, whilst being a very different car in some ways to the Spridget, gave its fortunate owners exactly the same sort of driving experience. The big difference between the two cars was that the production of the early car was very limited due to the early methods of construction, whereas the Spridget was produced in huge quantities.

The name 'MG' stood for 'Morris Garages', which was then a retail business selling Morris cars. Cecil Kimber, the General Manager of this retail operation and the 'father' of the MG marque, began to produce specially bodied versions of Morris cars from 1923 and, shortly afterwards, the MG name was adopted as a separate marque.

In 1935, the MG company was bought by Morris Motors, and the following year the first of the 'T' series MGs, the TA, was introduced. Although very similar in appearance to the earlier Midget, the car was powered by a cheaper 1292cc Wolseley pushrod engine which, fitted with twin 1¼″ SU carburettors, developed 50BHP. The TA possessed hydraulic rather than the mechanical brakes of the earlier Midget, and

had cam and peg steering and a cork clutch. The MG TB appeared three years later, still with the same general appearance but this time powered by a 1250cc, 54.4 BHP version of the Morris Ten four cylinder overhead valve pushrod engine which would remain with the 'T' series cars until the launching of the MGA in 1955. Perhaps just as importantly, the TB had a new gearbox with synchromesh on three forward gears and a conventional clutch.

As the 'T' series evolved to the 1250 cc, 54 BHP model TC (launched in 1945; 10,000 cars – all right hand drive – produced until 1949), export sales to the United States of America began in earnest, and the following 57 BHP model TD, which used a different chassis based on that of the Y-type saloon, saw the majority of its production sold to America during its 1950–1953 production life, during which time just under 30,000 examples were manufactured. The 'T' series ended with the TF, of which just over 6000 were produced with the 1250 cc engine, and 3400 with a larger 1466 cc unit, which boosted power to 63 BHP. The T series was manufactured until 1954. The British motor industry of the time noted the growing success of the T series in the seemingly vast North American market with more than passing interest.

In 1952, The British Motor Corporation (BMC) was formed from a merger between the Austin and Morris companies. The MG company found itself effectively ruled by the then head of Austin, a company which in many ways could have been considered its arch rival. MG were keen to develop new medium-sized sports cars like the TD, to take advantage of the North American market, but this appears to have been effectively spiked by corporate manoeuvres, the upshot of which was that Austin

collaborated with one Donald Healey to produce instead the Austin Healey 100/3000 series.

The MG 'T' series cars had all been based on a narrow chassis, which is a kind of sturdy steel (or wood) framework on which the engine, suspension and body are all mounted. Having narrow chassis', the body fitted in between the wheels rather than extending to the outer edges of the tyres as do modern car bodies. As a result, the cars were rather upright in appearance and had very limited cockpit width for the occupants. This type of car was still being produced in the late 1940s and, in some instances (the MG T series being a notable example), the early 1950s, although major changes in car design and production methods were about to change the small sports car for ever.

It is possible to build a wider car body onto a chassis by incorporating outriggers, which are simply sideways extensions of the chassis between the front and rear wheels, and in fact cars had been built in this fashion for many years. Much more practical wider bodied sports cars like the Austin Healey 100 and the Jaguar XK120 began to appear and the days of narrow upright cars were numbered.

The MG company had such a project car of their own in 1952, called the EX (EXperimental) 175, and nowadays any classic sports car enthusiast would recognise the body as being that of the MGA. The Austin-influenced BMC appear to have prevented MG from putting the MGA into production for three years, during which time the Austin Healey 100 effectively had the market to itself. Denied the opportunity to go ahead with the MGA, MG introduced the TF to try and counteract a drop in TD sales. The MGA was finally launched in 1955, and the production lasted up until the introduction of the MGB in 1962. 101,000 MGAs were built during this period and, like the Austin Healey 100, many were exported to the USA. Both cars possessed chassis. Interestingly, the Austin Healey 100/3000 range remained in production from 1953 until 1968, yet failed to sell anything like as well as the MGA did in its shorter production life – a case of corporate shooting oneself in the foot?

The first monocoque car to be produced by MG was the Z-type Magnette of 1954. The monocoque principle allowed cars to be constructed more cheaply and more quickly, certainly more quickly than in the case of the MGA. The MGA was immensely popular but could not be manufactured quickly enough to satisfy demand. The MGB of 1962 had a monocoque bodyshell, could be manufactured in great numbers quickly, and during the following eighteen years of its production life it became arguably the most commercially successful British sports car of the period if not of all time.

The partnership between Austin and Healey which had resulted in the Austin Healey 100 was to again bear fruit towards the end of the decade in the form of the first of the Spridget line, the Austin Healey

LEFT *Frogeye with the top up; an Austin Healey badge, but all 50,000 were produced by MG. (Photo: Andrew Morland)*

ABOVE *Austin Healy 'Frogeye' Sprite: the MX5 of its day? And then some. (Photo: Andrew Morland)*

'Frogeye' Sprite. Exactly why this powerful alliance came to design and build a smaller sports car when they already had the Austin Healey 100 and MGA might have had something to do with the 1950s phenomenon of the 'special'.

In the late 1940s and 1950s a number of what today we would call 'kit cars' but which were usually then referred to as 'specials' appeared on the market. These comprised a chassis and either a body or plans from which one could be constructed, usually from plywood and/or aluminium or steel sheet. Although 'specials' were by no means a new concept, the idea of commercially made kit specials – made possible by the development of plywood appears to be a 1940s-50s phenomenon.

GRP (glass reinforced plastic) bodied kit cars began to appear and, unlike the previous wood, steel or aluminium bodied kits, the bodyshells manufactured from GRP could be comparatively mass-produced in almost any shape or style. This is because GRP is moulded around a 'plug' (a full sized model of the car body), to produce a female mould, from which shell replicas of the original plug could then be made. Once the plug had been constructed and the mould taken from it, a relatively low skilled work force could mould (the correct term is to 'lay

up') bodies very quickly. Previously, all bodywork for non-mass produced cars had to be made by highly skilled craftsmen or by the enthusiast working at home; in either case, a painstaking business. In contrast to the new GRP process, the production speed of the old methods was very slow and the prices of the commercially manufactured bodies were very high.

Like the modern 'kit' or 'component' car, those of the 1950s used mechanical components from production vehicles. Amongst these, the Austin A30/A35 engine and gearbox were particularly popular. Some kit cars such as the Turner 950 (A35 engine, trailing arm/torsion bar rear suspension) look very similar to the small production sports cars of the 1960s and, in fact, the Turner bears an uncanny resemblance to the Mk.2 Sprite/Mk.1 Midget! Perhaps due to the popularity of small sports kit cars, larger motor manufacturers began to develop similar production cars of their own.

In May, 1958, the famous Austin Healey 'Frogeye' Mk.1 Sprite was launched. Unlike earlier mass-produced sports cars, the Frogeye Sprite was built on the monocoque principle, with strong 'chassis rail' sections built into a pressed steel welded body. In fact the Sprite did possess a chassis of sorts

Because the entire front end pivots up and out of the way, engine accessibility is excellent with the Frogeye Sprite.

The simple no-frills interior of the covetable Mk.1 'Frogeye' Sprite.

which ran from the front of the car back to the main central body cross member, although the rear half of the car was indisputably monocoque. This type of construction is more suited to mass production than the separate chassis method. Various sub-assemblies such as the transmission tunnel/heelboard assembly were built up individually on small jigs, then assembled quickly onto a large jig, so cutting the amount of time that the large jig was in use and speeding the production process. In the event, it was fortuitous that the new car could be built quickly in large numbers. So popular was this little car that nearly 50,000 of them were sold in the three years of production.

Although the Frogeye Sprite was badged 'Austin Healey', it was actually manufactured by MG (as was the 'big' Healey), having been developed by Healey. Thus the tie up between Austin Healey and MG began right from the start of production of the Frogeye.

The Frogeye Sprite housed a 948cc A series engine developing 42.5 BHP at 5500 rpm and 52 foot pounds of torque at 3200 rpm. A top speed of 81 mph and a nought-to-sixty mph acceleration time of 20.3 seconds might not sound much today, but in the late 1950s this performance, coupled with the style and handling of the little car, was enough to set the pulse racing! It was not only the enthusiasts who reacted to the car, but also other manufacturers, who were persuaded by the Frogeye's sales success that great potential existed for similar cars bearing their own badges. Triumph launched the Spitfire (staying with the separate chassis method of construction), Honda introduced their tiny S360 and S800, MG ditched the separate chassis construction methods which had held back production of the beautiful MGA, and launched the monocoque-bodied MGB then, in 1961, (perhaps inevitably, because they manufactured it!) their own badged version of the Sprite Mk.2, the MG Midget Mk. 1.

The Sprite Mk.2/Midget Mk.1 retained the 948cc A series engine of the Frogeye, but with 46 BHP it had a slightly increased top speed of 84 mph and a nought-to-sixty mph time of 19 seconds. This was the car which introduced the basic shape of all subsequent Sprites and Midgets and, as the last Midget was manufactured in 1979, the design certainly stood the test of time. The circumstances of the redesign were, to say the least, unusual. Healey was charged with redesigning the front end of the car, whilst responsibility for the rear end rested with MG! It is hardly surprising that the rear end of the Mk. 2 Sprite/Mk.1 Midget (square wheelarch) bore something of a resemblance to that which would later be seen adorning the MGB. Although the two design teams were allegedly supposed to work completely independently of each other, there seems little doubt that a series of unofficial meetings took place during the design stage of the car. The Healey prototype with its redesigned front end was completed before the MG version, and it appears that one or perhaps two cars with the Mk.2 Sprite front end and the Frogeye rear end were produced. These do not appear to still exist, although replicas are around.

In 1962 and 1963, the car took class wins in the Monte Carlo rally. Over 20,000 Sprite Mk.2 cars were manufactured, plus just over 16,000 cars with the MG (Mk.1) badge. In 1962 the engine size was increased to 1098cc, and disc brakes were fitted at the front. In this guise, the Sprite badged car sold just over 11,000 and the Midget 9,000.

The Sprite Mk.3/Midget Mk.2 launched in March 1964 retained the 1098cc engine which gave 55 BHP with better fuel economy than its 948cc predecessor. Top speed was increased to 89 mph and the nought to sixty mph time was cut to a more respectable 16.4 seconds. The car was fitted with wind-up windows and the rear suspension changed

from the earlier quarter elliptic to half elliptic springing. The cars were produced in roughly equal numbers, with just under 26,000 Sprites and 26,500 Midgets. Two years later the cars (Sprite Mk.4 and Midget Mk.3) were given the 1275cc version of the A series engine, developing 65 BHP, to again increase performance. In this version, top speed was increased to 93 mph and the nought-to-sixty mph time was cut down to 14.6 seconds. The car also gained a proper fold-down hood. Only 14,000 Sprite badged cars were produced, against 22,000 Midgets

The Sprite Mk.4 was discontinued in 1971, although production of the Midget Mk.3 continued until 1974. Some detail changes took place during this period, most notable being the switch to matt black grille in 1969 (both cars) the introduction of round rear wheel arches in 1972 (Midget only) and the standardisation of the previously optional anti-roll bar in 1972. Some 8400 Sprites bearing the matt black grille were produced before the model was discontinued, whilst 29,000 Midgets preceded the switch to round rear wheel arches and a massive 48,000 round wheel arch Midgets were manufactured between 1972 and 1974. Many enthusiasts felt and still feel that the round rear wheel arch is more attractive than the MG-influenced square wheel arch, and consequently, 'round wheel arch' cars, as they are called (look for the letters 'rwa' in advertisements), are today somewhat sought-after.

The dashboard of the 1974 Midget. Note that 'safer' rocker switches are now fitted. Pity about the non-standard steering wheel.

One of the, if not the most important market for all British sports cars at the time was the United States of America. Over the years, a series of laws in the US which limited exhaust emissions had forced British sports car manufacturers to fit extra emission control equipment into the essentially simple and efficient SU-based carburation fitted to not only the Midget but also the Triumph Spitfire and the enormously successful MGB. The effect of these changes was to slowly degrade the performance of the cars.

Further US legislation was aimed at improving safety for a car's occupants. Over the years, British sports car manufacturers had complied with the ever-tighter legislation by fitting padded dashboards, replacing toggle dashboard switches with rocker switches, and so on. Then crash collision regulations were introduced which forced the British manufacturers to drastically alter their cars. Along with its 'big brother' the MGB, the Midget Mk. 4 was fitted with huge black urethane bumpers, which concealed some sturdy and heavy steelwork underneath. Comparing the engine bays of this and earlier Spridgets, you will notice some fairly heavy-duty metalwork along each side in the rubber bumper cars. This is solely to support the heavy front bumper assembly, but of course, it adds again to the overall weight of the car. The new bumpers were fitted so that the cars could pass the US test of being driven into a concrete wall at 5 mph without impairing the operation of the lighting system.

The new US regulations also governed the height of the bumpers, the idea being that if all bumpers were at the same height from the road, collisions would all be bumper verses bumper. Unfortunately, most people brake immediately before a collision, an action which lowers the front bumper and raises the rear bumper, so that nose to tail collision could involve two bumpers at quite different heights irrespective of the relative heights of the bumpers whilst the cars were at rest. Furthermore, the new bumpers were so massively built that they caused severe damage to any bodywork which they hit in this manner.

The introduction of the new Midget bumpers had several serious implications. Firstly, the bodyshell had to be substantially reinforced to carry them. Secondly, the ride height had to be raised in order to get the bumpers to the regulation height. Thirdly, the car put on so much weight that the faithful 1275cc A series engine simply did not have the potential left to give enough power for a respectable performance

(especially as it had already been subjected to various performance-robbing modifications to comply with stringent US emission laws). The ride height problem was dealt with by altering the front cross member mountings at the front and fitting sturdier, re-cambered six leaf springs at the back. The A series engine was replaced with the 1493cc Triumph unit used in the Spitfire. It seems likely that the round wheel arches were not considered to be strong enough for the new, heavy Midget, and the square wheel arches re-appeared.

The 1493cc engine in US specification gave roughly the same power output as a home market 1275cc A series engine, with 57 BHP and 71 foot pounds of torque. For the UK and other markets, the engine had a higher compression ratio and twin SU carburettors to give 65 BHP and 77 foot pounds of torque, enough to give a respectable nought to sixty mph time of 12.3 seconds. The standard three-synchromesh gearbox gave way to the four-synchromesh unit also fitted to the Marina 1300. This gave better ratios, which contributed to the car's road performance and a new top speed of 101 mph. No less than 72,185 1500cc Midgets were produced. The total production figure for the Spridget (not including the 50,000 Frogeyes) was over 300,000.

The Midget Mk.4 continued in production until November of 1979, being survived by the MGB for eleven more months before it too was discontinued and the famous MG Abingdon factory was closed. In the following eleven years, the MG title was used by the Rover Group only to badge performance variants of its Metro hatchback, Maestro and Montego saloon cars. With the Midget, Triumph Spitfire and TR7, the MGB and the little Fiat X/19 all discontinued, it appeared that the phenomenon of the mass-produced and affordable small sports cars had disappeared for all time, yet the Japanese motor manufacturer Mazda saw fit to build the superb MX5 two seater convertible sports car and reaped a deserved reward in the form of instant commercial success. Lotus launched the front wheel drive Elan, and suddenly, the market

RIGHT *By the time that the 1500cc Midget came along, much of the uncomplicated character of the earlier Sprites and Midgets had undeniably been eroded as the cars became ever-more sophisticated – largely in response to North American legislative demands. Still, the UK 1500cc Midget remained a relatively simple car for its period.*

awoke to the fact that people wanted to buy small sports cars. As this is being written in 1991, the talk is of an all-new MG sports car, or two or perhaps even more. Published (informed?) reports suggest that the Heritage MGB bodyshell is going to form the basis for a new limited edition V8 which, with the believed 260–280bhp power, will be a supercar by anyone's standards. Sadly, the reports do not mention any similar plans for the Heritage Spridget shell . . .

The popularity of the Sprite/Midget (often referred to collectively and throughout this book as the 'Spridget') and the MGB is such that British Motor Heritage have seen fit to produce brand new body shells for both, rescuing much of the original tooling from scrapyards in the vicinity of the MG's Abingdon home! It is remarkable that both cars have survived the years in such numbers that this exercise is viable, and that the cars have survived is a great testament to their original build quality and to the enthusiasm and loyalty of their devoted owners.

Devotees of the original Frogeye Sprite have not been overlooked, either. That unique Frogeye body-shell has been recreated in a GRP bodyshell which sits upon a spaceframe chassis. There is nothing too surprising about that, because many classic sports cars, including the D Type and E Type Jaguars, the MGA and the 'big' Austin Healey have all been recreated in GRP. What makes this car different is the involvement of Geoffrey Healey and the fact that the car is known as the Healey Frogeye. For more details of the Healey Frogeye and the British Heritage Midget shell, see Chapter 6.

Between the efforts of dedicated restorers, British Heritage and the Frogeye Car Company, the Sprite and Midget should still be with us long after today's crop of characterless saloon cars and 'hot' hatchbacks have become a distant memory.

LIVING WITH A SPRIDGET

Many eulogies have been published about these little cars by their infatuated owners, some of which get rather carried away and claim varying degrees of practicality for the cars, which is not a realistic appraisal of the Spridget. The Spridget is NOT a practical everyday car. It can seat two people (and no more in the UK due to legal constraints) and also carry a limited amount of luggage, although even the average week's shopping can exceed the carrying capacity of the small boot and cause overflow on to the rear shelf and even into the passenger footwell.

The truth of the matter is that the Spridget was not conceived nor designed to be practical in any way, shape or form. The Spridget revels in being a delightfully impractical car. The Spridget is a fun car. You quickly come to realise this as soon as you climb into the driver's seat of any Spridget, let alone drive it. Manoeuvring anything but the smallest and slimmest human frame into or out of the car with the soft top raised or with a hard top in place with anything approaching elegance is near impossible. You quickly come to appreciate how much more difficult it is to enter the car when parked next to a tall kerb.

When you have clambered into the driver's seat, a touch of claustrophobia is understandable, because the steering wheel is within inches of your face. With the hood raised or a hard top in place, the cockpit can feel very enclosed to a larger person. The view to the front is not too spectacular through the low windscreen and there is a worrying blind spot caused by the windscreen frame side posts. The rear view through the perspex hood window is poor at the best of times. Through an old opaque screen it becomes worse. Better fold it down. Spridget drivers seem to pride themselves in having the top down on the coldest days when mere mortals are huddling indoors next to an open fire while their open sports cars are tucked away in a heated garage. Despite the tight fit of the average person in the Midget cockpit, the seating and the driving position are surprisingly comfortable, so that you will not end a long drive feeling stiff and sore.

Then you may start to wonder just how the driver is supposed to extricate him or herself from the snug cockpit with the hood raised. Open the door and drag oneself out on all fours? Not very elegant. Only time and practice can allow the taller driver to exit the car with dignity.

Then you start the engine and, if the right exhaust system is fitted, you hear that wonderful exhaust note and remember one of the reasons why you wanted a Spridget. Getting the first gear (which has no synchromesh on most Spridgets) from a standstill is not as easy as it might be, but, once on the move, the short and easy gearchange quickly endears itself. The fairly low gearing allows the driver to make the most of engine BHP, so that the performance of the car is better than you might expect for the engine power. It certainly SEEMS fast

A sight to gladden the heart of any classic car enthusiast – the craftsmen of British Heritage busy at work building a batch of square wheel arch Spridget shells. (Courtesy British Heritage).

from your position inches above the road.

In comparison with the handling vagaries of many other small sports cars, the handling of the Spridgets (the 1500cc Midget to a lesser degree) is superlative, completely predictable and fun. Perhaps a little too much movement can be induced at the rear end through 'S' bends (which could probably be dealt with by a light rear anti-roll bar) but when pushed towards the limit on a bend the car responds with nothing more dramatic than mild understeer. Of course you can go too far and get the rear end to break away, but with the light and responsive Minor steering rack the resultant oversteer is easily corrected. This is a very forgiving car. If you do get into trouble then the brakes of all but the earliest examples will be found to be more than up to the task of stopping the car quickly and without unnecessary fuss.

At the end of your first drive you will understand why Spridget owners are so fond of their cars. It is because they derive such great pleasure from driving what can only be described as a fun driver's car.

Out and about in the Spridget, you become aware that every other Spridget driver you encounter flashes his lights or waves a friendly greeting. It matters not whether your car is badged MG or Austin Healey, for most drivers of cars with either badge do not acknowledge any dividing difference between them (and, of course, they were all built by MG anyway).

This camaraderie also extends to the clubs. The two large UK MG clubs each have many local branches in the UK, and others in all major export markets for MG cars. It would be a strange MG local branch which did not welcome the owner of an Austin Healey Sprite or even a Frogeye with open arms as a kindred spirit. For those who want their very own dedicated club, the Midget and Sprite Club, based in Bristol, England, is exclusively yours.

One of the beauties of the Spridget is its low running and maintenance costs. The overall fuel consumption ranges from 27–28 mpg for the 1500cc Midget to 30 mpg for the 1275cc Sprites and Midgets, 37 mpg for the 1098cc models and 34 mpg from 948cc models. Whilst none of these figures can be considered especially frugal by today's standards, they are good for sports cars and especially good for classic sports cars. Miles per gallon fuel economy, however, is only a part of overall running costs, and in some of the other departments the Spridget outshines nearly every other car on the road.

The long-lived and reliable A series engine and the simple but effective ancillaries from the likes of SU and Lucas which are found on Spridgets mean that the cars are fully user maintainable and repairable, and will probably remain so for many years to come. Furthermore, the spares which are likely to be required are widely available and invariably they are very competitively priced.

Spridget owners have four choices of sources for spares. They can often find the spare they need at a breaker's yard and, because many of the components used on Spridgets were common to other British vehicles, the yard need never have broken a Spridget but still have the desired part, taken from another BMC/BL vehicle. Many of the components can be ordered new from Rover Group garages as they are still manufactured by the Heritage Unipart Division or by the original third party manufacturer. Your nearest motor factors will also be able to supply such spares and delivery is usually within one or two days.

Almost any component can be sourced from one of the many specialist dealers in Spridget spares. These businesses not only stock genuine and pattern spares, but some of them commission the manufacture of otherwise unavailable spares. If no specialist is within reasonable travelling distance of your home then they all operate efficient mail order services.

Insurance costs are kept low by special deals between insurance companies and owners' clubs, although the author believes that premiums could in some instances be still lower than is the case because the increasing classic value of Spridgets is ensuring that they are constantly being driven more carefully by more doting owners than may have been the case in the past when they provided low cost sports cars for youngsters.

In common with all classic cars, the Spridget should not depreciate in the manner of a modern car so that, despite its higher fuel consumption and more frequent need of maintenance and repair, the overall running costs of the Spridget can be far lower than those of the modern car. At the time of writing, five years' depreciation for some new cars can be more than the combined restoration and five-year running costs of a car like the Spridget.

Although not a practical car as such, when compared with other two seater open sports cars the Spridget is an immensely practical option. It has probably the lowest running costs and is still (at the time of writing) affordable to buy and not too expensive to restore. No car could actually improve on the sheer driving pleasure of the Spridget, and that is what it is all about. After all, this is a *fun* car.

2 · BUYING A SPRITE/MIDGET

The Sprite and Midget both have a character all of their own which is not to be found in any other sports car. Once you have made up your mind to buy one of these cars, then there can be no substitute. You will not be distracted by a Triumph Spitfire, a Honda S800 or an MGB, because, however good each of these and similar cars may be in their own way, they are not Spridgets. Your know that you want a Spridget; the question remains, which Spridget?

Basically, there are six essentially different cars to choose from irrespective of the badge on the grille. These are the Frogeye, the 948cc, 1098cc, 1275cc, 1275cc round wheel arch and 1500cc. The matter of which badge adorns the models sold under both Austin Healey and MG badges is purely one of personal preference, and an MG enthusiast might well actively seek a Midget, an Austin Healey fan might actively seek a Sprite. Most buyers will be happy with either, because there is very little difference (in some cases, only the badges – ALL Spridgets were manufactured by the same craftsmen and craftswomen at Abingdon) between a Sprite and a Midget for any given engine capacity. The MG badge, however, does sometimes sell for a little more than the Austin Healey, even though the cars are identical under the skin.

Of all the variants, the Frogeye is the most highly regarded by classic car enthusiasts. Although 50,000 Frogeyes were initially produced, many went for export and many have not survived over thirty years of use, so that rarity alone has probably helped to make this the most expensive of the breed. In addition to the pure rarity value of the car, the endearing and highly individual looks of the Frogeye ensure that it is sought-after by very enthusiastic buyers and hence that it commands the highest prices. Typically, you might have to pay between 50% and 100% more than any other Spridget variant for a Frogeye in equal condition.

Restoration costs for the Frogeye are also likely to be rather higher than for other Marks of Spridget because many of the repair and replacement panels will be manufactured in small quantities and be more expensive as a result, whereas new panels manufactured by Heritage should eventually cover virtually any requirement for any other Spridget. As an example, the complete steel bonnet assembly for a Frogeye costs very nearly as much (according to a well-known spares supplier's catalogue, which also lists a GRP alternative at a fraction of the cost) as the Heritage bodyshell complete with bonnet, wings etcetera for later Spridgets! Mechanically, the entire Spridget range is very well served with just about any conceivable spare and, because many components were also used on other contemporary cars, second-hand spares can be obtained cheaply from many auto-jumble events and from breakers' yards.

Those who seek a car with collector's values in mind will undoubtedly be attracted to the Frogeye because, as interest in old cars rises, this will inevitably be the best 'performer' financially. The fact that some enthusiasts do take the financial performance of a car into consideration should not be taken to imply that they are necessarily avaricious, because many people can only afford to buy the type of car they want by borrowing money, and it is no more than economic prudence to borrow only against an appreciating asset. However, there can be no guarantee that any car will rise in value, and buying these or any other cars for pure speculation is not recommended.

Many people believe that it is better to either pay

a very low price for a basket case Frogeye (and to be fully aware of likely restoration costs) or to pay top money for a car in very good condition rather than pay a seemingly attractive price for a car which needs some degree of work carrying out – the idea being that mid-priced cars will often be found to need very expensive body repair work in a few years time, so that the purchase price plus any restoration or repair costs can exceed the high prices demanded for cars in excellent condition. This approach has much to commend it and, incidentally, holds good for all years and Marks of Spridget.

The Mk.2 Sprite/Mk.1 Midget of 1961 to 1964 will undoubtedly be seen by many as the 'purest' form of the Spridget, because it like most other 'Mk.1' cars is the most basic and in many peoples' eyes the most unspoilt by later modifications. It is also now relatively rare, despite having been manufactured in fairly large quantities (948cc engine, 16,000 Midgets and 20,000+ Sprites, 1098cc engine, 9600 Midgets and 11,000 Sprites). These Mk.1 cars were widely considered to be simply 'old' cars rather than classics before the classic car movement started a huge growth in interest in 60s cars during the late 1970s, and many were scrapped in the intervening years. If the Spridget had been discontinued after 1964, then these cars would undoubtedly today be as highly sought-after as the Frogeye, and many of those which were scrapped would probably have been restored instead. The 948cc version does suffer rather sluggish performance (although the handling is of course fine), with the 1098cc being noticeably quicker and more pleasurable to drive at modern everyday speeds. The front disc brakes of the latter are also very welcome today, although the earlier all-drum brakes were quite competent.

The Mk.2 Midget/Mk.3 Sprite was the only version to have been manufactured in roughly equal quantities under both badges. Earlier versions saw the Sprites outnumbering the Midgets and later versions saw the numbers of Sprites decline and Midgets increase. These variations in relative production figures do not appear to be reflected in collectors' values, at least, at the time of writing. The relative 'rarity' of later Sprites, in other words, does not necessarily result in higher values. Published price guides (which it must be said are to be taken with a large pinch of salt) place the MG and Austin Healey versions of the car at roughly the same value for any given year. Perhaps the Austin-badged Sprite Mk.5, model number A.AN10 (manufactured during

1971) will at some stage in the future assume higher 'collectors' values due to the fact that only 1022 were sold in this form. Otherwise, treat Sprites and Midgets as having basically the same value for a given production year and condition.

The Mk.4 Sprite/Mk.3 Midget saw the 1275cc engine fitted into the range for the first time, with a noticeable increase in performance which will be appreciated by the modern driver. A nought to sixty mph time of 14.6 seconds will not allow many of today's vehicles to be beaten away from the traffic lights, but at least drivers will be better able to keep up with modern highway traffic. Because these cars were the last to be fitted with chrome grilles and because they had the extra performance of the 1275cc engine, many enthusiasts will consider them to be the most desirable of all Spridgets. It is purely a matter of aesthetics whether you like or dislike the matt black grilles of cars from 1969, but the Sprites sold until 1971 and the Midgets manufactured until the introduction of the 1500cc in 1974 do offer the benefits of good performance from the 1275cc engine plus pre-rubber bumper looks. Midgets from 1972 also have the much-liked round rear wheel arches which many enthusiasts believe to enhance the looks of the car greatly. Spridgets manufactured before 1972 had 'square' rear wheel arches reminiscent of those of the MGB, which is hardly surprising because the rear end of the car was designed by MG. The round wheel arches from 1972 were probably really 're-introduced', because they had featured originally on the Frogeye Sprite.

Many enthusiasts dislike the 1500cc Midget, mainly for its appearance with those heavy rubber bumpers but also for its handling. Nevertheless, this is the fastest of the production Midgets and its nought to sixty mph time of 12.3 seconds and 101 mph top speed mean that it can keep up with traffic almost anywhere and cruise at motorway speeds without having to work too hard. It is the most practical (if any two seater sports car can be called 'practical') of the Spridget range for the modern day. When you have decided which Mark and marque of Spridget you desire, the problems arise of where to look for your dream car and who to buy from. Classic cars are, of course, widely advertised in national classic car magazines, and this may appear a good place to begin your search. Unfortunately, because such magazines are distributed nationally, they attract advertisements from all over the country. If you are in the market for a comparatively rare Frogeye Sprite then the national press might offer the best solution because it will be the only place where you can find any sort of selection to choose from, but if you seek one of the more common Spridgets then you may as well begin looking nearer home. Vendors of Spridgets usually arrive at their asking prices by following one of the published 'classic car value guides' in a classic car magazine. These can cause problems. Firstly, the guides often differ from each other in the values they ascribe to particular cars (the author has seen two guides which were published at the same time give one valuation of 50% more than the other for the same car!) and secondly, they value the cars as belonging to one of three groups according to their condition. Group '1' or 'A' usually refers to very clean and original cars with little or no rust and reliable mechanical and electrical components (but excludes pristine concourse winners). Group '2' or 'B' usually refers to cars which run and possess the relevant certificate of roadworthiness (the MOT certificate in the UK) but which would benefit from a certain amount of mild mechanical repair and/or a small amount of bodywork attention. Group '3' or 'C' cars are described as those which may or may not be runners and may or may not possess a current certificate of roadworthiness, but which do require fairly extensive mechanical and body repair to make them really usable. A vendor often assumes that his group 3 or C car is actually a group 2/B, and asks the appropriate price as indicated in the guide. It will not be until you actually examine the car that the mistake or misrepresentation will come to light. This is not too annoying if you have travelled only a short distance to view the car, but following a long and wasted drive it can be infuriating.

If you are looking for a reasonably common Spridget variant then you will save much time, money and temper by only travelling to view cars situated fairly close to your home. In this case it is best to confine your search initially to notice boards, local newspapers and other local publications. Word of mouth is also an excellent way of finding a local car, because one of the people you inform that you want a Spridget might just know where one is available. This also brings the benefit of allowing you to make an offer on the car without having other potential buyers hovering in the background ready to outbid you, which can often happen if you and they both answer an advertisement and turn up for a viewing at the same time.

In the UK, regional advertisement-only publications which specialise in used cars offer another useful media to study. These usually feature far more classic and sports cars than local media, giving a far better selection at the cost of having to travel further to view likely cars. The author has noticed general pricing trends applying to cars according to which media they are advertised in. National magazine advertised cars tend towards the top end of their expected price range, especially cars which are advertised in the more 'up-market' magazines which have pages full of advertisements for affordable classic and classic sports cars yet glossy editorial features on Ferraris and Bentleys. There are some much more editorially down-to-earth, 'man in the street' type classic magazines, and the advertisements in these tend to feature less extravagantly priced cars.

The prices asked for cars in regional advertisement-only publications, in common with local newspapers, are in general realistic, although the occasional silly price creeps in from time to time. Before leaving the subject of Spridget prices, do not pay too much attention to insurance valuations given to the cars you view because most of these appear to be based on photographic evidence of a car's condition and, although they serve a useful role in the insurance field, for your purposes as a potential buyer, they are without substance.

There are five sources of classic cars.

1   The vast majority of classic cars which are bought and sold pass from a private vendor to a private buyer.

2   An increasing number of cars are sold by dealers who specialise in classic cars, a particular marque or even a particular model.

3   Very few classic sports cars like the Spridget nowadays find their way on to general car dealers' pitches.

4   The Classic Car auction is a relatively modern but growing phenomenon at which more and more classic cars seem to be traded.

5   General motor auctions very occasionally have a classic car.

Each potential source of classic cars has points in and against its favour, and each will be briefly discussed in the order in which they appear above.

PRIVATE

The private vendor is often sought by potential buyers because it is assumed that the prices involved will be lower than those asked by dealers. Not so, for many vendors, misinterpreting (genuinely or otherwise) classic car value guides, ascribe ridiculously high values for their cars. Many vendors are loath to sell their beloved classic car but are forced to by circumstances beyond their control and such people are prone to add a degree of 'sentimental' value to the actual value of the car when arriving at an asking price. Some private vendors are simply avaricious and are prepared to keep their cars on the market until they find a buyer silly enough to pay their inflated asking prices.

Buying from a private vendor can sometimes result in your getting a bargain, but the practice does carry huge risks. Private vendors of many products, certainly within the UK, are not subject to the stringent consumer protection laws by which a businessman selling the same item would have to abide. In the case of a motor vehicle it is still an offence to misrepresent it, but unless the misrepresentation has been published in an advertisement then there is no proof of any such offence. It is also an offence to sell a motor vehicle which is in a dangerous unroadworthy condition, but unless you can prove that the car in question was unroadworthy at the actual time of purchase then it is very difficult to take any action against the vendor. A private vendor will assume that, once the car is your property and you have driven it away, he or she has no further liability for the car. If the rear spring hangers crumple up into the body a week later then you will have great difficulty in gaining any form of redress. The worst liability from buying privately is the chance of buying a stolen vehicle or a vehicle on which there is an outstanding debt due to a Hire Purchase company. As the name suggests, in hire purchase (HP), the goods covered in the agreement between the company and the customer remain the property to the hire purchase company until the repayment has been received in full. If the car which you buy has such an outstanding hire purchase debt attached then the company can legally repossess the car and it will owe you nothing in the way of compensation because it is reclaiming its own property. The type of person who would sell you a car with an outstanding hire purchase agreement is not going to prove very helpful when you seek redress.

You can reduce the risk of buying a car with outstanding hire purchase repayments by seeing the receipt which was given to the vendor when he purchased the car. This also helps guard against inadvertently buying a stolen car. Classic cars are extremely tempting targets for thieves. Not only do the cars command high prices and often find a ready market, but even broken down for spares they are worth money. Most classic cars which are stolen and subsequently offered for sale (certainly in the UK) are the product of a type of organised crime called 'ringing'. In this, a car of a specific year and colour is stolen. In order to sell the car, the thief has to give it a new identity, which he can do in one of two ways. Firstly, he can take the registration document and number, engine and commission numbers of a scrapped example of the vehicle and merely replace the various identification plates on the stolen car (the 'ringer'). Secondly, he can apply for a duplicate registration document for an existing and perfectly legitimate example of the car, then buy number plates and other identification plates to create another seemingly legitimate example.

Ringing is far more likely to be used with the later and much more prolific rubber bumper cars, because there are so many still in circulation that finding a ringer of a particular year and colour is not too difficult. Of course, with the prices of Spridgets rising there could come a day when it would be financially attractive for a thief to respray a ringer (if he was unable to steal one in the right colour) to match the seemingly 'legitimate' documentation he possesses, but at the time of writing, the values of Spridgets (Frogeyes excepted as a borderline case) are so low that this does not appear to be happening.

Your best guard against buying a ringer is to ask to see not only the previous receipt of purchase but also a current or the last tax disc and insurance document pertaining to the vehicle and owner respectively. A vendor who can not immediately supply these for your perusal has obviously not used the vehicle in question for some considerable time, or he or she may never have run it at all if it turns out to be a ringer.

Never allow a vendor to bring a car to you for viewing, because this is the favoured selling method of thieves. Most 'cars for sale' advertisements carry a telephone number rather than an address, and it is important that you have the vendor's address and cross-check this against the telephone number, and that you actually visit the address and view the car there. Perhaps the safest private vendor to buy from would be a member of a local MG/Spridget club or a local branch of a nationally based club. Alternatively, few thieves would risk advertising in club literature, so that cars advertised through advertisements in club magazines should also, in theory, be safe buys. To summarise, buying from a private vendor rarely results in acquiring a car at a bargain price, and it can prove risky.

Specialist Dealers

The classic car dealer has been portrayed by some classic car magazine contributors as a profiteer who takes classic cars out of the hands of genuine enthusiasts and hoards them as an investment. This is utter rot. Firstly, a classic car dealer has to make a profit and hence to make sales in order to pay the business bills and in order to have an income. He can do neither if he hoards cars until their value reaches a pre-determined level. He can do neither if he over-prices his stock, because he would sell no cars. Classic car dealers are also blamed for pushing up the prices of classic cars and taking many beyond the reach of 'real' enthusiasts. Again, this is nonsense, because a dealer who over-priced his stock would sell no or few cars and eventually he would see his stock liquidated by a receiver and sold off at very low values when he could not pay his creditors.

Classic car values saw an unprecedented rise in the late 1980s, but it was not dealers who were to blame, it was a combination of the majority of people selling classic cars (the private vendors) asking the highest current value, and a lot of hype and nonsense which was published with the general media, including television, newspapers and even some classic car magazines. Classic car dealers have had an undeservedly bad press.

There are some rogues amongst classic car dealers just as there are in any other trade or calling, although the dubious classic car dealer is usually fairly easy to identify. A good dealer will have repair and possibly restoration facilities with which he can honour the terms of whatever guarantee he gives. A dubious dealer will not. A good dealer will usually have proper premises whilst a dubious dealer will often be found operating from a barn or sometimes from a small lock-up or even his own residential property. A good dealer will usually specialise in a particular marque, model or type of car which he knows well enough to properly appraise, whilst a dubious dealer will take anything which comes his way. Without specialist knowledge, the dubious dealer will be vulnerable to buying poorly restored cars, fakes and unroadworthy cars. A good dealer will avoid such cars, because he knows that to sell just one such vehicle on to a customer could cost him his reputation. It is important to establish whether a dealer is honest and reputable. You require the certainty of a worthwhile guarantee to the authenticity, legality and roadworthiness of a car before you part with money. If you bought off a seasoned rogue then you could find redress difficult.

There is another type of dealer who should be avoided at all costs. This is the person who trades from his own residential premises, usually unofficially. Such people often come from the ranks of classic car enthusiasts. Having bought and sold a few cars and made a profit from the activity, they try to build it up into a lucrative business. These people cannot offer guarantees and if they did then the guarantees would be worthless. These people are probably breaking various trading laws and avoiding taxes and, if they will happily defraud the authorities, they will just as happily cheat the customer. Avoid them at all costs.

General Car Dealers

General used car dealerships do not usually welcome having a classic sports car on their forecourts or in their showrooms for the simple reason that it would be the only one amongst a sea of modern vehicles and hence very unlikely to sell. Classic sports cars are sometimes taken in part exchange against modern cars by general dealers, but they are usually consequently disposed of through the trade, that is, they are sold on to another business which specialises in this type of car.

A surprisingly high percentage of the classic sports cars which do enter the car trade do so because they were previously purchased by the wrong people. A married couple with two small children or even a medium-sized dog to transport might be tempted to buy a Spridget for the same reasons as the rest of us, but they would not usually keep a small sports car for very long because it would be impractical for the job in hand. A husband might buy a Spridget for his wife or a father might buy one for his daughter, but the car could soon be back on sale if the recipient of the gift demanded rather more refinement and luxury than the Spridget would provide.

The fact that Spridgets do enter the used car trade can be put to good use by anyone who lives in or near a large town. Simply visit the car dealers and explain that you wish to buy a particular type of Spridget. The dealer will be certain to let you know the moment he has a Spridget, because he can sell it to you for a far higher price than he could get through the trade. The price in question, incidentally, would almost certainly be negotiable and you may be able to haggle the price down and obtain a bargain in this way.

CLASSIC CAR AUCTIONS

Classic car auctions have been going on for years, but it is only since the start of the 'classic car boom' of the 1980s that there have been so many auctions, or that auctions have dealt with cars like the Spridget. In the UK there seems to be a major auction taking place somewhere every Summer's week-end. The drawbacks to buying from an auction is that you do not have the opportunity to have a test drive, nor the opportunity to place the car on ramps or over a pit to have a close inspection. However, a practiced eye can rule out many cars on the grounds of poor bodywork with a minimal visual inspection, and most auctioneers seem to build a 'cooling off' period into their terms of business contract so that if the loom catches fire when you turn on the ignition to drive the car away, you can back out of the deal. Classic car auctions attract many very knowledgeable people (and a great number who merely kick tyres and check to see whether the ash tray is full). By listening to the comments of the more expert appraisals, you can glean much useful information about individual cars. Be careful not to get caught doing this, just in case the person giving you a free lesson in car appraisal notices you and starts giving out false information! Auctions are terrible places for impetuous people to shop. In the heat of the moment many buyers get completely carried away and really require an assistant to help them keep their feet firmly on the ground. Try to take along an experienced classic car enthusiast who can give you reasoned and level-headed advice, just in case your enthusiasm takes over your own sense of reasoning.

GENERAL CAR AUCTIONS

Nobody visits general car auctions expecting to see classic sports cars, and so nobody much bothers to enter them in general auctions. Occasionally, a company liquidation or the auctioning of goods and chattels from an estate might see a Spridget being entered into a general car auction, but in the main any classic cars at all which are found at an auction will be there simply because they proved impossible to sell elsewhere. Avoid these events.

FINDING THE RIGHT SPRIDGET

The Spridget buyer is lucky compared to buyers of many other classic cars, because the prices of the various years of Spridget are all fairly close. Compare this to the problems faced by an intending Mini Cooper S buyer, who has to be extremely careful not to spend a huge amount of money on a heavily disguised and modified Mini 850! There is great financial reward in obtaining a cheap 850 Mini and altering it to resemble (and selling it as) a Cooper S. There is no possible virtue in taking a Spridget of any year or Mark and trying to pass it off as anything else, save perhaps a well known and historically important competition car. Happily, such cars and their whereabouts and current owners are so well known that the chances of anyone getting away with such a deception are minimal. Anyone who is contemplating buying such a car can check its authenticity quickly by contacting an owners' club. The Spridget buyer is also fortunate in usually being able to track down a selection of cars from which to choose. The Spridget is so prolific that several possible cars can usually be gleaned from the pages of a classic car magazine or regional advertising magazine. Even a local newspaper can render a useful selection over a period of a month or two. The fact that there are usually so many Spridgets on offer means that there is no artificial pressure on the prospective purchaser to buy in haste for fear of missing the fabled once-in-a-lifetime bargain. Those who buy in haste, as the proverb has it, repent at leisure. Never was a saying more deeply rooted in fact. Never be pressurised into buying a car before you are 100% certain that it is exactly what you want, that the price you have negotiated is acceptable and that the car is neither stolen nor the subject of an HP agreement.

The ploys used to pressurise purchasers into making an unnecessarily swift decision are predictable, yet we can all get caught out by them in the heat of the moment. The vendor might suggest that he has a firm offer from someone who 'knows a lot about Spridgets' and who is very keen to buy; if we do not come up with a better offer here and now, the implication is that we have missed out on a real bargain. The vendor might suggest that he has been flooded with telephone calls since placing the advertisement and that you are the first person to be permitted to view the car; the implication is the same as before.

It is very easy to fall for this kind of trick; even expert high-pressure salesmen sometimes get caught out by them! The one thought which can always save you from making a hasty (and usually a wrong) decision is to remember that there are an awful lot of good Spridgets out there, and if you miss this one, then the next one might be even better, and cheaper. It is best to decline to come to an immediate decision, for often the car will still be found to be unsold a day, a week or even a month later, at which time you might care to make the failed high-pressure salesman an offer to 'take the car off his hands'.

Vendors who do push prospective customers for a hasty decision usually do so with good reason. Most often, it is because they know of some problem with the car which you are almost certain to discover if you spend enough time looking. If you can be persuaded that if you do not take the car now then you will have missed a golden opportunity, then the chances are that the car has some fundamental and expensive problem such as a twisted ladder chassis or bodyshell. If you subscribe to a certain type of classic car magazine then you may well have read a dozen sad articles of the 'Why I love my Classic Car' ilk. These sometimes begin with a story of how the author fell instantly in love with the car and just HAD to buy it there and then. The stories usually then detail the trials and tribulations which followed the impulse purchase. Make buying decisions with the head, not the heart. When you go to view a prospective car, *always* take along a companion. Obviously, it would be very useful to have a Spridget expert to accompany you, but even a complete novice might spot something wrong with the car which is so obvious that you miss it. For instance, while you are busy minutely examining the outer sills for signs of body filler, your inexpert companion might be standing back and comment that the bottom edges of the two sills are not in the same plane.

Decide on exactly what you will require of the car before you start answering advertisements. For instance, if you are looking for an engine-out restoration project car then there will be little point in paying extra for a car which has recently been re-sprayed. If you seek a car to use as reliable daily transport then there is little point in buying a very cheap vehicle with a predominance of tired mechanical and electrical components, because these will fail at regular intervals and the car will be anything BUT reliable. If you seek a quality car with good bodywork and excellent mechanical components, then you must accept that all such cars will cost a lot of money, and there will be no point in viewing cheap to middle-priced cars.

Before you begin looking for a car you should also obtain a parts catalogue from a major spares supplier (or preferably two). Familiarise yourself with the current price levels of spares and, if the catalogue and price list are separate and use the original MG/BL part numbers, take the time to actually write the prices of relevant spares in the catalogue. Take the catalogue along when you view a car, and you will be able to list those parts which obviously require replacement (you can not expect to find everything but list as many components as you can) and then quickly ascertain how much the necessary parts will cost you. Add this figure to the asking price then add on any envisaged labour charges at the current hourly rate and the final figure will be the cost of buying the car and getting it to the condition you require.

You may well discover that the innocent car you are viewing needs as much as the asking price again (if not more) added on for necessary repair or restoration work. This may help prevent you from inadvertently buying a car which you cannot afford to bring to the required condition. Many of the cars which you see advertised will have been placed on the market because the owner discovered that the costs of restoration or repair were too great for his or her pocket. You do not wish to repeat that mistake! There is another benefit to having current spares and labour pricing information when you view a car. By estimating the total purchase and repair/restoration cost as outlined above and by sharing this information with the vendor, you may be able to negotiate a substantial reduction in the asking price. Very often, the vendor will already be quite aware of what work the car needs and how much this would cost. In such cases you may be able to arrive at a compromise price well under the original asking price.

One factor which affects the pricing of classic cars on which a book such as the one you are reading can not be specific is the current state of the market. The prices generally of classic cars or of certain classic cars might be rising, stagnant or falling at any given time in the future. Knowing the state of the market could save you from buying at too high a price. The only way in which you can assess movements in classic car prices is to follow the value guides which are published in some of the classic car magazines, and to couple this information with your own observations of the prices asked for cars in advertisements.

Market values rise and fall according to many factors which no-one can claim to accurately predict, and so the only option is to discover the current trend and to base any pricing judgements you make on that. One point worth bearing in mind is that irrespective of market pricing trends, open top sports cars enjoy a better sale in the Summer and are very difficult to sell in the Winter, BUT that restoration project cars sell better in the Autumn and Winter than in the Summer.

ASSESSING CARS

When you have decided the condition of the car you require and the amount which you can afford and believe fair to pay to both buy the car and then bring it to the desired condition, you are in a position to begin assessing cars.

In addition to the aforementioned spares catalogue(s) and paper and pen to make up your list of components which need attention, you will require a trolley jack and axle stands to raise the car so that you can examine the underside in safety, a torch to enable you to see into dark crevices, a screwdriver with which you can poke dubious metal to discover whether it is rotten, protective clothing (leather gloves, overalls etc.) and a magnet to test for excessive use of body filler.

Most advertisements for cars will carry a telephone number, which is your first point of contact with the vendor. By asking pertinent questions when you first make telephone contact, you should be able to rule out some cars unseen and so save yourself wasted journeys. Firstly, when the vendor answers the telephone say that you are calling about 'the car' without mentioning which car you are referring to nor whether you are buying or selling. If the vendor asks 'which car?' then you are probably speaking to a part-time dealer. These people should be avoided at all costs.

They trade in second-hand cars and in doing so some break planning and tax laws (if the advertisement for the car does not state that the vendor is a trader then this in itself is illegal in the UK). A person who willing breaks such laws will not pay too much attention to consumer protection laws, and dealing with such people as at best risky. If the vendor correctly guesses the car to which you refer but adds that a. he can offer a choice of two or more or that b. the car is sold but there is another 'coming in' next week, then you are talking to a part-time dealer.

Pay little attention to the written description of the car in the advertisement, but ask the vendor directly whether the sills, floor and heel board etcetera are sound. Many vendors who pen quite fanciful advertising descriptions of cars will be far more honest when actually speaking to you, and many can be persuaded to give a more factual appraisal of the car when they are actually speaking to someone. Asking a few direct questions along the lines of 'Are any of the gears noisy?' or 'Are the sills sound' can often bring a surprisingly revealing answer from a vendor whose written advertisement made the car seem immaculate. The cost of the extended telephone call will be recouped many times over if it saves you a wasted journey.

A car appraisal can be broken down into three separate areas. These are a. the bodywork, b. the mechanical, hydraulic and electric components, and c. the ancillaries and fittings. But first, take a general look at the car.

Look in the engine bay to see whether it is clean and workmanlike or filthy dirty and covered with oil (which denotes an engine oil leak and possibly severe consequences). Look at the interior and quickly assess the state and originality of the trim and carpets. Step back to look at the car from both sides to see whether it sits square to the ground.

Try to form an opinion of the vendor if you feel this may help you to reach an eventual decision (the author does). If you are unhappy with the vendor's attitude or actions then weigh this along with allother considerations before reaching a buying decision. Some people may not think such amateur psychology necessary, but the author knows that when a vendor suddenly calls you over to view some fascinating and worthy feature of the car then he or she is often merely drawing your attention away from a fault which you were dangerously close to discovering!

BODYWORK APPRAISAL

Exactly what constitutes 'acceptable' bodywork on a Spridget will vary according to the requirements and aspirations of the individual buyer. The person who wants a car to completely restore (if not to concours condition then very close to it) will waste money by looking at a car whose body has been partially repaired by the fitting of new sills or perhaps new A posts, because most such people will find the standards of such repair work lacking and they will replace poorly fitted new panels along with old. Furthermore, it is common practice to place new sills on a car which has a dubious floor (and even a floor with a little pitting will not be good enough for the person building a concours car), rear spring hanger box assembly, A post and so on. In such cases, the work will prove so much easier with the sills off that most restorers will replace them as well. The same person would be wasting money buying a car which had recently been resprayed. Such buyers might be tempted by cars which qualified for the name 'basket cases'. What could prove tempting is a car on which the previous owner had lavished vast sums of money on mechanical repair only to discover that a full bodywork restoration was needed, because such a car will invariably come cheaply, it will save the restorer a small fortune in replacing mechanical, electrical and trim components and it will provide a low cost bodyshell which can be rebuilt from scratch or re-bodied with a Heritage shell.

A potential buyer who was seeking a car which could be used on the road but which needed limited restoration work or generally tidying up might find the bodily repaired car ideal, provided that the repairs were carried out properly and that the car was mechanically sound enough for the purpose. The problem with trying to find this type of car is that nearly all medium-priced examples of Spridgets (and more so in the future) will have at some time received some body repair, and of these, some will have been expertly 'bodged'. Putting right such bodges can prove as time-consuming and expensive as a full

restoration. Some buyers seek cars which can be used on the road immediately and which are in such good condition that they will require no attention save maintenance for many years. Such cars will never come cheaply, so always ask for photographic evidence of the restoration of the car, so that you can adjudge the quality of work which has been carried out.

Each of the buyers described will set out with a target price for the acquisition and, as already described, very different ideas of how their ideal Spridget will look when they find it. It would therefore be wrong to advise the reader not to buy a car which had such-and-such a fault, or to advise that an example in a certain condition would cost too much.

Compared to many cars, the body construction of the Spridget is reasonably simple. This does not mean, however, that repairing or restoring a rotten Spridget body shell is any easier or any cheaper than restoring any other monocoque body shell. In order to quantify the difficulties involved in the repair of bodywork problems, each is graded as it appears in the text. A Grade One problem is easily dealt with by the amateur with welding equipment and a reasonable level of skill in using it. A Grade Two problem is approaching the limits of what the more enthusiastic amateur might contemplate, and a Grade Three problem really requires extensive knowledge and skill to rectify; the kind of problem which could best be tackled by a professional, preferably with a body jig. In order to understand why certain parts of the body should be especially scrutinised, it pays to have a knowledge of how the Spridget is put together.

The body construction method used for the whole Spridget range is based on a comparatively early implementation of the Monocoque principle. This is in fact a kind of 'halfway house' between chassis and full monocoque construction, because the front end of the car incorporates a small chassis of sorts. Two chassis rails or legs extend forwards from the main central cross member (visible from inside the cockpit) and are joined to a heavy cross member which is situated in the engine compartment which carries the engine mounting brackets and elements of the front suspension. Many of the forces generated when the car is on the move by the suspension, brakes, steering and engine are transmitted initially into this framework.

The centre cross member to which the chassis

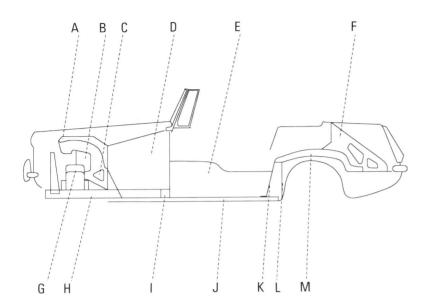

The internal structure of the Spridget. A. Inner front wing. B. Reinforcing plate. C. Triangular box section. D. Footwell assembly. E. Transmission tunnel. F. Wheelarch/ boot floor strengthener. G. Damper bracket assembly. H. Chassis leg. I. Cross member. J. Floor. K. Inner heelboard. L. Outer heelboard. M. Rear chassis rail. Black bumper Midgets have extra strengthening members built-in; check these for distortion.

rails are joined extends each side of the car to meet the sills. The sills are a box section comprising an upright inner panel (the inner sill) and a pressing (the outer sill). The outer sills can be seen from the outside of the car, extending from wheelarch to wheelarch underneath the wings and doors. The sills provide the rigidity for the centre section of the car, and their integrity is vital on any open car.

A fairly complex combination of welded panels incorporating sturdy spring housing boxes and reinforcers joins the rear of the sills to the rear chassis rails. These run to the rear of the car, and may be seen from within the boot. They follow the line of the inner wheelarch. Body rot in any of the body members already mentioned will weaken the car considerably, and so the soundness and integrity of these panels is the first consideration when assessing the car.

Begin by checking that the body is not sagging in the middle (a consequence of thoroughly rotten sills) by checking the door gaps at either side. When a Spridget sags in this way, the gaps at the top sides of the door will close up and the gaps at the bottom will open up. A Spridget which is suffering body distortion in this way is repairable, but unless the greatest care is taken to properly true up the body before welding on the sills (rating Grade Two/Three difficulty) then the body shell will be forever twisted, the handling unpleasant and the roadholding unpredictable. If the doors appear to be mounted at a diagonal to the door apertures (one top side gap closed and the other open, ditto the bottom gaps), then the lower hinges are

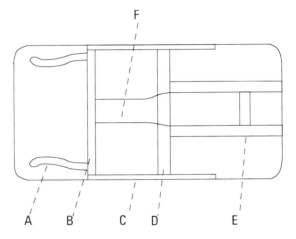

Spridget structure seen from top. A. Rear chassis rails. B. Heelboard assembly. C. Sills. D. Cross member. E. Front ladder chassis. F. Transmission tunnel.

probably either very badly worn or might even have moved due to a rotted lower A post.

The outer sills may appear quite sound if they have recently been replaced, but this in itself is no guarantee that the equally if not more important inner sill has also been replaced! Many backstreet bodyshops and some amateur 'bodgers' will happily place a new outer sill onto the rotted remains of the inner, and some will simply knock the old outer sill inwards rather than go to the trouble of cutting it away. The problem with these practices is that placing clean metal near rusted metal causes the

If you open the door and gently raise and lower it, you might see the lower hinge moving freely into and out of its (rotten) mounting area within the inner A panel. This repair is neither simple nor pleasant but, more importantly, if the inner A post is rotten then either the sill and foot well side panel will be thoroughly rotten or they will have recently been replaced by someone who could not be bothered to attend to the A post.

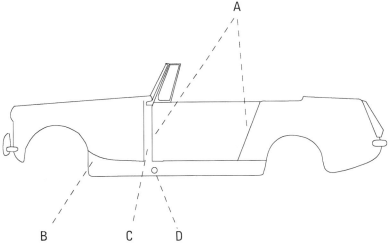

*Checking for a sagging bodyshell.
A. Door gaps. B. Line between front wing/sill top. C. Door hinges.
D. Jacking point (two on 1500).*

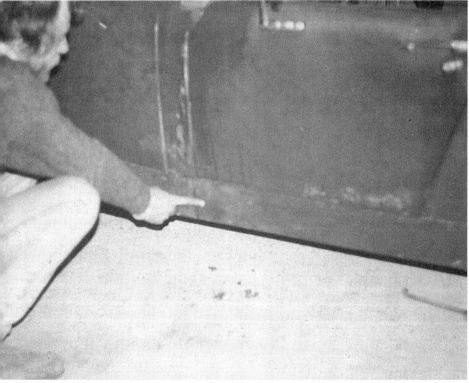

LEFT *Er, there should be a jacking point hole here somewhere... The use of such poor quality repair panels is now largely a thing of the past, because good quality panels (with jacking point holes where applicable) are widely available at reasonable prices. The black bumper Midgets, incidentally, should have two jacking point holes per side.*

LEFT *These stainless sill covers are supposed to prevent the sills from rotting; unfortunately, the sills rot from the inside rather than the outside. If water was allowed to lie in between a sill cover and the sill, however, then the sill would most certainly rot away underneath far more quickly than would otherwise be the case. When assessing a car fitted with sill covers, the author would either insist on being able to examine the steel underneath them, or budget for sill replacement.*

RIGHT AND BELOW *A thoroughly rotten outer sill reveals another hazard – the seatbelt mounting is bolted through the inner sill: one gentle tug and out it comes. In the UK, (or anywhere else) no vehicle in such condition should ever be granted a certificate of roadworthiness (MOT). Do not believe everything you read on such certificates, because the theft of blank certificates and the forging or alteration of certificate details are by no means a rarity.*

former to rust through in record time.

If one sill has a jacking point (or two, in the case of the 1500cc Midget) and the other does not, then the second has been recently (and shoddily) applied. Expect great problems from any car which lacks one or more jacking points, because it will have been very poorly repaired. An outer sill without a jacking point is probably a poor quality panel, and the fact that the 'restorer' concerned could not be bothered to deal with the jacking point is a sure indicator that he or she was a real bodger. Sill replacement on a Spridget is not too difficult or troublesome a job, (Grade One on our scale) although rotten sills both indicate and can hide further problems which are both difficult and troublesome to deal with. One such example is the lower seat belt mounting, which passes through the inner sill. If the mounting is rotten, then (in the UK) the MOT tester can easily pull it out. Worse, you could pull it out (with terminal consequences) in the event of a front-end collision! From inside the car, lift the carpets (they may be glued, in which case you can peel away one corner) and examine the centre cross member. If one section of this essential component is rotten (Grade One/Two repair) then the rot in the pressing is probably extensive and will have spread to the floorpan. (Grade Two repair).

Remove (if the vendor will permit this) one or both footwell side trim panels. The underlying metal performs a role in maintaining the rigidity of the body, although it is arguably not quite so important as the main chassis rail members. Rot along the lower edge is quite common, but quite easily dealt with (Grade One), but with the cover panels off, you will be able to see just how bad the inner sills are, as well as

ABOVE LEFT *This is what can happen if you give the rear end of a sill a gentle tug! The lower edge of the rear wing adjacent to the sill has rot to match.*

LEFT *Tug a little harder at a really rotten sill, and this is the result. Inside was a mass of large rust flakes, which had all dropped off the insides of the inner and outer sill, weakening them to the point at which the 'A' and 'B' posts are effectively detached and capable of moving independently of each other. Jack this car up in the middle and the door gaps will widen before your very eyes. It is not unknown for an open car with rotten sills to flex so much that the steering wheel moves towards and away from the driver on braking and acceleration respectively!*

TOP *Remove the footwell side panel covers if the vendor will allow, because they could be hiding the likes of this not untypical example of a bodge. Rather than rebuild the rotten footwell side panel and inner sill, someone has crudely tacked over a thick sheet of steel. The author has seen many similar 'repairs' which have been carried out by back-street 'body repairers'.*

ABOVE *Although the top edge of the steel sheet has not rotted, the area adjacent to the rotten inner sill and footwell side panel soon gives way under the merest pressure to reveal advanced rot; this is what happens when new metal is welded over rotten metal. If you discover this sort of bodge on a car you are viewing then expect any other work which has been carried out to be of a similarly abysmal standard.*

RIGHT *Check the rear edge of the boot floor, the metal surrounding all brackets and the side quarters. If a small hole like this opens up easily then expect the rot to be widespread.*

ABOVE LEFT AND LEFT *The areas around the lights and any other chrome trim are favourites for bodged repairs in an attempt to deal with rusting. Use the magnet to reveal GRP and body filler. Removing (if the vendor allows) the carpets from the rear parcel shelf and heelboard might reveal apparently limited areas of body rot. Do not be deceived, because if the top of the heelboard assembly and the front end of the rear chassis rail are rotten, then the important heelboard area is almost certain to be in need of rebuilding. Rebuilding the heelboard assembly entails cutting away so many surrounding panels that you may as well call the job by its real name – 'complete body restoration'.*

the floor edge. You will also be able to see the results of shoddy 'repair' work, such as welding heavy gauge steel plate over a hole in the inner sill. Move the seats as far forwards as they can travel, then (where applicable) hinge the seat backs towards the front of the car. The heel board will normally be covered with carpet, as will the 'parcel shelf' panel to the top and rear of it. Remove the carpets. If the heelboard carpet is glued into position then peel back the four corners. In the lower corners lie the spring mounting box assemblies. The strength of these is vital, because they house the front end of the rear spring on all Spridgets excepting the Frogeye, Mark One Midget and Mark Two Sprite, in which cases they house the thick end of quarter elliptic springs. The state of the floorpans surrounding the spring mounting box assemblies is also of great importance, so poke quite vigourously with a screwdriver to test for rot. Repairs to this area can be very difficult, especially if the majority of metal seems to be badly rotted. The repair will entail some very careful measuring in order to get the spring mounting box assembly precisely placed, and this repair is Grade Two, bordering on

Grade Three. At each side of the parcel shelf run the rear chassis rails, more properly referred to as inner wing to boot floor reinforcers. These will not normally be extensively rotten but localised rot at the front ends and rot on the underside (for which repair panels are available) is very common and would rate a Grade Two on the scale of difficulties.

From within the boot, examine the chassis rails and the reinforced areas which form the tops of the rear spring mounting brackets on all cars with semi-elliptical springs. Poke around the rear and sides of the boot floor to check for rot. This may be patch repaired (Grade One work) or replaced (Grade Two). The final section of the 'skeleton' of the car to check is the front chassis rail assembly. This requires inspection from underneath the car, which in turn requires that the car is raised.

If your inspection to date has disclosed that the sills, floor, cross member and rear spring mounting box assembly are all rotten, then bear in mind A. that repairs will be extensive and expensive based on what you already know about the car, B. that jacking up such a weak car carries the threat of distorting the

ABOVE *Rot such as this is all too apparent, but don't take it at face value. Behind every rotten sill lies rotten innards, as proved to be the case here. Although the bottom edge of the front wing looks passable, it proved to be quite badly rotted.*

LEFT *If you can remove the door aperture edge trim, it will enable you to see both how many thicknesses of metal there are in the sill top welds and the method of welding used to join them. There should be two thicknesses, and they should be spot welded. Three layers as shown could indicate either that a new outer sill has been tacked onto the edge of the previous one (which was cut away) or that it has been tacked onto the edge of a hammered-in predecessor. Both indicate shoddy workshop practice because a. any remaining rusted metalwork underneath the new sill will rot away in double quick time and b. it is foolish to weld on a new outer sill but to leave the old inner sill (which is bound to be rusted if not rotten) intact.*

body and C. that the author would be very reluctant to climb underneath such a car for fear that it could disintegrate!

Chock the rear wheels (handbrake on and in gear) then raise the front end and support it on solid axle stands which themselves must be on a solid, crumble-free surface. Armed with some form of eye protection (loose rust flakes falling into your eyes can have serious consequences), a torch and an old screwdriver to poke into suspect metal, get under the car and examine the chassis rail/suspension assembly. If any rot is discovered here, get out from underneath the car immediately. Check whether the two chassis rails appear straight and parallel, if not, then the car has been involved in a hefty front-end

collision and will require straightening (preferably on a jig) and may have weaknesses elsewhere which can not be seen. The work will be undoubtedly of Grade Three calibre, and would be so expensive that the car would best be considered as a candidate for re-shelling. Do not confuse the slight upwards bend which can be seen in the chassis legs with collision damage – they are supposed to be like this. If rot is found in the front chassis assembly then other parts of the car will be far worse, so double check for rot and for bodged repairs.

A Spridget with any of the faults listed above (excepting a straightforwards case of surface rusted – not rotten – sills) should not be used on the road until such time as all necessary repair work has been

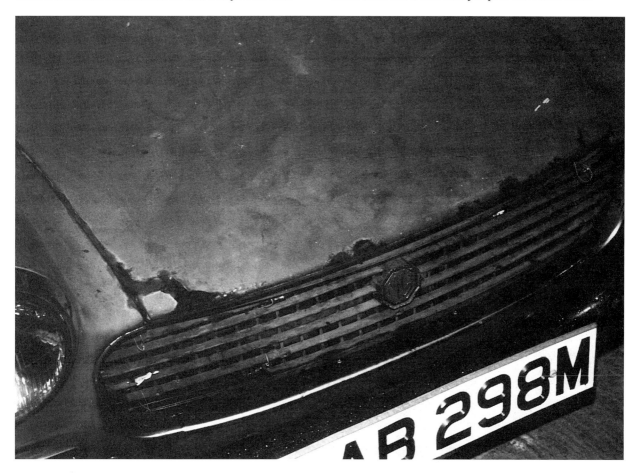

A rotted bonnet leading edge is expensive (if the whole bonnet is replaced) or extremely difficult (if a repair panel is used) to deal with. Little wonder that many apparently sound bonnets will be found on closer examination to consist largely of GRP. Check for this with a magnet. A complete GRP front end (wings and

bonnet, which hinge up together rather like the bonnet assembly of a Frogeye) costs roughly the same as a new steel bonnet, which explains their popularity on older Spridgets. There is nothing actually wrong with GRP front ends, although purists will usually replace them with steel.

Looking for body filler. A. Rear wing top fillet. B. Valance, areas around lights. C. Lower front wing. D. Bottom of A post. E. Bottom of door. F. Rear wing bottom. G. Rear wing bottom. H. Around tail lights, boot inner edge.

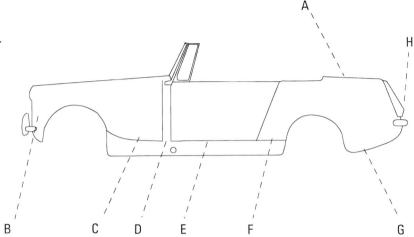

Behind this footwell front panel (or toe board) lives another panel inside the car, creating a box section which naturally rusts from the inside-out. Have a good probe with an old screwdriver blade if the wheelarch area has been freshly undersealed.

carried out.

Secondary in importance to the panels and pressings already listed are the more cosmetically important panels such as the valances, wings and doors. The front wings merely bolt on and off, so the only consequence of their condition is a replacement bill. If just the lower rear edges are rotten, then repair panels are available and although easy to fit (Grade One) they are difficult to fit so that they do not show (Grade Two).

The doors rot badly at their bases and also along the trailing edge and at any point where the body or skin of the door is breached by a fitting such as a screw. Repairs to the door frame are not too difficult, bordering on Grade Two, and door skinning is to be considered a Grade One task in terms of difficulty. If the door rot is extensive, though, bear in mind that replacements, although available, are not cheap. The lower halves of the rear wings rot badly, and are usually 'treated' to large doses of body filler as a

Check the lower front end of the rear wing for body filler (using a magnet) if no rust is to be found; this is a favourite area for bodging and, although it is not in itself structurally important, it covers some extremely important metal which might well be rotted.
A degree of light surface rust here is acceptable, though rot is most certainly not.

Expect the bottoms of the door skins to have some rusting; this in itself is no great problem because doors can be re-skinned. If the frame underneath is also rotten, the repair becomes far more complicated.

41

consequence. Use the magnet to reveal this.

The top edges of the rear wings present special problems, because they are internally spot welded onto the boot lid surround (rear shroud panel) seam and also incorporate a fillet between the two. Rust here can entail cutting away the entire rear wing along a line next to the fillet, drilling out the spot welds and parting the remainder, then cleaning up the remaining metal and welding on a new wing from the inside of the boot, something which is not too physically difficult but which can be at best unpleasant and at worst dangerous due to the danger of welding fires and the fumes given off by MIG welders. This repair qualifies as a Grade Two. The A posts are very prone to rust and, on cars with advanced body rot, can become so weak that the hinges all but part company. Open each door and (not too vigourously) pull it upwards and downwards to reveal weakness in the hinge assembly. Repair sections are available, and fitting them borders Grades One and Two. The A post covers are very prone to rot but are not too difficult to replace. As you examine the bodywork, list those panels which require attention. If you intend to restore the body yourself, add up the cost of necessary panels and add that to any other component replacement costs which become apparent when you assess other aspects of the car. This will help to prevent you from inadvertently buying a car whose restoration costs are bound to exceed its resultant value. If you are having the restoration carried out professionally, show your list of problems to the restorer and ask his opinion of the likely costs. If the car is really bad then the restorer may be able to himself find you a better one. If you are looking for a car to use immediately and the viewed car shows any of the chassis/sill/spring box problems listed above, then forget it!

Frogeye

When assessing a Frogeye Sprite, there are other considerations of great importance. First amongst these is the state of the bonnet. At the time of writing, a new Frogeye bonnet assembly in steel will cost around 70% of the price of a complete Heritage bodyshell. An alternative assembly made from GRP will cost around 6% of the price of the steel assembly – it is little wonder that many people fit GRP bonnets to old Frogeyes! If you view a Frogeye with an unsalvageable bonnet then the cost of replacing the

RIGHT *It pays to closely examine areas such as the rear wing fillets and the surrounding metal. Although rust holes may be small, they can be very difficult to deal with properly.*

FAR RIGHT *The only way to find rusting like this is to remove the rear lights; this is of course impractical, and you will have to judge many such areas by the condition of the rest of the bodywork.*

BELOW RIGHT *A goodly thickness of body filler had previously disguised the advanced rot in this nearside A post outer cover. Be sure to check this area using a magnet to reveal such cover-ups.*

bonnet should greatly influence the price which you are prepared to pay. If you view a Frogeye fitted with a GRP bonnet assembly then take this into consideration when making an offer for the car. Other Frogeye panels are also generally more expensive than the equivalent panels for later Spridgets (though not so spectacularly as the bonnet assembly). Because of this, many Frogeyes will have been fitted with various GRP panels. These all reduce the likely value of the car and, in many people's minds, they also reduce its desirability. Bodywork restoration on the Frogeye is likely to be rather more difficult than on later Spridgets, because the repair panels commercially available may not be so accurately manufactured as the Heritage panels now available for other Spridgets.

ALL SPRIDGETS

Look along outer body panels, with your eye positioned two or three inches from the surface. If you see rivelling, then you may be looking at poorly corrected accident damage, or at a poor quality repair. Check the affected panels with a magnet to test for bodyfiller and GRP repair. Take a look inside the boot lid, using a torch if necessary. You might be surprised to discover that areas inside are of a different colour to the rest of the car, indicating that the car has for some reason been resprayed in a different colour. It seems to the author that many people who have their Spridgets resprayed (especially later Midgets) opt to have them resprayed in red – which is not always appropriate to the year. There is a chance that the change of colour has a more

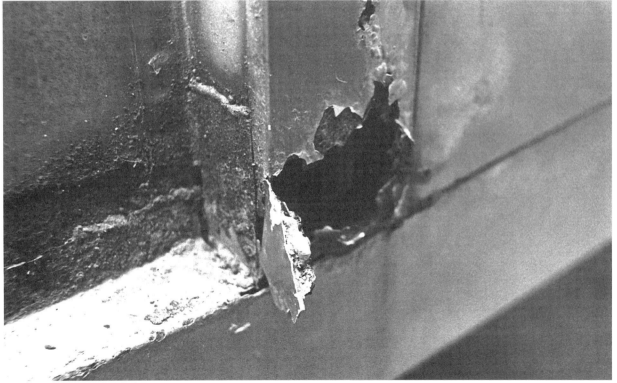

sinister reason, so be extra careful to establish the car's credentials. Look at the suspension, petrol tank and within the wheel arches for signs of overspray. This could indicate that the car has been hastily smartened up for sale, or it could indicate a 'quickie' repair to a major problem, such as bodyrot or accident damage. The purchaser will have to discover which.

Look for fresh patches of underseal within the wheelarches or underneath the car, which could indicate a recent repair or a cover-up of uncured bodyrot. Check that the paint colour is the same all over the car, and that the paint all shows the same signs of ageing. If you find that some of the paintwork is dull, but other areas are shiny, then the car has obviously received bodywork attention, and the reason should be investigated.

On rubber bumper Midgets, pay especial attention to the two rails which run either side of the engine bay. If one of these shows the slightest rivelling, then the car has probably been involved in a heavy frontal or side collision. The author was called upon to investigate a Midget which had one normal front wheel, and one with negative camber (it sloped inwards at the top). The rail referred to had cracked paintwork and slight rivelling and, coupled to the fact that the front wing had been resprayed (the engine bay side channel/wing bolt heads were sprayed, whereas on the other side they were not), this pointed to a heavy side collision which had somehow pushed the damper mounting assembly inwards fractionally. Further investigation revealed the presence of overspray on one or two components within the engine bay.

Had the author been viewing this car alone with

ABOVE LEFT *Taken part-way through the restoration, this photograph does show just how weak a Spridget can get. The centre section of the sill assembly simply pulled away from the floor by hand!*

LEFT *The two banes of the Frogeye restorer's life; the one piece bonnet/front wing assembly and the rear end of the car. Both are available as one-piece GRP mouldings and, because these cost but a fraction of the price of steel panels, many Frogeyes will nowadays sport them. There is nothing wrong with GRP panels so far as their strength is concerned, although a car with these will fetch rather less than a car in the same general condition which is panelled in steel throughout.*

a view to buying it then he would probably not have noticed the damage. This is why it is so important to have a companion at such times; whilst the main appraiser is busy going through the motions and checking on the usual problem areas, the second person can take a detached view and often find such problems. Check the bonnet front edge for rust (expensive to replace or difficult to repair), and the boot lid for rusting around the lip.

MECHANICAL/ELECTRICAL ASSESSMENT

The entire Spridget range is so well served with low cost mechanical and other spares, and the cars are so easy to work on, that the financial consequences of mechanical problems are relatively insignificant in comparison with those of bodywork faults. This does not mean, however, that mechanical or electrical faults are to be taken lightly, because the consequences of such faults can leave car and occupants in danger. For instance, if the lights were to suddenly fail when the car was travelling on an unlit road at speed the consequences could be terminal for car and passengers – if the braking system were to fail the results could be the same. The importance which you attach to the mechanical aspects of a car will to a large degree depend on what you want of the car. Those who seek a car for a complete restoration might well accept faults which the person who wants the car to use on the road immediately would find unacceptable. When appraising cars, be sure to have a spares price list with you. This will allow you to quickly add up the costs of rectifying various mechanical and other faults.

Begin with an external examination of the engine and its compartment. It should be fairly clean on a well-maintained example, and the oil filter and distributor cap should be rather cleaner than the rest (indicating regular maintenance). If oil is to be seen anywhere on the engine then the source of the leak should be established, and the likely rectification costs taken into account. If the entire engine bay is very clean, then the chances are that it has recently been steam cleaned, and it will be essential that you again inspect for oil leaks following the test run. Also, examine the ground underneath the engine for signs of oil leaks. If oil is found and the vendor insists that the oil came from another car, then slip a piece of card over the existing oil to see whether oil leaks during the inspection period. Because few vendors would wish you to view their cars parked over oil-stained ground (most will move them to clean areas before the viewing), it is as well to check the ground under the engine bay after the engine has been running for some minutes, just to be sure that oil is not being lost.

Remove the oil filler cap and look to see whether there are any signs of water in the oil within the rocker box cover (the mixture emulsifies), and also remove the dipstick and check for correct oil level and for the presence of water. If there is water in the oil, this could indicate a blown cylinder head gasket (a minor problem) or a cracked cylinder head or block (expensive). If the engine is run or if it has run with water in the oil then expect to find serious problems inside the engine.

Examine the wiring within the engine bay. Look for cuts, splits, abrasion, perishing or signs of scorching of the insulation on all visible wiring. If serious insulation damage is found, then bear in mind that a new loom is expensive and rather a chore to fit. Any sign of scorching or burning of the insulation is to be taken very seriously indeed, and unless a thoroughly convincing explanation is found from the vendor, anticipate that wiring within the loom will also be damaged, so that the loom ideally needs replacing. Look for any lengths of non-standard wire, both wires contained within the wiring diagram (the actual colour must match that within the wiring diagram) and extra wires. Extra wiring indicates the presence of an extra accessory; check that the new circuit is properly fused and powered from an appropriate source.

Check the battery for signs of leakage and to ensure that it is properly held and unable to move whist the car is under way. Check the non-earthed battery terminal insulation.

Examine the state of the various hoses and pipes, which are within the cooling system and the fuel delivery system. A perished water hose could fail at any time and should be replaced; a cut, abraded or rotting fuel line could fail and spray neat fuel over the hot exhaust manifold with obvious results, and *must* be replaced before the engine is run. Examine the state of all visible screw and bolt heads and nuts. If these are damaged, then the car has been worked upon by someone who did not possess the appropriate tools, or who possessed very low quality tools. In

either case, the state of the interior of the engine will reflect the standard of work shown by this check. If, for instance, the valve clearances have been set using poor quality tools then the slots in the tops of the adjusters will probably have opened up and it will be very difficult to accurately set the clearances unless the adjusters are firstly replaced.

Check the levels of clutch/brake fluid in the master cylinders, and look for the (fairly obvious) signs of leakage or spillage on the surrounding paintwork. Low fluid levels obviously warn of possible leakage, but also indicate poor maintenance.

Remove the radiator cap and check that the coolant level is correct. If it is low then losses could occur from a hose, a connector or from the radiator (the latter expensive to rectify) or, more seriously, from a blown cylinder head gasket or cracked cylinder head or block. If the level is acceptable, check that there is no oil in the coolant, indicating a blown cylinder head gasket, cracked cylinder head or cracked block. If the coolant can be seen to be plain water, then the lack of anti-freeze should be taken seriously. At best, lack of anti-freeze shows lamentably poor maintenance; worse, it could indicate that work has recently been carried out on the engine or cooling system, and that the owner could not even be bothered to replace anti-freeze; at worst, in cold weather the coolant could have frozen and cracked the block.

Check that the engine is cold. If the car usually proves difficult to get started, then a vendor will normally warm it up prior to your arrival – if so, let it cool before trying to start the engine. Start the engine yourself, but do firstly ask the vendor how much choke the car likes, to be fair to him or her. As the engine fires up be ready to look and listen. Look through the rear view mirror for a cloud of either blue smoke (oil seepage past the valve stems) or steam (cracked cylinder head or blown cylinder head gasket) from the exhaust. Listen for untoward starter motor noises which can highlight problems with the starter dog (easily repaired, although problems might also lie with the ring gear) or the ring gear (engine out repair), and as the engine fires up but before the oil pressure has time to develop, a deep rumbling noise which tells you that the big end bearings are on the way out. Watch the oil pressure. On fast tickover just after starting up, you should see 50 psi or more registered, settling down to perhaps 40 psi on normal tickover when the engine has warmed.

When the engine has reached normal operating

temperature, switch off and wait until pressure in the top hose has dropped (squeeze this to feel for pressure). When no pressure remains, remove the radiator cap and check that the coolant is A. still there and B. still free of oil. If the coolant has disappeared from sight, then obviously it was topped up for your benefit and there is either an internal or external leak. If no external leak can be found then coolant is being lost internally, probably through a faulty cylinder head gasket or a crack in the head or block.

Climb back into the driver's seat. Holding the steering wheel firmly, try to pull and push it. Any movement reveals problems with the steering column. Attempt to lift and lower the steering wheel, which will highlight any problems with the column mountings. Turn the wheel and note how much movement there is before the front wheels begin to turn. If there is more than 1″ at the circumference, then the car will fail the UK MOT test because there is far too much play in the steering system, usually within the steering rack, although other faults could be to blame and these will be tested for in the next part of the examination. Press the brake pedal and hold it down. If it feels spongy then there is air in the hydraulic system, which will need overhauling. If the brake pedal slowly sinks to the toeboard, then there is probably a fault with the master cylinder.

Grab the brake then the clutch pedals, and feel for excessive side play. This is not too serious and indicates worn bushes. Check the amount of travel of both brake and clutch pedals.

Before setting off on a road test, the author prefers for his own peace of mind to check that all is well with the suspension and braking systems. The alternative is to opt for the road test first, during which problems might come to light which lead you to turn the car down before you have to crawl underneath it and get yourself dirty. The alternative is to set out on a test drive and discover the faults on the road, which is not a good idea. Whichever you choose is up to you.

Engage the handbrake, chock the rear wheels, raise the front of the car and support it on axle stands.

Check the tyres for cuts, abrasions and bulges. Grip each front wheel in turn top and bottom, and try to rock the wheel whilst listening and feeling for wheel bearing play, loose wires (wire wheel cars only), or wear in the kingpin assembly. If you hear knocking noises as you carry out either of these checks, then the cause should be traced, and could include something as simple as loose damper bolts.

Gripping the sides of the wheel, turn the steering from lock to lock. Listen for roughness and feel for stiffness in the steering rack. Spin the wheel and listen for bearing roughness. If the wheel will not spin freely, then the brakes are binding badly. Whether drum or disc brakes are fitted, rectification can be expensive. Try turning the brake adjusters (front drum brakes only) to check for maladjustment or seizure of the adjusters. With disc brakes, binding means that a piston caliper is seized, necessitating either an expensive reconditioned unit or a far from easy DIY repair. Check the thickness of the material on the brake pads, if this is allowed to wear too low, the backing metal will come into contact with the discs and score them, necessitating replacement. Visually, check the brake pipes for damage, and also the earth strap.

Lower the front end of the car to the ground, move the chocks to the front wheels, disengage the handbrake and place the car in neutral. Raise the rear of the car and support it on axle stands. Check the rear tyres for damage. Apply the handbrake and see whether either wheel can be turned by hand under the maximum force you can exert – if one will turn then suspect brake fluid contamination or badly worn brake shoes, although the problem could turn out to be maladjustment. Using the correct tool, try turning the brake adjusters (which can reveal maladjusted brakes).

If the stud refuses to turn at all then freeing it will usually entail removal of the backplate. If wire wheels are fitted, try to determine whether the outside of the wheel turns before the hub, in which case the wires are loose.

Check the brake backplate for oil or brake fluid leakage, and the brake pipes for damage. Whilst under the car, check the fuel tank for dark stains which reveal leakage, check the fuel line for damage and check the security of the exhaust mountings. If no serious safety-related faults are apparent, then it is time to road test the car.

ROAD TEST

Firstly, ensure that both you and the car are road legal, and if not, check that the vendor (who will of course have to drive) possesses appropriate insurance and that the car is taxed. If you are caught by the Police in a car which is not road legal (even as the passenger during a road test) then you are technically aiding and abetting in the offence, and liable to prosecution. The author and publishers can accept no responsibility for the consequences of any advice given in this section. It is up to the reader to reconcile the advice with local conditions and laws, and to ensure that all actions are taken with due attention to safety and, if they cannot be undertaken in safety then do not attempt them. Always check that the road ahead and behind is clear before attempting any manoeuvre, and if any problem with the suspension, brakes or roadholding manifests itself then discontinue the test immediately.

Drive gently as the car comes to normal operating temperatures, and during this period, gently assess the braking system and the car's roadholding. If either are suspect, then proceed only at slow speed or terminate the test if you feel that the car is unsafe. With the engine thoroughly warmed, slow down in top gear to 20mph and then accelerate, listening for pinking, which could indicate maladjusted timing or air induction. If left unattended, pinking will eventually wreck the engine.

In all gears, accelerate and decelerate hard, checking to see whether the car jumps out of gear (gearbox rebuild). Listen for knocks in the transmission, which could be either worn universal joints or problems within the axle. If the gearbox seems noisy then this is not in itself necessarily a fault, and many people drive cars with noisy gearboxes for thousands of miles – it just depends on whether you can put up with the noise! However, some gearbox noises could have serious consequences, and any noise other than a whine probably indicates that a gearbox rebuild will be needed before long.

If the rear end of the car veers left or right during hard acceleration or deceleration, then the axle is loose. As you change gear, particularly towards the top end of the revolutions range, check that the synchromesh is functioning correctly (gearbox rebuild). From 20mph or so, gently apply the handbrake (keep your thumb on the button and only engage the handbrake for a second or so) and note whether the car veers, which indicates maladjusted or perhaps contaminated rear brakes. When you use the footbrake also, note whether the car veers to one side. If all seems well with the braking system, increase speed to normal road speed. Does the car appear to 'float'? If so, then the dampers are in need of

replacement. This will have an adverse effect on roadholding, so do not drive at speed, especially around corners.

If the car appears to lose poise (either end tends to twitch or jump to one side) when being driven over a bump or hole in the road, then faulty dampers or some other aspect of the suspension could be to blame, but there is also a strong possibility that the car body is out of alignment following unjigged crash repair. Unless the fault can be proven to lie with a specific area of the suspension, and this can be corrected and the car re-tested – DO NOT BUY THE CAR. A Spridget with a bent body is nowadays best considered only as a re-shelling candidate. Stop off the public highway. Engage the handbrake.

Place the car in second gear and slowly release the clutch pedal, pressing it in again the moment that the engine starts to labour. If the engine does not labour then the clutch is slipping; if the car begins to creep forwards then the handbrake is not efficient. If you encounter a hill during your test, try climbing it with a very light throttle setting. If the engine protests and splutters or coughs then the chances are that the mixture is too lean, which can cause (or which may have already caused) engine damage over a period of time. When you return from the road test, re-check for external engine, gearbox and axle oil leaks, and re-check the oil and coolant for correct level and contamination.

Super Quick Check List

These first checks are intended to quickly rule out the very worst examples of bodily damaged, badly restored or rotten cars. The only economic way to deal with such cars could be to re-shell them.

1   Door gaps both sides of car. If the gaps are not even then the door hinges could have moved in a rotten A post, so check this by partially opening each door and lifting its rear edge – if it will lift much then the chances are that the lower hinge mounting in the A post is rotten; alternatively, the body could be sagging or otherwise distorted. Measure the two door gaps both top and bottom – differences between the two sides indicate a distorted body.

2   Check visually that the tops of the doors are level. If the tops of the doors appear out of alignment, then an A post may be rotten (re-try previous check); alternatively, one side of the body could be distorted. This can be proved by checking the level across the

tops of the B posts with a spirit level and straight edge (hood frame removed) and comparing this with the level of the front chassis rails. See Chapter 5 for details of checking these important levels.

3   Wheels within wheelarches. Check that the relative positions of wheels within their wheelarches are the same on both sides of the car (steering straight ahead for front wheels). If not, the difference could be due to poorly fitted external panels, or to movement of the suspension and hence the main chassis sections of the body.

4   Wheel camber (front wheels). Both wheels should be in the same plane. If one is angled in or out top or bottom, then crash damage has probably distorted the ladder chassis and so moved the damper mounting.

5   Sills. Both sills should have jacking point holes (two per sill on 1500cc Midgets). Absence shows use of shoddy repair panels and shoddy attitude by repairer. Tug sharply on both lower seat belt straps; these are fitted to the inner sill and can be pulled out from rotten inner sill members.

6   Heelboard/rear side chassis rail. Lift carpet from parcel shelf ends and check condition of tops of spring hanger assembly. If rot is discovered then expect worse rot in the vital lower section of the hanger assembly.

7   Paintwork. Check for patches of new paint and for signs of overspray (paint on mechanical or other components). This could indicate a hasty and perhaps shoddy or unsafe 'repair' to bring the car to saleable condition. An explanation should be sought from the vendor – if this is not entirely convincing, then the area in question must be checked thoroughly.

8   IF IN DOUBT THAT THE BODY IS TRUE: Either reject the car (unless you intend to re-shell it) or obtain a straight edge and spirit level and carry out the alignment checks detailed in Chapter 5 – Bodywork restoration. These should show up a twisted shell, the mark of an unroadworthy car which is to be avoided at all costs.

General Checklist – Bodywork

These checks are in addition to those in the super-quick list, and are intended to weed out cars which are basically straight but which require or will shortly require expensive bodywork repair. Check all visible panels for rivelling (sight along panel with eye 3″ from surface), paint blemishes (which could mean taking the area concerned or the entire body back to clean metal and respraying if the paint was contaminated when it was applied) and use of GRP/bodyfiller (a magnet will reveal this). Areas for special attention are as follows:

1   Sills. Check the ends, the underside and (as far as possible) the tops of the insides.

2   Rear wings. Check the lower front portion (adjacent to the sill), the lower rear portion and the area by the fillet along the top.

3   Front wings. Check the gap between the wing and the sill (an uneven gap indicates poor fitting of the wing or possibly the outer sill). Check the areas around the lights and the lower and rear edges.

4   Doors. Check the bottoms and lower skin.

5   Bonnet. Check the front end.

6   Seat belt mountings. Pull on the lower strap of each seat belt as hard as you can. If the mounting can be moved then this reveals rotten inner sills.

7   Seats. Sit in each seat, hold the sides and try to rock it side to side/front and back. Check that both seats move freely in their mounting rails. If the seats fail these tests, then the floorpan is weak.

8   Top shroud/A post outer covers. Check the top shroud and the A post covers with a magnet to reveal GRP/filler.

9   Boot. Check the rear side chassis rails (boot floor to wheelarch strengthener). Bounce rear of car and look for any flexing of the boot floor in the vicinity of the rear spring mounting points. Check along rear edge and side pockets of boot floor for GRP/filler.

10   Under bonnet. Visually check alignment of the ladder chassis members (it would have to be very bad to be visible), but concentrate on looking for any signs of rivelling in the sides or tops of the two main rails, which can reveal previous heavy side impact. Check the footwell assembly panels for rusting, especially the top panel on which the brake and clutch cylinders are mounted. Check the battery/heater platform assembly. Battery acid can attack the top surface of the assembly, and if water is allowed to lie undisturbed inside the air intake assembly then rust will sooner or later result.

GETTING SERIOUS

If the car has passed all of the checks already listed, then it is time to don overalls and closely examine the underside.

1   Rear spring hanger assemblies. The heelboard sandwich which surrounds the heavy gauge rear spring hanger assembly rots unseen both from the inside, and from the outside if the underseal and paint covering is breached. The inner heelboard is usually covered by carpet; remove this if possible and check the metalwork underneath for rot. From under the car it is possible to prod the outer heelboard end with a sharp implement to also reveal rot.

2   Front ladder chassis. The closing panels on the underside of this assembly rot, and the panel under the main forwards crossmember (under the engine) also gets damaged when it is used for jacking up the car. Check all with a sharp implement.

3   Floorpan. Originally a single pressing, this is usually repaired with half panels which cover one side of the car. Lift the edges of carpets and prod the metal with a sharp implement to reveal rot, especially near the four edges adjacent to the sill, transmission tunnel, toeboard and heelboard.

4   Rear chassis rails/wheelarch. Prod a sharp implement into the sides and base of the rails from within the wheelarch to reveal rot. Treat the top inner seam and edges of the wheelarch in the same way.

5   Boot floor. From under car, prod the boot floor edges with a sharp implement to reveal rot.

General Check List – Mechanical

The first set of checks will reveal unroadworthy cars, which are not safe to be driven until mechanical rectification work has been carried out. It therefore follows that such cars should not be road-tested.

1   Brakes. Press the brake pedal and hold it down. If the pedal slowly sinks to the floor then the master cylinder is probably in need of replacement. If the pedal feels soft and spongy then there is air in the system. This could merely need bleeding, although a component could be faulty and have allowed the air to enter.

Engage the handbrake. Start the engine and place the car in second gear, then slowly release the clutch until the engine begins to labour – immediately push the clutch pedal back in. If the car crept forwards then the handbrake is faulty, contaminated or maladjusted. Test the footbrake in the same manner. Examine all visible brake pipes for leakage or signs of damage.

2   Suspension. Bounce each corner of the suspension. The body should rise and then fall back to its normal position. If it bounces up and down a second time, the dampers are faulty. This can reduce roadholding to dangerously poor levels.

3   Lights/Electrical. Check that all lights (including indicators) function. Check windscreen wipers for correct operation.

4   Fuel. Check for smell of petrol under bonnet, within boot and generally around car. If there is a strong smell of petrol then the cause should be established and rectified before the car is driven.

Main Mechanical Check List

Engine Check visually: state (clean, dirty, oily); general condition of hoses, electrics; state of coolant; oil level and condition; state of bolt heads, nuts and screw slots; cables; fan belt, fan blades; oil leaks; non-standard components.

Audible/Visual Checks; starter motor/ring gear noise; exhaust – blue smoke on starting; exhaust – steam on starting; top hose temperature rise; tappet noise; timing chain tinkle; bottom-end rumble; temperature; oil/coolant loss under car.

Electrics; batteries, levels, security, terminal insulation; main feed to solenoid; brown permanent live wires; under-dash wiring; all lights and equipment; fuses; uninsulated spade connectors; instrument originality.

Steering/Suspension/Brakes; Steering column; kingpins tightness/play; state of wishbone bushes; steering column universal joint play; steering rack wear/roughness; effectiveness of dampers; state of rear springs/fittings; state of tyres; handbrake effectiveness; front brakes effectiveness.

On The Road. Tendency to float or pull; steering self-correcting after bend; straight line acceleration/ hard deceleration; wheel wobble; oil pressure/ temperature gauges; gears – noise in, jumping out of, synchromesh; transmission clonks, whine; handbrake; footbrake; clutch; engine – pinking, spluttering, knocking.

3 · MAINTENANCE

The Spridget is without doubt one of the easiest of all cars to maintain properly. The mechanical components are simple, sturdy and long-lived; the ancillaries are usually user-repairable or alternatively new or exchange reconditioned replacements can be obtained easily and at low cost. Access to most of the components for servicing is better than on many cars.

Maintenance comprises a number of procedures which should be carried out at fixed intervals which are determined by the number of miles travelled since the last service or the amount of time which has lapsed since then. Most maintenance procedures are concerned with preventative measures to prolong the life of the car and its components, some are concerned with making adjustments to maintain good fuel economy, smooth running and so on; many are checks to ensure that certain components (particularly the brakes, fuel and electrical systems) are functioning perfectly for safety reasons.

The price of ignoring proper service routines is that the car can become less safe to drive due to decreased braking efficiency, insulation breakdown on electrical wires or fuel leaks. Furthermore, failure to check oil levels and to change both the oil and its filter, to check the ignition timing and carburation will shorten the useful working life of the engine. The same applies to other mechanical components if maintenance is skimped.

With an old car like the Spridget range there can be no hard and fast service intervals, because too much will depend on the condition of the individual car and the way and conditions in which it is driven. A car which lives in dusty, very hot or very wet conditions or a car which is driven hard will require attention on a much more frequent basis than a car which is kept in a garage and driven carefully. The service intervals given in this chapter are a general recommendation which should be taken as a minimum requirement for a car which is driven hard or in adverse conditions, and as having a margin of safety for cars which are driven gently.

The most frequent recommended service routines are concerned only with checking the efficiency of components and maintaining lubricant and other fluid levels. These are intended to give a framework which will ensure that potential problems are spotted at the earliest opportunity. A small, apparently insignificant problem, left unattended, can often quickly develop into a large and expensive to rectify problem. The most obvious illustration of this is when the oil level is allowed to fall to the point at which the big ends start knocking. Do not worry if you do not understand the terminology at this stage, for all will be made clear later in the book. Suffice to say for now that for the sake of topping up the oil, the engine has to be removed from the car and stripped down for an expensive repair.

For weekly and monthly services, little specialised equipment is needed. With each service interval, the list of necessary equipment grows a little. However, all of the tools and equipment necessary to carry out all servicing on a Spridget can be bought at a fraction of the cost of one year's servicing from many franchised garages, so the expenditure is easily justified. It is a great help to have a warm, dry and well illuminated place in which to work, although all servicing can be carried out in the open. Avoid carrying out work in the rain, because water can cause problems with the ignition and electrical systems. A strong concrete surface over which you can park the car, raise it on a jack and support its weight with axle stands is essential.

Whenever you drive

Every time you drive the car, listen to the engine (which makes a sweeter sound than that coming out of any car radio!) and try to detect whether there are any unusual noises. If any strange noises occur then investigate as soon as you can. If an oil pressure gauge is fitted, check it periodically (or otherwise check the low oil pressure warning light) and monitor the coolant temperature gauge. If the coolant temperature suddenly rises or the oil pressure drops then stop the car as soon as it is safe to do so and do not drive again until the problem has been identified and rectified. It does not take many miles to damage the engine of a car with low oil pressure or extra high coolant temperature. Try to detect any change in the 'feel' of the brake pedal. If the amount of travel alters or if it seems to be becoming soft or springy, then attend to the problem at the earliest opportunity. See chapter four.

WEEKLY

You will require a jack and axle stands. The trolley jack is far preferable to scissors, wind-up or bottle jacks, and the extra expenditure is well worth while (although if you cannot afford a trolley jack then the bottle jack is the next best choice). Axle stands are essential. A jack is a lifting device rather than a device intended to hold weights for any length of time and, if the car was to for whatever reason suddenly lower or fall to the ground with you underneath then you would be severely injured. Axle stands are widely available from motor factors.

You will also require an accurate tyre pressure gauge and some means of inflating tyres. Most people use a foot pump for inflating tyres and some of these have a built-in dial gauge, as do tyre inflation attachments for compressors. Use a separate gauge, as this will be far more accurate than the built-in dial gauges.

Certain consumables are necessary. Keep a gallon (or 5 litres) of good quality engine oil 'in stock'. Obtain distilled water, which you can either collect when you de-frost a refrigerator or buy from most garages and service stations. You will need a grease gun and general purpose lithium-based grease, both of which can be obtained from motor factors. A small pumping oil can and a selection of Imperial spanners, pliers and screwdrivers will be needed only if work is found to be necessary.

With the engine cold, check the engine oil level. The dipstick, which is situated on the left hand side of the engine when viewed from the front, has two lines scribed on it which show the maximum and minimum oil levels. If the oil level is low, remove the rocker box cover mounted oil filler cap and top up, taking care not to pour in too much oil in one go. Check the level again and top up further if necessary. Be careful not to over fill the sump with oil. If you do this then you will have to drain off the excess through a drain plug situated in the sump.

Again with the engine cold, remove the radiator cap and check the level of the coolant. If none is visible or if the level appears low, refill using a mixture of water and anti-freeze in the appropriate proportions for likely temperatures. These are 25% anti-freeze for temperatures down to -13 degrees C, 33% antifreeze for temperatures down to -19 degrees C and a 50/50 mixture for temperatures down to -36 degrees C.

Check the tyre pressures (including the spare tyre) and re-inflate them if necessary.

Check that no hydraulic fluid is leaking from the brake calipers, drums (early cars only) or the flexible hoses or their joints. Slacken the wheel nuts or spinners on the front wheels. The front end of the car must now be raised, and it is essential that the wheels which remain on the ground are unable to turn. This is achieved by using chocks; either purpose-made wedges or bricks are placed both in front of and behind the tyre. Chock the rear wheels, apply the hand brake (and place the car in gear, too, if you like) and raise the front of the car and support it on axle stands. Remove the front wheels, and check the tyre tread for depth and uneven wear. Check the tyre for damage and the walls for bulges. If the tyre has started to wear more on one side than the other then the tracking probably needs attention. This is best carried out by a professional garage business. If damage is apparent then the spare wheel should be fitted in place and the tyre taken to a specialist for repair or replacement as appropriate. Check that no hydraulic fluid is leaking from the brake calipers, drums (early cars only) or the flexible hoses. Re-fit the wheels, lower the car to the ground and finally tighten the wheel nuts or spinners. Chock the front wheels, slacken the rear wheel nuts or spinners, then raise the rear of the car and support it on axle stands. Repeat the previous checks.

Remove the caps from the clutch and brake master cylinder reservoirs and check the level of the clutch/brake fluid. Top up if necessary. If the level has dropped appreciably, then the cause should be investigated and the problem rectified at once, in the case of the brake fluid, before the car is driven on the road again. It is wise not to drive the car if a fluid leak is suspected from the clutch hydraulic system, because the fluid is highly inflammable, and if ignited by a hot exhaust system or a spark then a fierce fire will quickly ensue. The brake master cylinder is the larger of the two and situated on the offside.

Unscrew the black top from each carburettor and lift the dashpot piston damper out. There should be oil visible within ½″ of the top of the bell housing centre tube. If the level is low, then top it up with new SAE 20W/50 engine oil. Check the operation of all electrical accessories including, the lights, indicators, windscreen wipers and horn.

MONTHLY (OR EVERY 1000 MILES)

Carry out all of the checks and operations listed previously under weekly checks.

Remove the screw caps from the top of the battery and visually check the battery electrolyte level. This should be just above the plates. If low, top up with distilled water. If the level is very low, then one of the cells is leaking and the battery should be replaced and the battery platform thoroughly cleaned of the leaked electrolyte. If any of the plates are beginning to buckle, then the battery will begin to lose efficiency, and replacement will be inevitable, sooner or later.

The front end of the car must now be raised, and it is essential that the wheels which remain on the ground are unable to turn. This is achieved by using chocks; either purpose-made wedges or bricks are placed both in front of and behind each tyre. Firstly, slacken the wheel nuts or spinners. Chock the rear wheels, apply the hand brake (and place the car in gear, too, if you like) and raise the front of the car and support it on axle stands. Remove the roadwheels. Check the tyre tread for depth and uneven wear. Check the tyre for damage and the walls for bulges. If the tyre has started to wear more on one side than the other then the tracking probably needs attention (although such wear can be caused by improper inflation – under inflation causes rapid wear of the

outside of the tread, over inflation causes rapid wear of the centre section, and both adversely affect handling and roadholding). This is best carried out by a professional garage business. If damage is apparent then the spare wheel should be fitted in place and the tyre taken to a specialist for repair or replacement as appropriate. Check the brake calipers (disc brakes) or drum backing plates for brake fluid contamination. If fluid is found to have escaped, then the cause must be sought and the problem remedied before the car is used on the road. Visually check the dampers for fluid leakage, and the steering rack for oil loss and for splits in the gaiters. Replace the wheels, nuts or spinners (tighten them as far as possible), lower the car to the ground and finally tighten the nuts or spinners.

Chock the front wheels, take the car out of gear and disengage the handbrake. Slacken the rear wheel nuts or spinners. Raise the rear of the car and rest it on axle stands. Remove the road wheels. Check the rear tyres for bulges, cuts, abrasions and to ensure that they have nothing sticking into them, such as a sharp stone or nail. Check the brake backplates for any signs of contamination, and the brake hoses for leakage. Visually check the rear dampers for fluid leakage. If the handbrake operation is suspect, take the opportunity to adjust this (see Chapter 4). Replace the wheels, nuts or spinners, lower the car to the ground and finally tighten the nuts or spinners.

With the car back on its roadwheels, grasp the steering wheel and see by how much the perimeter is able to turn before the front wheels respond. If there appears too much play then the rack should be attended to at the earliest opportunity (see Chapter 4).

Check the fan belt deflection. If the belt is too slack, slacken the nuts which secure the dynamo/alternator, tension the belt (use a lever acting against the dynamo or alternator) and tighten the nuts.

Check all fuel lines for signs of leakage. Check that the seat belt mountings are solid by tugging sharply on the belt straps. Check the condition of the windscreen wiper blades, and renew if necessary.

EVERY 6 MONTHS

Carry out all of the checks listed previously. Change the oil and filter – never one without the other. The engine should either be cold and not have run for several hours so that the oil has plenty of time to

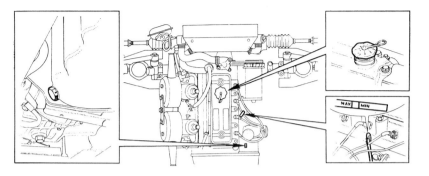

LEFT *Draining and refilling the engine oil. (Courtesy Autodata)*

BELOW LEFT *The renewable element oil filter assembly. (Courtesy Autodata)*

BELOW *The oil filter cartridge of the 1500 Midget. (Courtesy Autodata)*

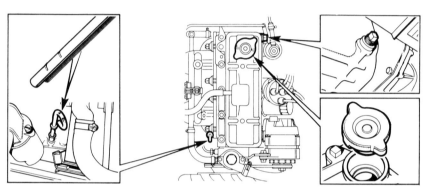

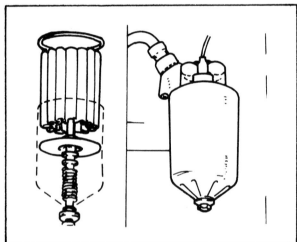

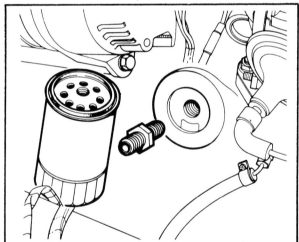

drain down to the sump, or it should be warmed to thin the oil and so help it to drain more effectively. Do NOT try this with the engine hot – the oil will cause burns if it touches your skin! You will need a receptacle for the old engine oil, and a five litre oil can with one side cut away is ideal, although you can obtain specialised containers for the purpose if preferred. Place the receptacle under the sump drain plug (it may be necessary to raise the front of the car slightly for this, undo the plug, then remove the oil filler cap allowing thc oil to drain. This will take quite

some time, so allow fifteen minutes or more in order to let as much as possible drain. While this is happening, you can get on with changing the oil filter.

Earlier cars are fitted with cannisters which contain replaceable oil filter elements. The cannisters are held by a single bolt, undo this, and lower the cannister, taking care not to spill the oil contained within. Discard the old element and wash out the cannister with neat petrol. Replace the sealing rings (new rings come with the filter element), replace the filter element, part-fill the cannister with new engine oil and replace the unit. On the 1500cc Midget the oil filter is of the cartridge type, and replacement is rather easier. Use a strap wrench if necessary (these are available at any Motor Factor's, although you might get away with simply wrapping a piece of old inner tube around the filter to gain extra purchase) and undo the old filter. Be sure to place a little oil on the sealing ring of the new filter before fitting it.

Disconnect the earthed terminal of the battery. Pull the spark plug leads from the plugs, and remove the distributor cap by pressing simultaneously on the two spring clips and lifting the cap away. Pull the main coil lead from the coil, and lift the distributor cap and leads complete out of the engine bay. Remove the sparking plugs, and note the condition of the ends, which should be light fawn/grey in colour. If the plugs are an oily black then oil is being lost to the combustion chambers, probably past worn valve guides/stems. If the plugs are a sooty black then the fuel/air mixture is set too rich. If the plugs have a glazed appearance then the engine is running hot for one of a number of reasons, including a weak mixture setting, air induction or badly set timing. Clean the plugs and re-set the gap using feeler gauges to test and the correct instrument to alter the gap. Do not replace the plugs until the points gap has been set or

RIGHT *The distributor and contact breaker assembly of the 1098cc and 1275cc cars. (Courtesy Autodata)*

BELOW *The distributor and contact breaker assembly of the 1500cc Midget. (Courtesy Autodata)*

after the timing has been set if you are to time the ignition statically.

Check the condition of the contact breaker points. If they are dirty then clean them. If they are pitted or one side has a bulge and the other a corresponding hollow, replace them. In any case, check the gap and re-set if necessary. To alter the points gap, firstly place the car in fourth gear (handbrake off) and rock it backwards and forwards until the cam lobe opens the points to their maximum gap. Undo the large screw in the plate, then use a screwdriver in one of the notches provided to move the plate until the points gap is correct. Re-tighten the screw. Remove the rotor arm and examine this; if

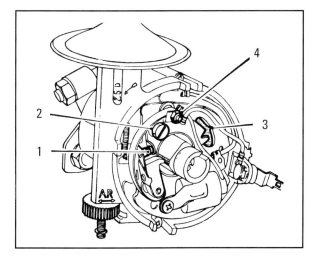

| 1. *Points gap* | 3. *Screwdriver cutout* |
| 2. *Securing screw* | 4. *Spring securing nut* |

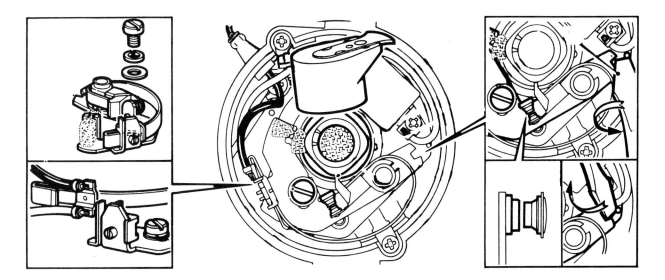

the contact is loose or badly pitted then replace it. Place a few drops of motor oil through the hole in the top of the cam.

Rather than buy in the various ignition components separately, it is often better to buy an 'ignition service kit', which will contain all of the components needed for a major service. Those spares which you do not use during this service can be used in the next major service. Rebuild the distributor assembly, replace the spark plugs and connect up the high tension leads to the spark plugs and the coil. It is now time to check the ignition timing.

There are two methods of checking and setting the ignition timing; static and dynamic. The advantage of static timing is that it does not require any specialised equipment, the drawback is that it is not so accurate as dynamic timing. Before delving into this subject, it is worth stating that it is often far better to have this work combined with setting the carburation and carried out at a service centre which is equipped with a Crypton tuner or, even better, at a business which also possesses a rolling road. A Crypton-type machine with an exhaust gas analyser can tell the operator what is coming out of the exhaust, whilst a rolling road also tells the operator what power is being transmitted to the driving wheels. Armed with such knowledge, the operator can not only set ignition and carburation to the optimums, but also trace weaknesses which would not otherwise be apparent.

Static timing

Remove the sparking plugs and the distributor cap. The engine has to be turned over, which can be accomplished by taking the car out of gear and manually pulling on the fan belt, or by placing the car in fourth gear and rocking the car. The best method is to raise one rear wheel (car in gear) and turn it.

When following the instructions do not leave the ignition switch turned on for any longer than is necessary. Turn the engine over until the notch in the crankshaft pulley is aligned with the correct timing mark. Connect a 12 volt test lamp between the low tension (LT) lead and earth. When the ignition is switched on, the lamp should light, indicating that the contact breaker points are open. Rotate the crankshaft against the normal direction of rotation until the lamp goes out, then forwards until you find

the exact point at which the lamp lights up. If this happens before the crankshaft pulley notch is correctly aligned then the ignition is too far advanced, and vice versa.

If the ignition timing is not correct, turn off the ignition. Set the timing marks then slacken the pinch bolt on the distributor so that it may be rotated. Turn

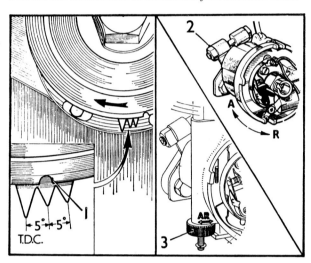

1 The timing marks. 2 Adjusting the timing. 3 Fine adjustments using the vernier adjuster.
(Courtesy Autodata)

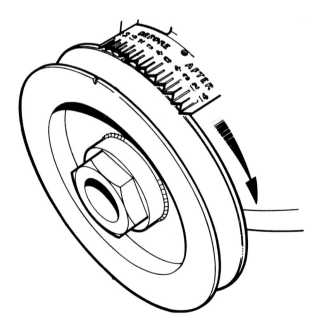

Setting the ignition timing of the 1500cc Midget. The arrow shows the direction of rotation.
(Courtesy Autodata)

on the ignition, and move the distributor firstly anti-clockwise then clockwise until the point at which the light comes on, then tighten the pinch bolt. Check that the timing is correct by turning the crankshaft until the timing marks are again aligned, and re-testing. Switch off the ignition, disconnect the test lamp and reassemble the distributor cap and leads.

Finally, take the car for a test drive. In top gear, accelerate slowly from around 20mph. If the engine pinks, retard the ignition slightly and then re-test.

Dynamic timing

For dynamic timing, you will need a stroboscope. These are relatively low cost items, and well worth having. Try to gain a recommendation for a make which has a reasonably bright light output; some are so dim that they are only of use in very dark conditions.

Connect one lead from the stroboscope to the number one cylinder spark plug, the other lead to the spark plug lead. Disconnect the vacuum advance from the inlet manifold. Using typists' correction fluid, highlight the correct timing mark and the notch in the crankshaft pulley, to make both easier to see. Ensuring that the strobe leads cannot become entangled in the fan blades(!), start the engine and shine the light onto the timing marks. The light should flash very briefly every time the timing marks are aligned, in effect 'arresting' the motion of the pulley and making it appear to be static.

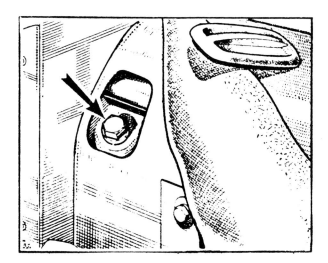

The gearbox filler level plug of the 1500cc Midget. (Courtesy Autodata)

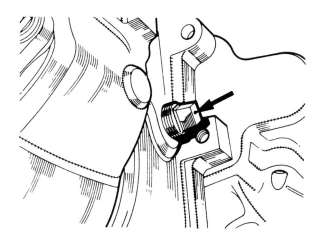

The gearbox filler level plug is accessed through a hole in the offside of the transmission tunnel. (Courtesy Autodata)

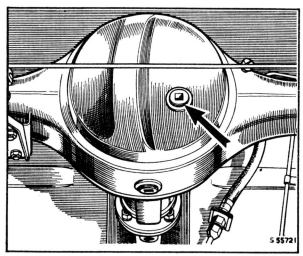

The axle oil level plug (Courtesy Autodata)

Adjust the distibrutor as in static timing until the crankshaft pulley notch appears stationary against the correct timing mark, then rev the engine a little. As the revolutions pick up, so the mechanical advance mechanism in the distributor should slightly advance the timing and the crankshaft pulley mark should appear to drift – if not, the distributor will have to be overhauled. Repeat the test with the vacuum advance pipe connected, and the timing should show a further slight advance.

ANNUAL SERVICE

Carry out all checks and jobs already outlined, plus

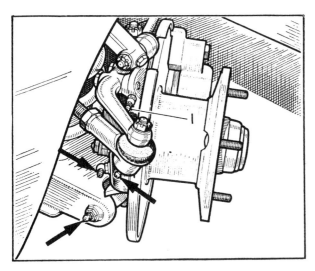

LEFT *The front suspension grease points, which cannot be given attention too frequently! (Courtesy Autodata)*

BELOW *The handbrake cable grease points. (Courtesy Autodata)*

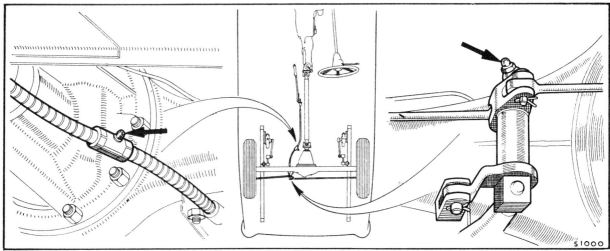

the following.

Change the gearbox oil and the axle oil. Drain the coolant and replace with fresh, using anti-freeze in the appropriate quanity. Renew the sparking plugs and air filters. Lubricate the steering rack (where appropriate).

Check the following (see chapter 4); the valve clearances, the braking system, all pipes, hoses and wires. All gaiters. All breather pipes.

BODYWORK PREVENTATIVE MAINTENANCE

No matter how badly rotted a Spridget bodyshell is allowed to become, it can be salvaged or, of course,

re-shelled. The expense and inconvenience of a restoration or re-shell should, however, be enough to convince anyone that rust prevention is better than cure. You can extend the life of your car's bodywork considerably through a little regular maintenance.

GENERAL CARE

In order for metal to rust it needs only to be exposed to the slightest amount of moisture (including moisture in humid air). Paint scratches and chips which expose bare metal will obviously permit this to happen, and so any such breaches of the paintwork should receive immediate attention, preferably before any moisture which comes into contact with the metal has sufficient time to let rust gain a foothold.

Very shallow scratches which do not go through to the metal may be gently cleaned out and hand painted with a small brush. If bare metal has been exposed (to all intents and purposes corrosion begins the moment metal comes into contact with air which contains moisture) then it is usually best to take a small area of the surrounding paintwork down with wet 'n dry (used wet) to reveal a little more metal than was originally exposed. The existing paint at the edges should be 'feathered', that is, there should not be a discernible shoulder around the area. This should be dried and thoroughly de-greased before being treated with Finnegan's 'Number One' primer or Bondaglass Voss 'Bonda Prima'. Either of these products should stop any tiny traces of rust which remain on the surface of the metal from spreading. If necessary, high-build primer can then be applied and flatted down before top coating.

All original Spridget paint colours are readily available from any car paint shop with mixing facilities. Do not expect the shop to guarantee to supply the correct colour by name alone, but find the manufacturer's code and quote that as well.

Old paintwork will usually be faded, so that the new paint stands out from the surrounding area. If this is the case then cutting the old and new paint (allowing a suitable period for the new paint to harden first, which varies according to the type of paint used) with a proprietary mild cutting compound will remove accumulated road dirt and take a very thin layer off the old paint to lessen the difference, as well as improving the surface of the new paint. If you are unsure about the hardening period for the paint you have used, it is best to leave any new paint to harden for at least a fortnight before cutting it back.

Underneath the car, particularly within the wheel arches but also along the bottom of the sills, the springer hanger assemblies and the floor, mud accumulates and should be cleaned off at regular intervals. Mud not only holds moisture in contact with the car body for long periods but it holds the salt which is used on roads in the U.K. in winter. Little accelerates rusting faster than salt, as can be witnessed in cars which are regularly exposed to salt-laden coastal air.

Steam cleaning is the very best way in which to remove mud from the underside of the car, although most people make do with a powerful jet of water. Even a garden hose which has a 'choked' fitting to give a pressurised jet of water will remove the majority of mud, although specialised high-pressure cleaners will do the job much faster and more thoroughly. If the paintwork of the car was applied badly, they can also remove paint, so take care! High pressure cleaners can also remove underseal which no longer adheres to the metal due to the spread of rust underneath. Far from being a problem, this is a great help because it gives you a fighting chance of dealing with the rust at the earliest opportunity. You can hire such washers by the hour or day from many DIY and equipment hire businesses. If you do use one then firstly make sure you have rust-arresting primer and some underseal to deal with the rusted areas which will be exposed!

Washing the car regularly not only keeps it looking good but also helps to show up any scratches or minor dents which could, if left untreated, lead to the onset of corrosion. It is a good idea to begin by washing the underside of the car and the wheels, since the use of a hose or high-pressure water device can splatter mud all over the place, including onto the paintwork you have just washed if you did things in the wrong order. The head of a stiff broom can be a help in removing mud from under the sill, where it can be difficult to direct a jet of water. After the underside, switch attentions to the bonnet and boot and then work downwards.

Never use ordinary washing-up liquid to wash the car, because many liquids contain industrial salts! (Do not use them in the windscreen washer bottle, either, because some of this soapy water will find its way onto the paintwork). It is always safest to use a proper car shampoo. Begin by hosing the car down with fresh water to get as much dirt as possible into suspension and off the body. On very hot days work on just one section of the car at a time, because if you try to hose down the whole car at once then the roof will be dry and the dirt will have re-settled before you can begin to use a leather or sponge. If you take the wash leather or even a sponge to bodywork covered in gritty dirt then the dirt will grind at the surface of the paint! Begin with the horizontal boot/bonnet surfaces, down each side and lastly do the lower wings and valances.

After this initial hosing or washing down it is as well to use a chamois leather and repeat the exercise, gently helping all dirt from the surface with the leather. Then shampoo the car and hose or wash the lather away. When the bodywork is really clean then you can dry it off with a spotlessly clean chamois.

At this stage you should thoroughly inspect the paintwork for any signs of damage and attend to these before polishing. If the paintwork is very dull then you might consider cutting it back before you polish it, using one of the several products for the purpose which are widely available from motor factors. Finally, polish the paintwork. Car polish repels water, so that water which is kicked up from the road (and which contains dirt) will wash away before the majority of the dirt has an opportunity to come out of suspension and adhere to the surface.

DEALING WITH RUST

New panels. Whenever a replacement panel which is a part of a box section has to be welded into position, the opportunity should be taken to give as much protection first to the side which will end up inside the section. Obviously, the area of metal which is to be the actual join will have to be cleaned bright and de-greased, but the majority of the panel can be treated to several layers of primer. Some of this paint protection will probably burn off during the welding process, but, as they say, every little helps!

The maximum protection against rusting will be gained by using one of the better 'rust arresting' primers rather than normal primer. The two rust-arresting products previously mentioned also perform very well on clean metal; better, in fact, than normal primers.

The Spridget, depending as it does on combinations of metal panels welded together for its strength, has a lot of box sections, most of which can (and usually do) rust from the inside. When a panel or panels from a box section is repaired the opportunity to give further protection to the metal should not be missed. As soon as the welding is finished and the metal has cooled, Waxoyl or a similar substance should be applied. In the case of the sills this will entail drilling a ⅜″ hole in order to gain access to the enclosed section, and the hole should afterwards be sealed with a rubber grommet. Alternatively, you can apply Waxoyl through the jacking-point holes.

The Waxoyl is applied either with one of the hand pumps supplied by the manufacturer or via a compressor-driven 'parafin' or underseal spray gun. When cold, Waxoyl is of too thick a consistency to spray properly, and so it should be warmed until it becomes thin enough by standing the tin in a bowl of hot water. A cheap alternative to Waxoyl is old sump oil, which will have to be thinned in order to get a fine spray.

Areas which particularly benefit from such preventative maintenance are the sills and the main chassis sections.

Underneath the car

Not only the bodywork but also items from the suspension benefit from protection against corrosion. Even the heavy ladder chassis can suffer from rust to such an extent that the car will fail an MOT. There are various ways in which the suspension and associated components may be protected.

If the underside of the car is steam cleaned, then components previously covered in a layer of mud will be revealed to possess a covering of rust underneath. It is not always practical to clean and repaint such components nor to partially clean and then use a proprietary rust arrester. Many people slow the corrosive process in such cases by spraying or painting on old engine oil.

When oil is applied to a ferrous surface, it spreads to form a thin protective layer which offers the considerable advantage of remaining 'self healing' for a period of time insofar as if the layer is breached by a scratch then the oil will again spread to re-cover it as long as it remains thin enough to do so. In time, the oil not only thickens of its own accord but also because it is absorbed by dirt, so that in order to work consistently the process should be repeated from time to time. If oil is used thus then be very careful not to let any come into contact with the front brake discs or the rear drums!

Proprietary wax products such as Waxoyl are used by many in place of oil (which can be very messy to apply), mainly in the protection of the underbody. Waxes remain reasonably fluid during the summer months and so can be self-healing, but in colder winter climates this will not happen.

Underseal is the usual product utilised for underbody protection. It is a very thick substance which can go some way to absorbing the impact of stones kicked up by the road wheels which would otherwise expose bare metal to the elements. Underseal forms a thick and hard 'skin' over the metal, and here lies its greatest drawback. Any rust which exists before the application of underseal or rust which forms afterwards can spread rapidly and virtually unopposed, unseen under the surface of the underseal.

Underseal works best on new panels which already have some form of rust protection, and is best considered a form of protection for the actual anti-rust protection.

Arresting rust

When rust is discovered on thin body metal or even on sturdy chassis or suspension components there are two options for dealing with it. Preferable is the complete removal of all traces of rust from the surface of the metal, followed by primering and top-coating. This can be a time-consuming process, however, and many people prefer to utilise rust arresting products. Sometimes, the body panel metal can be so badly rusted and thin that completely removing the rust would result in a hole. In such circumstances a good rust arresting product can prolong the life of the metal, provided that it is not a structurally important panel.

The car accessory market usually offers a wide range of chemical treatments which are all 'guaranteed' to arrest existing rust and ensure that the metal never rusts again. Not all appear to actually work in the experience of the author and also according to various published reports of independent testing. Rather than list the many products which do not work, the two which in the author's experience do work are Finnegan's 'Number One' primer and Bondaglass Gloss 'Bonda Prima'.

Unlike many other products, Bonda Primer is not claimed to chemically alter the composition of rust. It is stated to work by infiltrating and encapsulating rust particles in a resin. Finnegan's Number One, on the other hand, is claimed to convert rust into 'black mangenite' and to contain particles of glass which give the primer function a tough and smooth finish. Both certainly work.

In order to work properly, rust arresters should be applied only to flake-free, grease-free and dry surfaces, which should ideally have no more than a thin coating of corrosion. Finnegan's Number One is available either in a spray can or a tin, and the former is recommended for most car bodywork as it is much thinner than the paint contained in the tin (the manufacturers recommend that this is not thinned), which is itself best suited to use on heavier sections.

It is useless, incidentally, to use any rust arresting primer on metal which is to be filled. If you are straightening out a dent, for instance, then you have to remove all traces of rust before applying the filler, because the filler will not normally adhere strongly enough to such paint and it will drop off rusted metal in next to no time.

To arrest rust, you should begin by thoroughly cleaning and de-greasing the section in question. When it has dried then it may be firstly wire-brushed and finally rubbed with emery cloth or paper in order to remove any loose rust and to key the surface. Follow the instructions (with whichever product you choose) to the letter. In the case of Finnegan's Number One, this entails applying two separate coats with a two hour drying interval in between. The work should be carried out in a warm, dust-free and dry building if possible; otherwise on a hot and dry day outside. Bonda Prima also comes in a spray can or a tin for brushing or spraying with a compressor. After treatment, cellulose should be applied either within 6 to 24 hours or after seven days, other paints may be applied after four hours.

Areas which can really benefit from rust arresting maintenance are body panels on the underside of the car, such as the boot floor, the wheel arches and the floor pans. If underseal on such panels shows any signs of lifting then the following can greatly increase their lifespan (assuming that they have not rusted right through).

Firstly, all traces of old underseal and paint have to be removed. The easiest way in which to achieve this is to use an electric drill (or an air drill powered by a compressor) fitted with one of a selection of wire brushes and 'flap wheels'. Protective clothing, especially goggles, must be worn to avoid personal injury from flying rust flakes! If the panel being treated is anywhere near the petrol tank then this should firstly be removed (see page 150).

Next, as much rust as possible should be removed using emery cloth or paper (to work right into corners) in addition to the drill and wire brushes and flap wheels. No more than a very thin coating of rust should remain. Apply the rust arrester, followed by a second coat and a topcoat at the recommended intervals. Underseal may then be re-applied if desired to finish the job.

Areas for Special Attention

On the hottest, driest day of the Summer it is a good idea to remove the seats, carpets and interior trim from the car, and to give as much of the newly exposed metal as possible anti-corrosion protection.

A thin coating of a moisture-inhibiting wax may be applied under footwell rubber mats to protect the floor and inner sill sections. Even with this protection, if the carpets (where fitted) get wet then they should immediately be removed and dried out.

Chromework presents special problems. The tiniest pin-hole will enable rust to become established under the surface of the chrome, and it spreads unseen until large areas begin to 'bubble' and eventually to flake off. New chromework could be polished to provide some protection, but because the bumpers and other items with a chrome finish are vulnerable to stone chipping, there remains very little which can be done in the way of protection. The non-chromed side of such fittings does benefit from either wax or oil protection.

Where small chrome fittings meet painted bodywork, problems with rusting can arise. The chrome light surrounds and side chrome strip are all able to trap and hold water in contact with the bodywork, and furthermore, the bodywork paint is often breached as the pieces of trim are fitted into place. If a small piece of self-adhesive plastic tape is fitted under such chromework, then paint damage

and consequent rust damage is far less likely to occur. Especial care should be taken when fitting items such as wing mirrors, as this entails making holes through the body metal underneath and some bare metal will almost certainly be exposed.

Surface rusting

Some areas are especially prone to surface rusting which, if left unattended, will slowly but surely eat its way into the metal. Surface rust should be dealt with at the earliest opportunity, as the longer it is left, the more difficult the repair becomes, which probably isn't the biggest surprise you've had this year.

Prime areas are the fillets at the tops of the rear wings and the areas around the light clusters. The first step in dealing with such rust is to remove the paint from all suspect areas, then to remove every trace of rust using a wire brush. A cup brush mounted on an angle grinder makes light work of this. If the rust proves indeed to be light then the surface may be primed and any tiny undulations filled using body stopper.

If the surface turns out to be pitted, then when every trace of rust has been removed, body filler should be used to smooth over the surface before primer is applied. Finally, the entire area should be flatted, cleaned, degreased and primed.

4 · MECHANICAL REPAIR/RESTORATION

From a mechanical viewpoint, the entire Spridget range is simple, straightforward and comparatively easy to maintain, repair and restore. Spares are widely and usually cheaply available, because the Spridget in all its guises benefits from having a majority of components which were also used on other cars. If the asking price for a fully reconditioned engine, gearbox or even an ancillary such as a starter motor or SU carburettor is beyond your pocket and you do not feel confident enough to recondition your own, then many breaker's yards will be able to furnish one taken, if not from a Spridget then from another contemporary British car.

Because this chapter describes mechanical repair from the restoration viewpoint, full details of certain specialised repair work is omitted. For instance, it is possible to change the big end bearings or to work on the timing chain gear without removing the engine from the car, and such tasks are usually described in detail within a good workshop manual. If you do not have access to a workshop manual, then it will usually be possible to carry out the work following the instructions given in this chapter, but using common sense to work out the differences between the described routines for working with the engine removed from the car and the necessary routines for working with the engine in situ.

Always carefully consider safety before starting work. Disconnect the battery and preferably remove it from the car. If you have to work under the car, ensure that it is properly held aloft by solid axle stands and that the wheels which are left in contact with the ground are properly chocked so that the car can not roll and tumble off the axle stands. If you are starting work on a job which may involve using a naked flame on the rear of the car (welding or using

heat to help 'start' a reluctant nut or bolt) then begin by removing the fuel tank.

ENGINE/GEARBOX REMOVAL

It is possible to remove the engine separately from or in conjunction with the gearbox. If the engine alone is removed, then the gearbox can be removed separately afterwards, although there is nothing to commend working in this manner, and there exists a small and unnecessary risk of damaging the gearbox should the weight of the engine be taken by the gearbox input shaft. Engine-only removal is not described separately in great detail because it comprises essentially the same routines as removing both engine and gearbox, without those tasks which specifically apply to the gearbox, clutch slave cylinder and propeller shaft, and with the addition that the starter motor (which bolts through the engine backplate into the clutch bell housing) has to be removed, and the other nuts and bolts holding the engine back plate to the bell housing must also be removed.

You may wish to remove the engine separately in order to work on the clutch or on certain engine components such as the crankshaft or its bearings. It is little more difficult to remove both units than it is to remove just the engine, and the author would recommend that, given the choice, the two units are removed together. The restorer will usually remove both the engine and the gearbox as a single unit, because he or she will wish to clean or recondition both as required.

When a car which has a substantially weakened

body through rotten sills and rear chassis rail members undergoes body restoration, it is as well to begin by removing the engine and gearbox as described here because the two units are very heavy and can easily distort a weakened body if it is not supported properly. In fact, the engine/gearbox removal photographed was carried out specifically due to this reason, and the text recommends certain routines for man-handling the car which will help to prevent body distortion from occurring whilst this work is carried out.

Disconnect the battery and preferably remove it from the engine compartment. Drain the engine block and radiator. The engine block drain plug is situated behind and to the rear of the exhaust manifold. Coolant from here will fall onto the chassis leg and will splash around somewhat, so that a wide receptacle will be needed to ensure that it is all caught. Some models have radiators fitted with drain plugs; if not, then disconnect the bottom hose connection to the radiator. Again, the coolant is not easy to catch and a wide receptacle (such as a washing up bowl) will be needed.

Remove the bonnet. On all cars except the Frogeye, mark the positions of the hinges to aid reassembly then undo the eight bolts which secure the bonnet to its hinges whilst an assistant steadies the bonnet to prevent it from falling. On later cars it will be necessary to unbolt one end of the bonnet stay. On Frogeyes, the bonnet and front wings are a single unit. Disconnect the wires to the lights (make up identification tags to ensure correct reconnection), remove the wiring loom securing clip from the bonnet hinge, then remove the screw from the top end of each bonnet support. It will require two people to lift away the bonnet/wing unit.

If a Spridget other than the Frogeye is to undergo body restoration, it is a good policy to remove the front wings and the grille surround before removing the engine, to reduce the chances of damaging either. See Chapter 5 for details of this.

Remove the radiator. On early cars, simply remove the bottom and top hoses and the temperature gauge sender, then remove the grille then undo the two bolts either side of the radiator which run into captive nuts. On later models, removing the radiator will also entail removing the surround, because it incorporates a large lip which

Remove the bonnet before trying to remove the engine. It pays to have an assistant to steady the bonnet whilst the nuts and bolts are removed.

fits right over the radiator, preventing its removal alone. With later cars, remove the bottom and top hoses plus the small hose which runs to the expansion tank. Remove the grille. Remove the two nuts and bolts securing the radiator surround to the bonnet slam panel, then slacken off the two nuts and bolts securing the surround to the air intake panel. Remove the two bolts which run into captive nuts either side of the radiator and which secure it to its upright side brackets. The radiator and surround can now be lifted clear of the car.

Remove the throttle and choke cables from the carburettors. Remove the fuel feed pipe from the front carburettor. On models fitted with the mechanical fuel pump, remove the fuel lines from either side of the pump. If the standard exhaust manifold is fitted, then undo the manifold to down pipe clamp bolts. Although not essential, the author prefers to remove the carburettors to minimise the chances of damaging them as the engine is lifted out. This is essential if a long centre branch (LCB) exhaust is fitted (the exhaust manifold and down pipe are a single unit on LCB systems), because it gives access to the exhaust manifold nuts. Undo the two nuts which secure each carburettor, then lift away the two carburettors and their linkage as a single unit. Remove the heat shield, then the nuts which secure the inlet and exhaust manifolds. Lift away the inlet manifold then pull the exhaust manifold clear. Remove the manifold from the down pipe or, if a LCB system is fitted, simply tie the unit away from the engine.

Remove the spark plug leads and pull the lead from the distributor to the coil. If you are unsure about which lead runs to which spark plug, then mark the leads before removal by painting bands on them (one, two, three or four to denote the cylinder in question) or make up temporary tags from masking tape and write the number on this. If you subsequently forget to do this and can not remember which lead runs to which spark plug, remember that the longest runs to cylinder number one, that the direction of rotor arm rotation is anti-clockwise and

ABOVE AND RIGHT *Removing the grille surround assembly is not too time-consuming, and would make engine removal that bit easier. More importantly, removing it means that there is one less obstacle to damage with the engine. Drill out the pop rivets which hold the trim in position, then remove the bolts and lift the assembly out of the way.*

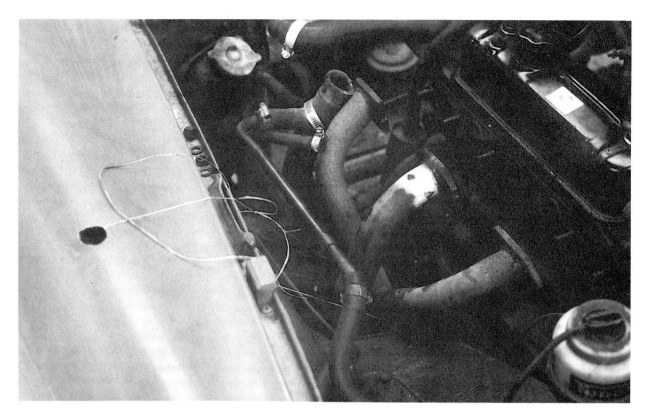

The project car was fitted with a non-standard LCB manifold, the down pipe of which was hopelessly seized into the exhaust. To save time and temper, the lot can be tied out of the way.

that the firing order is 1-3-4-2. You can then easily work out which lead goes where. Remove the distributor cap and the rotor arm, because these are easily damaged otherwise during engine removal. Disconnect the low tension lead from the distributor. Remove the wires (or the moulded plug) from the dynamo/alternator, the thick wire from the starter motor and, on some cars, the wire from the low oil pressure warning lamp switch.

Remove the temperature gauge sender unit. If this is seized, do not be tempted to use excessive force because the unit is easily damaged. If it will not easily start to turn, clean up the exposed thread with a wire brush, then leave the threads soaking in a penetrating oil until the unit can be removed easily. Remove the oil pressure gauge pipe.

The following text is split into three types: instructions for removal of the engine alone, instructions for removing the engine and gearbox together, and instructions which apply to both.

PREPARATION FOR ENGINE ONLY REMOVAL

If the engine alone is to be removed, undo the bolts which hold the starter motor and remove this. Drain the engine oil from the plug at the rear offside of the sump. Take the weight of the gearbox by placing a jack underneath it, then undo the nuts and bolts which secure the clutch bell housing to the engine backplate. Find and remove the earth strap, and if a return spring is fitted to the clutch lever, remove this.

PREPARATION FOR ENGINE/ GEARBOX REMOVAL

On Spridgets there is a flat plate which runs underneath the transmission tunnel from the crossmember backwards. This prevents access to the front propeller shaft universal joint flanges, so that the propeller shaft front universal joint cannot be unbolted in the usual way. It is necessary to unbolt the two flanges which connect the propeller shaft to the differential instead.

Chock the front wheels of the car, release the

handbrake and ensure that the car is in neutral, then raise the rear of the car and support the axle on axle stands. It helps access if the rear of the car can be raised high, although it is only necessary that the wheels are off the ground so that the flanges can be rotated to allow access to each of the nuts and bolts which hold the two flanges together. Drain the gearbox oil through the central plug. From underneath the car, make a mark across the rear propeller shaft universal joint flange and the differential assembly flange so that they can be correctly aligned afterwards. Propeller shafts are balanced to reduce vibration, and it is essential that they are reassembled in the original relative positions. Remove the nuts and bolts which pass through the rear propeller shaft/differential flange. These may be very stiff and two ½″ ring spanners are needed, because there is insufficient clearance for a ratchet drive and sockets to be used. Turn the propeller shaft to bring each nut and bolt in turn into view.

The rear of the propeller shaft may now be lowered and the internally splined end of the propeller shaft may be pulled from the gearbox mainshaft (third motion shaft) end and out of the transmission tunnel.

Lower the rear end of the car and chock the nearside wheels. Raise the offside. If the sills are badly corroded, it will be wise to spread the load by placing a long piece of sturdy timber or some box section steel on top of the jack so that it bears against the main crossmember and the rear spring mounting box assembly. If the car is so weak that even this is deemed liable to cause body distortion then either chock the rear wheels and raise the front of the car and support this on axle stands, or work with the car on its roadwheels. The latter is very difficult because you will be working by feel alone. The author can personally vouch for this, having done it on the project car.

Undo the two bolts which hold the clutch slave cylinder in position, then pull the cylinder away from the pushrod. On some models, the engine earth strap may be situated underneath one of these bolts, in which case you should wear gloves because loose wires from the earth strap will otherwise stick into your hands! Before lowering the car, remove the two lower gearbox mounting bracket bolts. Also, pull apart the two bullet connectors on the wires running from the reversing light switch (where applicable), and pull the speedometer drive from the securing clip on the gearbox casing.

From inside the car, remove any carpet and sound-deadening matting from the transmission tunnel front end. Remove the gear lever knob, the screws from the gear lever boot surround, then pull the boot away from the lever. Ensure that the gearbox is in neutral, then remove the three bolts from the anti-rattle plate and remove the plate and gear lever together. Pull the inspection cover rubber bung from the nearside of the tunnel and, using a small self-gripping wrench, start the speedometer drive. This can then be removed from underneath the car. Either side of the transmission tunnel is a bolt which passes into the rear gearbox mounting. Remove these.

Take the weight of the engine with the lifting gear, then unbolt the two engine mountings.

Lifting gear

The A series engine is very heavy, surprisingly so for its compact size. The lifting gear used to remove the engine should preferably comprise a proper engine crane or chain hoist of the type found in most professional garages. Crane hoists may be hired in some areas, and because these are mobile units (they have wheels) the crane and engine can be pushed around the workshop and the engine hence carried and lifted onto a bench.

The author uses a small 'block and tackle' set which is slung from a very strong steel beam and, although this has always proved satisfactory, he freely admits to some trepidation when he sees an engine and gearbox suspended on the flimsy-looking gear over an engine bay! DO NOT use lightweight ratchet winches because some of these are so poorly manufactured that the mechanisms have been known to break under loads far less than that of the A series engine. They are intended for horizontal pulling rather than vertical lifting, and are not intended to support weight, but just to pull. The winches referred to are sometimes offered for sale within the UK by car accessory dealerships without the caveat that they are unsuitable for vertical lifting, and if in doubt, don't buy.

If you use a roof beam to hold a block and tackle or chain hoist, it should go without saying that the beam must be immensely strong. Wooden beams, unless very solid, should be avoided. If in doubt, you could test the beam first by trying to lift the engine before the engine mounts are disconnected.

The lightweight lifting gear is attached to an immensely strong steel beam. With the radiator assembly removed, all that remained was to clear the spectators to a safe distance and begin lifting. It helps to have an assistant to manoeuvre the engine off the gearbox input shaft (engine only removal) then to angle it so that it can be lifted clear, or to manoeuvre the gearbox over the cross member and to angle the engine/gearbox for withdrawal.

Obviously, do not actually raise the car body in this way, but stop the moment that you see the slightest upwards movement of the engine and bodywork. At this point, the lifting gear is supporting more than the weight of the engine/gearbox. If the beam makes creaking noises during this exercise then discount its use; the last thing you want is for the beam or lifting gear to give way whilst the engine/gearbox unit is suspended above the engine bay.

Set up the lifting gear. Either run strong ropes or straps around the engine unit or bolt brackets (which can sometimes be found on Austin A30, 35 and 40 engines, or alternatively fabricated from heavy gauge steel) on to the rocker studs and attach chain or rope to these. The engine/gearbox if removed as a unit have to be angled backwards so that, as the engine is

raised, the gearbox can clear the heater/battery platform. This is achieved by shifting the lifting device bias so that it is towards the front of the engine, or by having an assistant to angle the assembly for you. Failure to correctly guide the assembly can result in the clutch bell housing hitting the heater/battery platform, which can crack the top of the bell housing and distort the platform, so be careful. The author intended to replace the rocker gear and so as the photographs show, he passed strong rope around the rocker shaft to lift the engine/gearbox assembly.

ENGINE ONLY REMOVAL

It is vital that the weight of the engine is never allowed to rest on the gearbox input shaft. There are two methods of working, of which the latter is recommended.

Place a jack and wood packing underneath the gearbox but do not begin to raise it at this point. Enroll the help of at least one reasonably strong assistant.

Raise the engine as far as possible, and raise the jack underneath the gearbox at the same time so that it is supported at an angle at which the engine can be drawn straight forwards or the car pushed backwards. Keep the gearbox at this angle if possible to make re-fitting the engine easier when the time comes.

The alternative method of working reduces the chances of damaging the gearbox input shaft when the engine is both removed and refitted. With the weight of the engine taken by the lifting gear, remove the engine mounts, so that the front of the engine can be lowered slightly and so that the engine lines up with the gearbox input shaft. The engine can then be drawn forwards until it is free of the gearbox input shaft, then lifted vertically out of the engine bay.

ENGINE/GEARBOX REMOVAL

Although this can be achieved by a person working alone (the author has done this but does not recommend it because it is far more likely that either the engine/gearbox assembly or the bodywork will be damaged) it is better to seek assistance from a reasonably strong adult (and preferably two) to help manoeuvre the heavy engine/gearbox unit. Place padding on the bonnet slam panel to protect the paintwork or, if the car is to receive a full bodywork restoration, remove the grille surround assembly.

Raise the engine as far as possible then, using a sturdy length of wood, raise the gearbox rear mount to clear the main crossmember. Pull the two forwards before again raising the engine and angling the gearbox downwards (a length of wood may be used for this) to clear the heater assembly platform. Continue to raise the engine until there is sufficient clearance to either pull the lifting crane away from the car or to push the car away from fixed lifting gear.

Relevant to both operations

Fixed lifting gear brings the question of how to move the very heavy engine or engine/gearbox assembly around the workshop. Trying to lift this bodily, either by yourself or with assistants, is inviting serious back injuries and is not recommended. The author nearly always works alone and lowers the unit on to two sheets of plastic-faced hardboard (plastic faces against each other) which can slip over one another easily. The engine can then be pushed quite easily for a short

distance in the desired direction. It is then possible to swing the lower sheet of hardboard around so that the engine can be pushed further. Alternatively, special mobile engine stands may be purchased, or a stand could be fabricated from strong angle iron and fitted with industrial castors so that it could be moved.

Hooray and up she rises! A smarter person would have removed the front wings and grille surround assembly first, since these would later have to be removed on a car undergoing a full body restoration. The engine/gearbox removal sequence captured here was accomplished single-handed, just so that the author could prove to himself that it was possible. The conclusion reached was that it is best to get the biggest assistant you can.

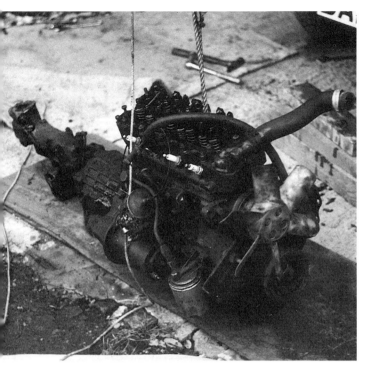

LEFT *To manoeuvre the engine gearbox around the workshop, the author placed it on a sheet of plastic-faced hardboard, and slid it along as necessary. Getting the engine up onto a bench is not so easy.*
The author managed to lift the engine (minus gearbox, head etc) by himself, but came dangerously close to injuring himself in the process. Again, get help.

RIGHT *The principles of 1500cc engine removal are exactly the same, although the type and number of connections to be removed vary considerably. (Courtesy Autodata)*

BELOW *With the engine out of the way, you can step into the engine bay for easier access to the various components which have to come out during a full restoration.*

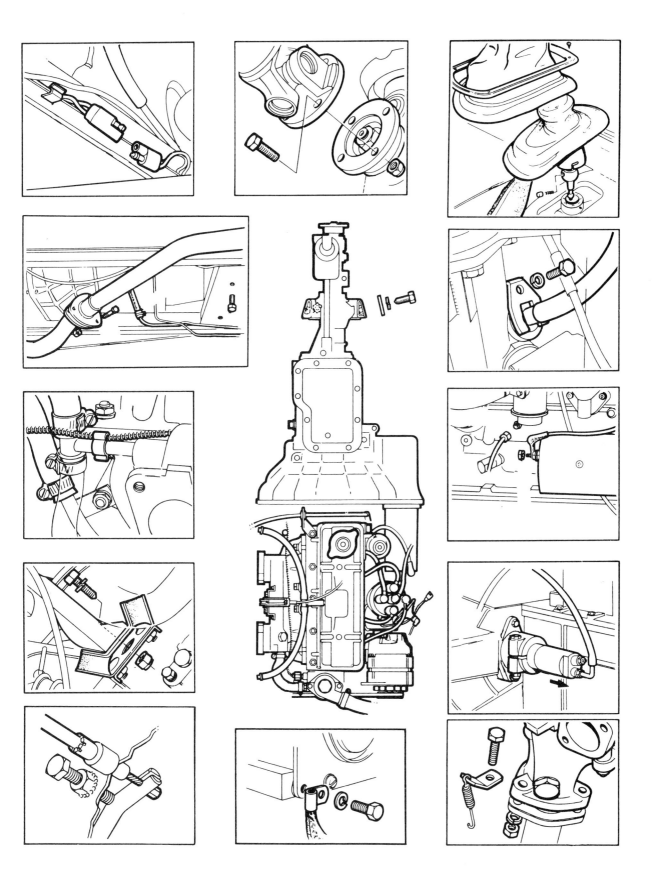

At this stage in the proceedings you will be covered with a mixture of oil, grease and dirt. It is a shame to waste the full potential of the monumental bath or shower which you are now due, so take this opportunity to clean down the unit. If you were to strip a dirty engine then some of the dirt from the outside would become dislodged and invariably find its way into the inside of the engine or gearbox, where it would quickly do considerable damage when the engine was re-started. The best way to clean the unit is using a steam cleaner, although various proprietary products such as 'Gunk' or paraffin may be used with equal success if more labour on your part. Be sure to seal every aperture on the engine before cleaning it, especially those which lead to the lubrication system.

Place the engine on a very solid bench of about waist height if you intend to work on it, or, in the absence of a bench and at risk of backache, on a suitably covered floor. The most important consideration is that the work area and its atmosphere are very clean and free from dust and air-borne dirt. Some people take the unit into their house to rebuild it rather than try to work in a dirty garage. Unfortunately, one of the very worst environments in which you could attempt an engine rebuild is the restorer's workshop. The cleaning, sanding and flatting operations that are part and parcel of the restorer's art fill the atmosphere with countless tiny particles of dust.

ENGINE REFITTING

Refitting the engine unit alone is essentially the opposite of removal, with special attention being given to aligning the engine and gearbox input shaft correctly by either angling the gearbox or leaving the fitting of the engine mounts to a later stage so that the engine can be lowered down into line with the gearbox input shaft. Those who have restored their Spridget's bodywork should fit the engine and gearbox as an assembly and carefully consider at which stage they refit them.

The recommended option is to spray the engine compartment and spray the wings and grille surround off the car, then fit the engine and gearbox before fitting the wings and grille surround. This reduces the chances of damaging the new paintwork to a minimum and gives the best possible access.

To refit the engine/gearbox assembly, lower it into the engine bay, then raise the gearbox so that it can enter the transmission tunnel. Refit the propeller shaft into the transmission tunnel and push its splines into the gearbox, working through the transmission tunnel gear lever aperture, then lift the engine and gearbox sufficiently to enable them to be moved backwards into the correct position.

ENGINE STRIP. A SERIES

The A series engines must be one of the most prolific car engines in the world; in the UK it probably outnumbers all other engine production figures, having been used in Minors, A40s and A35s, the 1100cc series and not least, the evergreen Mini in addition to all Austin Healey Sprites and MG Midgets up to 1974. The consequences of this are a wealth of spares, new and second hand, for the Spridget owner to take advantage of, a wealth of knowledge about performance tuning, and the fact that every garage mechanic in the UK (and most probably in many other countries as well) is intimately familiar with the engine and able to offer a local source of advice to the DIY engine builder who runs into difficulties.

The A series engine is very simple in construction and easy to take apart, work on and rebuild. No special tools other than those required for stripping any other engine are needed. You will need such tools as universal circlips, a piston ring compressor, valve spring compressor etc. These are covered in the following text.

Although the A series engine is relatively easy to work on, there is a strong case for opting for an exchange reconditioned engine rather than working on your own. This is because the cost of a good exchange unit can be surprisingly little more than the costs of bringing a poor example to good working order yourself; not only are engine spares rather costly, but there may emerge a number of machining operations which will require specialised (and expensive) attention. For instance, you could discover that your engine requires the crankshaft re-grinding and balancing (or replacing), that the block and

RIGHT *The internal components of the engine. There are detail differences between the various engines fitted to Spridgets. Refer to a workshop manual for more details where necessary. (Courtesy Autodata)*

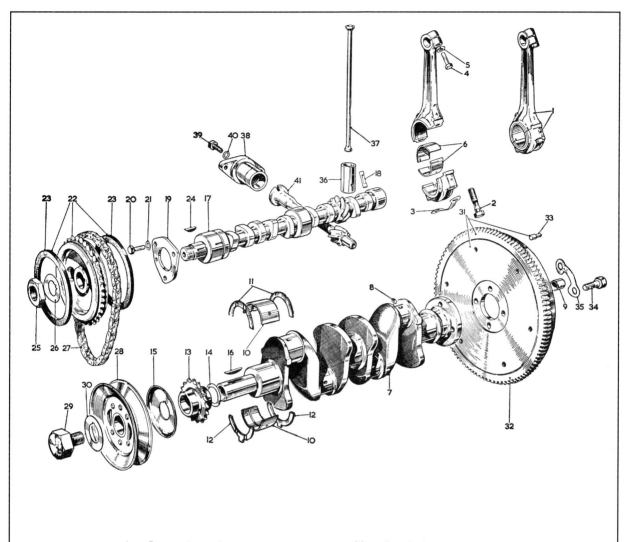

1. Connecting rod cap
2. Cap bolt
3. Lock washer
4. Clamping screw
5. Spring washer
6. Big-end bearing
7. Crankshaft
8. Oil restrictor
9. First motion shaft bush
10. Main bearing
11. Upper thrust washer
12. Lower thrust washer
13. Crankshaft gear
14. Packing washer
15. Oil thrower
16. Gear and crankshaft key
17. Camshaft
18. Oil pump driving pin
19. Locking plate
20. Screw
21. Shakeproof washer

22. Camshaft gear
23. Tensioner ring
24. Gear key
25. Gear nut
26. Lock washer
27. Camshaft driving chain
28. Crankshaft pulley
29. Pulley retaining bolt
30. Lock washer
31. Flywheel
32. Starter ring
33. Dowel
34. Screw
35. Lock washer
36. Tappet
37. Pushrod
38. Distributor housing
39. Screw
40. Shakeproof washer
41. Distributor driving spindle

cylinder head require skimming or that either are cracked, that the cylinders require re-boring and that new, oversized, pistons and rings will have to be fitted. If you oversee the work yourself and commission each engineering job separately, then the company you select to undertake the work will have to set up their machinery specifically for each task – all adding to the cost. The exchange engine, on the other hand, is reconditioned on almost a production-line basis. Costs are kept low by working on batches of engines, batches of components.

Don't think that engine reconditioning is simply a matter of stripping the engine, buying in the necessary new components and bolting them into place, and something which you can do at home entirely without need of outside specialist help – it is not. You will at the very least need the services of a good engineer to examine the bores, pistons, crankshaft journals etc for wear, ovality and (in the case of the crankshaft) straightness, to assess whether the cylinder head is warped and in need of skimming.

Exchange reconditioned engines can be acquired in various guises. The most basic exchange is the SHORT engine, which includes everything except the cylinder head (the alternative FULL engine includes the cylinder head). In the case of the exchange full engine, various performance versions are available; these are usually called 'fast road', half race' and 'full race' , depending on the state of tune and number of types of modifications – although other descriptive terms may be encountered. See chapter seven for more details of performance engines.

All in all, the exchange engine offers many advantages over DIY, not least of which is a written guarantee in the case of units from better companies. However, because many enthusiasts enjoy working on mechanical units, the stripping, examination and (the important bit) the rebuilding of the A series engine are covered in detail. Stripping the Triumph 1500cc unit entails essentially the same operations.

Begin by splitting the engine from the gearbox. Place chocks under the gearbox or, better still, wood packing on top of a trolley jack. This will keep the gearbox at a constant height as it and the engine are parted, to prevent the weight of the engine being taken by the gearbox input shaft. Remove the starter motor retaining bolts and the starter motor. Remove the remaining nuts and bolts which fasten the engine backplate to the clutch bell housing. When all have been removed, pull the gearbox back from the engine, taking care not to allow the gearbox input shaft to take any weight.

Remove all engine ancillaries. The dynamo or alternator will probably have already been removed to improve access to the right hand engine mounting when the engine was removed from the car. Undo the four bolts which pass through the cooling fan and remove the fan and its pulley. Undo the four water pump retaining bolts and lift the pump from the engine. Remove the old oil filter (which must be renewed, as must ALL gaskets and oil seals which are disturbed during the course of the work), and undo the large nut at the oil return pipe banjo fitting. Undo the two oil filter bracket bolts, and remove the oil filter housing and the pipe complete.

Undo the distributor clamp and pull out the distributor body. Undo the distributor housing bolt and withdraw the housing, then using a $\frac{5}{16}$" UNF bolt pushed down and rotated to engage with the internal thread of the top of the distributor driveshaft, pull (whilst slowly turning the bolt to disengage the driveshaft from the camshaft gear) the driveshaft out.

To remove the cylinder head, undo the nuts and rocker post nuts in the sequence illustrated on page 77, turning each nut very slightly on the first 'circuit' then progressively by more with each subsequent circuit until the pressure has been removed from the cylinder head. This sequence is to stop the cylinder head from warping as it is released. Undo the nuts fully.

The cylinder head is often reluctant to part company with the block, usually because it sticks on the threaded rods. DO NOT use any kind of lever in between the two mating surfaces, but instead, gently tap the underside of the thermostat housing and the sides of the cylinder head with a soft-faced mallet until it can be lifted off. Remove the pushrods and place them in a numbered rack (See 'Cylinder Head' for more details of removal and stripping).

Remove the clutch (see under a separate heading within this chapter). At the front end of the engine, fold back the tab on the tab washer which holds the pulley nut, then lock the engine to prevent it from turning by holding a screwdriver blade in the starter ring aperture against the flywheel ring gear teeth, and remove the nut. Probably a better way to lock the crankshaft is to remove the cylinder head studs, turn the engine upside down, remove the sump, and place a piece of timber between the crankshaft and crankcase see photo on pages 78. The pulley nut may require a lot of force to start it, and it is better to use a hexagonal impact socket than an ordinary twelve

RIGHT *When the gearbox and engine have been split, the engine becomes rather easier to move. Don't be deceived by its diminutive size; it is a very heavy unit best lifted by two or even three people.*

RIGHT AND BELOW *Before you begin chucking the engine around, it is best to remove ancillaries to avoid damaging them. The oil pipe banjo union bolt is removed, followed by the oil filter housing bolts.*

Slacken off the distributor pinch bolt, then withdraw the distributor.

You can then remove the clamp if desired.

sided socket. If the nut will not start, then try to borrow a compressor and impact wrench or transport the engine to a local garage and let them remove it. Lever off the pulley using a proper puller or, if this is unavailable, two large screwdrivers. Take care not to damage the pulley during this operation. Remove the woodruff key and store this safely.

Remove the bolts which hold the timing gear cover and remove the cover. This exposes the timing gears and chain.

A gear on the end of the crankshaft is linked by a chain to another gear mounted on the end of the camshaft, so that the camshaft rotates along with the crankshaft. The camshaft lobes bear against the cam

followers (tappets) which in turn act upon the pushrods which open and close the valves by bearing against the rocker arms.

Remove the oil thrower from the crankshaft end, noting that it fits with the concave side facing away from the engine. Bend back the lock tab on the camshaft nut washer, then remove the nut and washer.

The camshaft and crankshaft gears, complete with their chain, can now be removed as a single unit. Use a proper puller if available; otherwise, use two large screwdrivers to move each gear in turn a little before moving the other. Note that there are a number of thin shims underneath the crankshaft

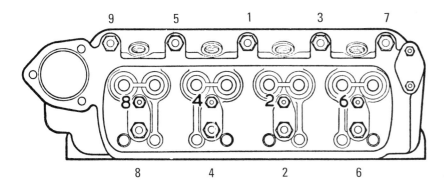

It is important that the cylinder head nuts are slackened in the order shown to avoid distorting the cylinder head. (Courtesy Autodata)

gear; these must be retained and refitted when the engine is rebuilt to line up the two gears properly.

The camshaft can be removed at this stage from all units excepting the 1275cc engine. Remove the camshaft locking plate by undoing the three bolts and lock washers which retain it. Remove the two covers from the engine side to expose the camshaft followers, and lift out each by pushing in a finger so that the tappet grips it like a thimble. The camshaft can then

It is as well to remove the cylinder head studs in order to prevent then getting damaged. Simply screw on two nuts and pinch them together. Don't use mole grips on the stud shafts, because these will invariably mark them.

be removed. Keep each camshaft follower in such a way that it can be returned to its original location. The author uses masking tape and a biro to mark each tappet. (On 1275cc engines, the camshaft should be removed with the engine either on its side or upside down, because there are no covers through which the tappets can be removed, and if you try to remove the camshaft with the engine upright the tappets will fall down and lock the camshaft, preventing its removal. Normally, with the 1275cc engine, the camshaft would be removed with the engine inverted only if the camshaft alone was to receive attention or be exchanged for a higher performance variant. If the engine is being completely stripped down, leave the camshaft in position until

Removing the clutch. Slacken off the bolts in a diagonal sequence to release spring pressure evenly.

Sump off. A piece of timber is being used to lock the crankshaft whilst the crankshaft pulley bolt is undone.

The pulley was reluctant to part company with the crankshaft end, and so a three-legged puller was employed to encourage it. Note that the crankshaft pulley bolt has been partially screwed back into position to give the puller something to push against.

ABOVE *With the timing gear cover off, the timing chain and gears can be removed together.*

BELOW *When replacing the timing gears and chain, ensure that the two dimples are facing each other. Be sure to replace any shims before fitting the gears, and place a straight edge across both gears to check that they are level. (Courtesy Autodata)*

the crankshaft has been removed, then turn the engine onto its side, remove the camshaft and push out the tappets using a pushrod).

Undo the bolts which hold the back plate, and remove this. If it is not easily separated, check again that you have undone the central bolt; the back plate on the project car had a split, almost certainly caused by someone trying to hammer off the back plate with the central bolt still in situ.

Again lock the crankshaft to prevent it from turning, and remove the flywheel fixing bolts. The flywheel should come off the end of the crankshaft without too much trouble, although a large three legged puller or flywheel puller should do the trick if it sticks.

The sump can now be removed by undoing the various fixing screws and giving the side of the sump a sharp tap with the heel of the hand to free the gasket.

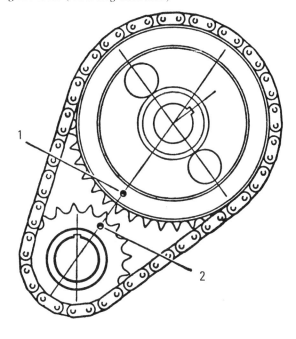

ABOVE *It may have been possible to grind out this crack in the backplate into a 'V', to fill with weld and machine flat. Simpler to get another one.*

Oil pump

The oil pump is situated at the end of, and is driven by, the camshaft. It is held by four bolts which are secured by tab strap washers. Bend back the tabs, undo the bolts and pull the oil pump from the engine. To check the oil pump, use a feeler gauge to measure the clearance between the lobes as shown in the photograph. If the clearance is excessive or if the internals show the slightest signs of wear or damage then take the opportunity to replace the pump whilst the engine is out of the car.

Crankshaft

With the engine either on its side or upside down, remove the bolts, which are held by tab washers (or the multi-sided nuts in the case of the 1275cc engine) holding each big end bearing cap, then remove the caps. Each cap must be replaced on the appropriate

LEFT *Whilst the engine is out of the car, it makes sense to check the oil pump as shown and described in the text, even if this is the only part of the engine you work on.*

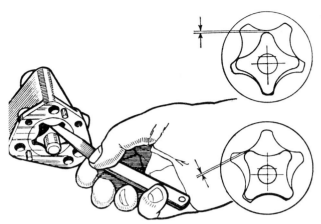

Checking the oil pump clearances in this case .006″ (.15mm). (Courtesy Autodata)

connecting rod when these are removed, so store or mark them in some way to prevent them getting mixed up.

The crankshaft bearing caps are held with six bolts. Remove these, then lift off the lower bearing caps. Again, mark each so that it can be replaced in the correct position. The crankshaft may now be lifted out, along with its bearings. The pistons and connecting rods may now be pushed upwards out of the cylinders. Mark every component as it is stripped to aid correct reassembly.

The pistons are held to the connecting rods by a variety of methods. With early engines, simply undo the small end bolt. With some later engines, the piston pins are floating and retained by circlips at either end. Remove the circlips, and then press out the piston pin. If the pin is tight, try immersing the piston in hot water to expand it slightly. On still later engines, the piston pin is an interference fit on the small end and should preferably be removed at an authorised workshop.

Clean all traces of old gasket material from mating surfaces.

WEAR AND FAULTS

Specialised measuring equipment, some of which is described here, is needed for a thorough examination of the engine internals. It is a good idea to take the major components (block, pistons, crankshaft etc.) along to an engineering works or an engine rebuilders' premises and ask the staff to check everything for you.

Examine the crankshaft bearing surfaces visually for signs of scoring. If any damage is apparent, then the crankshaft will have to be reground. Many companies will undertake such work, but not all will give equally good results. To locate a good business for the work, take advice from your nearest performance car preparation company. You should ideally use a micrometer to check that none of the journals or crankpins are oval. You should also have access to a flat metal plate and two machined steel blocks with large 'V' cuts machined from the tops. The outer main journals sit in these, and a dial gauge assembly is used against the centre main journal as the crankshaft is rotated slowly by hand. This is necessary to check that the crankshaft is not bent. If you cannot obtain such equipment, then have the crankshaft checked at a machine shop.

If the crankshaft is bent or if it has already been ground to the extent that you are advised by the company you have chosen to carry out the re-grinding not to remove any more metal, they may be able to supply you (at slightly higher cost) with a reground crankshaft from a competition car. These will often be deemed unfit for competition work by their owners even though they still have plenty of 'meat' on the mains journals. The author once took this option, and the cost was 30% higher than that of a straight re-grind of his old crankshaft. A new crankshaft would have cost 3 to 4 times as much.

Examine the cylinder bores for scoring and other marks, tapering and ovality. You require a bore gauge for this, and if you cannot gain access to one, it is best to have the bores professionally checked. If the taper in the bore exceeds .006″ top to bottom then the cylinders must be rebored and oversized pistons fitted. Also check your pistons for ovalness. The piston rings should be replaced as a matter of course. If the bores are satisfactory, use a glaze-buster tool or alternatively fine emery cloth (clean the bores thoroughly afterwards) to remove the glaze.

Insert a piston ring squarely into each cylinder (use an inverted piston for this) and measure the gap. If this is above that listed in the specifications for your particular engine, use another set of piston rings. Also, check the clearance of the grooves with the rings fitted.

If the crankshaft, cylinder bores and pistons are all suspect, then you may be better advised (and it may well be far cheaper) to make the best of a bad job and reassemble the unit and acquire an exchange 'short' engine.

ENGINE REBUILD

It is essential that the engine is rebuilt in very clean surroundings and it is advised that all components are thoroughly cleaned then lightly oiled immediately prior to re-fitting. All oilways in the cylinder block should be cleared, either by compressed air or by poking a piece of wire through them.

Refit the crankshaft bearings, ensuring if the original bearings are re-used that they go back into the positions from which they came. Ensure that the locating tags are properly engaged. If you find that half of the bearings do not have oil holes, then fit these into the bearing caps and fit the bearings with the oil holes into the top (crankcase). It is not unknown to some people to fit the blank bearings into the crank case side and so block off their oilways!

Apply oil generously to the bearings before fitting the crankshaft, then oil the crankshaft journals before fitting the caps. Fit the upper and lower thrust washers each side of the main bearing cap so that the oilways face away from the bearing. Tighten the main bearing bolts down to 63 ft lbs. The crankshaft should rotate easily and smoothly. If there is any roughness or drag then dissemble the crankshaft and bearings, clean everything thoroughly and reassemble. Check the crankshaft endfloat using a feeler gauge inserted between a thrust washer and the crankshaft face with the crankshaft pushed firmly in one direction, if this exceeds .005″, obtain and fit thicker thrust washers.

The piston rings should be replaced using the proper compression tool. Naturally, the author did not possess one and so quickly fabricated an alternative from 20g steel strip. Some rings may have 'Top' marked on one face and, if so, this face should be uppermost in the engine. If the top ring is stepped (for use in worn bores) then ensure that the step is at the top of the piston when the ring is fitted. The step is there to avoid the wear ring in the bore, and if these rings are fitted upside down then they will probably break up when the engine is started up. Before fitting the pistons, move the piston rings so that their gaps are evenly spaced on the non-thrust side of the piston.

Ensure that each connecting rod will have the correct offset when fitted (see illustration). Oil the bores and piston rings with clean engine oil, then re-fit the pistons and connecting rods, ensuring that the arrows on the pistons point towards the front of the engine. The connecting rod and piston can be fed into the cylinder and gently tapped home. Ensure that the

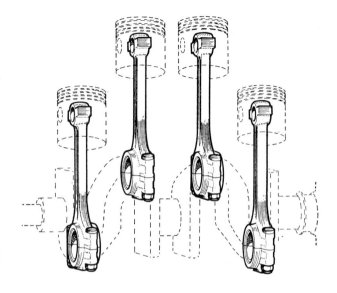

When re-fitting the pistons/connecting rods, ensure that the conrods will present the correct off-set. (Courtesy Autodata)

connecting rod does not lodge against the crankshaft by turning the latter before you tap the piston down.

Fit the bearings in the connecting rods and caps, then apply oil to the crankpins before pulling each connecting rod down fully into position and attaching the cap. Tighten the nuts (33 ft lbs) or bolts (37 ft lbs) and, in the case of the bolts, knock down the locking tabs.

On 1275cc engines, refit the cam followers, then the camshaft. On other models, fit the camshaft alone, because the cam followers can be added later through their inspection panels. Fit the engine front plate using a new gasket, then the camshaft locking plate so that its white metal face is towards the camshaft journal. Fit the dynamo/alternator adjuster bracket on to the cylinder block. Turn the crankshaft so that its keyway is at the 12.00 o'clock position and turn the camshaft so that its keyway is at the 2.00 o'clock position. Reassemble and fit the timing gears and chain as a single entity, then check the timing gears for correct alignment by placing a straight edge across them. Ensure that the dimples in the gears are opposite each other (see illustration on page 79). Secure the camshaft with the nut and lock washer, then refit the chain tensioner (where applicable) and the timing gear cover.

THE CYLINDER HEAD

The cylinder head contains the valves, the rocker gear, oilways and coolant galleries. It channels fuel mixture from the inlet manifold into the cylinders and burnt exhaust gasses out into the exhaust system. The cylinder head is thus the 'busiest' part of the engine and that which most frequently requires attention.

The restorer has several alternatives when dealing with the engine unit. The simplest route is to opt for a full exchange engine, which includes the cylinder head. Many will instead choose a 'short' exchange engine – which does not include a reconditioned cylinder head – and either recondition the cylinder head themselves or have cylinder head work carried out separately by a specialist.

Cylinder head problems are sometimes merely symptoms of real problems which lie with the carburation or ignition (although if you insist on putting unleaded fuel into a standard A series engine cylinder head, this will cause terminal cylinder head problems in next to no time). Running the car with too rich a mixture can cause the head to become fouled with heavy carbon deposits, running with badly set ignition timing can cause overheating, which in the long-term can have dire consequences. Always find and cure the cause of such cylinder head problems.

The most common fault which entails the removal of the cylinder head is a blown head gasket. Between the block and the cylinder head run a number of connecting water and oil galleries. The gasket seals each of these and also the cylinders themselves. Damage to the gasket allows either water or oil into the cylinders when the engine is at rest (steam or blue smoke respectively will dominate the exhaust gasses when the engine is re-started), or it can allow water and oil to mix, which is even more unpleasant for the engine and which should be immediately rectified. A damaged head gasket can also allow combustion fumes under very high pressure to escape into the oil galleries or the coolant galleries, or into other cylinders. None are desirable.

Sometimes the cylinder block or the head can crack, giving the same results as a blown head gasket, albeit at far greater expense!

Many faults can occur to components associated with or covered by the cylinder head, the rectification of which entails the removal of the head. Exhaust valves and seats can burn and lose all compression,

valve guides can wear and allow oil to enter the cylinders (blue exhaust smoke on starting – also caused by worn piston rings and bore damage). The head can warp (same results as a blown gasket). Even stripped spark plug hole threads require the removal of the head.

Removing the cylinder head

With the engine in the car, you will need to firstly obtain a new head gasket set, because old gaskets should never be re-fitted. Disconnect the battery. Drain the coolant from the radiator bottom hose. Remove the rocker box cover. Remove the air filters. Disconnect the throttle and choke cables, springs and vacuum advance pipe from the carburettors. Remove the distributor vacuum advance pipe clip from the heater control valve. If emission control equipment is fitted, remove this also.

Slacken the clip holding the top hose to the thermostat housing, and pull the hose free. Remove the heater control cable from the valve (if fitted), and disconnect the heater hoses. Disconnect the high tension leads from the sparking plugs. If you are not sure of your ability to replace the leads on their respective spark plugs, mark each using masking tape tags or by painting the corresponding number of bands with typist's correction fluid. Disconnect the wire from the water temperature sender.

Remove the nuts securing the carburettors to the inlet manifold, then remove the carburettors and their linkages as a single unit. Keep the carburettors upright at all times, because sediment in the fuel bowl will otherwise be disturbed and may foul the main jet on re-assembly. Disconnect the exhaust down pipe from the manifold.

With the engine in the car or removed: slacken the cylinder head nuts in the order shown previously, turning each by no more than one or two flats at a time to avoid distorting the cylinder head. When all of the nuts are slack, remove them. The rocket shaft nuts may now be removed and the rocker assembly lifted away. Lift out the pushrods, placing them in a numbered rack (a piece of cardboard with holes punched in it and numbers 1–8 written on will suffice) in order that they can be replaced in the correct order.

Lift off the cylinder head. If it sticks, do not use any kind of lever in between the block and head, but tap the cylinder head using a rawhide mallet until it is free. Discard the old cylinder head gasket.

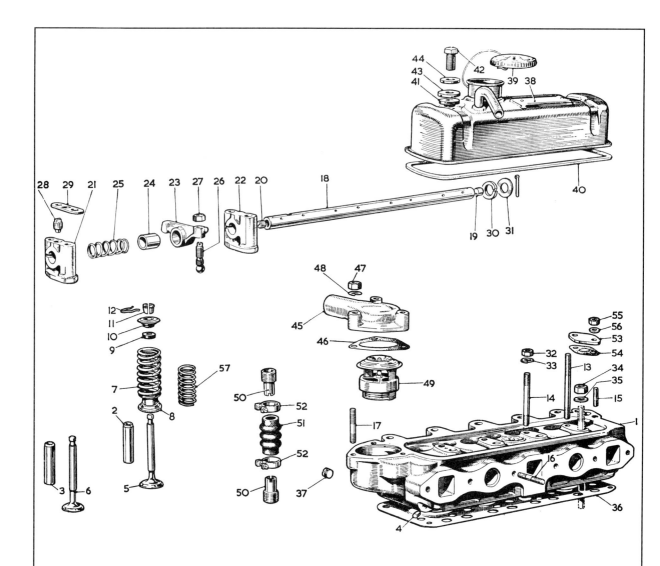

1. Cylinder head with valve guides	20. Rocker shaft plug (screwed)	39. Oil filler cap
2. Inlet valve guide	21. Rocker shaft bracket (tapped)	40. Cover joint
3. Exhaust valve guide	22. Rocker shaft bracket (plain)	41. Cover bush
4. Oil hole plug	23. Rocker (bushed)	42. Nut
5. Inlet valve	24. Rocker bush	43. Distance piece
6. Exhaust valve	25. Rocker spacing spring	44. Cup washer
7. Outer valve spring	26. Tappet adjusting screw	45. Water outlet elbow
8. Shroud for valve guide	27. Locknut	46. Joint
9. Valve packing ring	28. Rocker shaft locating screw	47. Nut
10. Valve spring cup	29. Rocker shaft bracket plate	48. Spring washer
11. Valve cotter	30. Spring washer	49. Thermostat
12. Valve cotter circlip	31. Washer	50. By-pass adaptor
13. Rocker bracket stud (long)	32. Nut	51. By-pass connector (rubber)
14. Rocker bracket stud (short)	33. Spring washer	52. By-pass clip
15. Cover-plate stud	34. Cylinder head nut	53. Cover-plate
16. Manifold stud	35. Washer	54. Joint (plate to cylinder head)
17. Water outlet elbow stud	36. Cylinder head gasket	55. Cover nut
18. Valve rocker shaft (plugged)	37. Thermal indicator boss screwed plug	56. Spring washer
19. Rocker shaft plug (plain)	38. Valve rocker cover	57. Inner valve spring

Cylinder head repairs

Remove the spark plugs, the thermostat housing cover and the thermostat. Tap each valve cap sharply in case it is sticking to the valve stem. Using a proper spring compressor, compress each spring in turn, lift out the collets, pull off the oil seal then release the spring pressure slowly. The valve may now be withdrawn from the cylinder head. It is important that the valves are replaced in the correct sequence, so either place them in a numbered rack or stamp them with a number of dots according to whether they came from cylinder 1, 2, 3 or 4. Early cars may have small spring clips fitted over the collets, and these should be removed before the spring compressor is used.

Carefully clean all carbon deposits from the cylinder head, using a proper scraper, NOT an old screwdriver, which can score the head. If very heavy dry carbon deposits are found then the engine could have been running far too rich. If oily black deposits

LEFT The cylinder head of the A series engine. (Courtesy Autodata)

BELOW When cleaning off the cylinder head and block mating surface, use a flat scraper which will not mark either. The impoverished author is here making do with the back of an old hacksaw blade.

are found then oil is leaking into the cylinders, most probably past the valve stems/guides. After cleaning the cylinder head, examine it for cracks, which usually run between two valve seats or between a valve seat and a coolant gallery. These can be repaired, although it may prove cheaper and it is recommended that you obtain a replacement head from the breaker's yard instead.

At this stage you should check that the cylinder head is not warped by placing an engineer's straight edge along the lower face – any distortion should be apparent, and has to be dealt with by having the head skimmed.

Examine the valve seats and valves for deep pitting, and if this is found, the valves should preferably be replaced as a set along with the guides, and the valve seats will have to be re-cut (work best placed with a professional, although valve seat cutting equipment is available for the DIY enthusiast). Place each valve stem in its guide from the topside of the cylinder head, and feel for play between the valve stem and guide. There must be a reasonable amount of contact between these two, because the valve dissipates excess heat partially through its contact with the guide. If a valve begins to stick within its guide at some point of its travel, then the valve stem will be bent and the valve and its guide should be replaced; preferably, all valves and guides should be replaced together as a set.

If the valves and guides are to be replaced, then it will pay to ask whoever re-cuts the valve seats to also fit the new guides. These can be drifted into position, but it is better to have them pressed in using a hydraulic press. At this point you have the option of fitting an exchange cylinder head, including those which have been altered so that they are suitable for use with unleaded fuel. The valves of the 1275cc unit are felt by some to be too large for the inserts necessary for use with unleaded fuel to be safely fitted. (See Chapter 7 Engine Modifications).

The valves may now be lapped in. You will need a very low cost tool (a stick with a rubber sucker on the end) and some grinding paste. Wet the rubber sucker, then attach the tool to the centre of the valve face, smear some of the coarser paste to the seating area, then place the valve into position. Rotate the tool between your hands, frequently lifting it and turning it through ninety degrees. Clean the paste from the valve and seat, then inspect both. You need to be able to see an unbroken circle with the matt finish produced by the paste, so repeat the process until this is achieved, then use the fine paste. When the valve and seat are properly lapped, the valve will bounce if dropped into its seat from a height of 1½″ or so.

Make sure that the block and head mating surfaces are spotlessly clean. Turn the engine over by hand until two pistons are at the tops of their travel, then stuff clean rags into the other two, in order to prevent carbon from falling into them (because it can lodge on the top piston ring grooves and score the bore). Also, mask off all water and oilways using masking tape for the same reason. Use the correct scraping device rather than a chisel or screwdriver blade: the correct scraper is fashioned so that it will not score the surface, whereas it will easily be scored with makeshift tools. The piston crowns should be cleaned.

Lightly wipe a little engine oil around the bores of all cylinders and double check that none are scored.

Place the new head gasket onto the block. It should be marked "Top" and "Front" but even so, make sure that none of the oil or coolant galleries will be blocked when the gasket is fitted, just to ensure that you have the correct gasket and are fitting it the right way up/round! Some authorities recommend that a small amount of 'instant gasket' sealant is placed around each of the water holes each side of the gasket, to help prevent water loss. This should not really be necessary if both the head and the block

faces are true, and the head nuts are tightened to the appropriate torque.

Lower the cylinder head into position. If tightness against the studs is encountered then they should be cleaned lightly. Replace the pushrods into the correct holes so that each locates correctly with its tappet. Replace the rocker assembly, ensuring that the ball end of each screw adjuster locates correctly in the pushrod top.

Fit the eleven cylinder head and four extra rocker assembly nuts to finger tightness, then turn each of the cylinder head nuts half a turn in the correct sequence until they can be finally set at the correct torque using a torque wrench. Reset the valve clearances.

Reconnect all hoses, cables, manifolds and associated gear and coolant/heater connections in the reverse of the stripping sequence. Run the engine until it reaches normal operating temperature, watching for signs of leaks from around the head gasket. Re-torque all cylinder head nuts in sequence. It is as well to re-torque the head after a hundred miles' use.

SETTING VALVE CLEARANCES

Tools: Ring spanner. Screwdriver. Feeler gauge. Proprietary valve adjusting tool optional.

With the battery disconnected and the cylinder head reassembled onto the block, remove the sparking plugs so that the engine may be turned over either by hand (via the fan belt), by pushing the car with 4th gear engaged, or by raising one rear wheel off the ground, engaging 4th gear, then having someone turn the raised wheel.

The valves should be checked in the following sequence (which saves the engine having to be laboriously turned over too much).

Valve fully open.	Test/adjust valve no.
8	1
6	3
4	5
7	2
1	8
3	6
5	4
2	7

Note that the sum of the valve number to be open and the one to be checked is always nine.

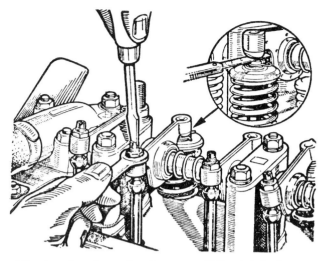

Adjusting the valve rocker clearances. If the slots in the top of the adjuster screws have opened, it may prove difficult to set the clearances accurately, in which case replacement adjuster screws should be fitted. There are special tools which make this adjustment rather easier, although it is up to the individual to decide whether the expense is justified for a tool which will be used so infrequently. (Courtesy Autodata)

Holding the ball-end adjusting screw with a screwdriver, slacken the locking nut using a ½″ ring spanner. Insert the correct feeler gauge(s) and adjust the screw until the gauge is very lightly gripped but may still be moved. Holding the adjusting screw still, tighten the locking nut. Re-check. Do not be tempted to reduce the valve clearances too much to cure noisy tappets, but always adhere to the recommended gaps.

If the adjuster screw slots are badly distorted, then it pays to renew them, as this will allow more accurate re-setting. The rocker gear has to be removed, which entails draining the coolant, slackening each cylinder head nut in the correct sequence and then removing the four which hold the rocker posts and the four nuts on the head studs.

When the cylinder head has been replaced and the ancillaries re-connected, the engine may not run very evenly. As the ignition has not been disturbed, check the carburation. If the engine requires copious amounts of choke to run, suspect an induction air leak. Check that the various connections to the inlet manifold and carburettors (distributor vacuum switch, breather pipe etc) are all in position.

There is always a danger that removing or re-fitting the carburettors disturbs sediment in the fuel bowl, allowing some to foul the main jet. Dismantle the carburettors and wash, then blow out the system.

GEARBOX. STRIPPING, EXAMINATION AND REBUILDING

Although it is perfectly feasible for the DIY enthusiast to strip, repair and rebuild his own gearbox, there are powerful arguments for opting instead for an exchange reconditioned unit. Firstly, you never know exactly how many parts will require replacement until the gearbox is stripped, and if the number of worn or faulty components is great enough then their replacement costs could outstrip the price of an exchange unit. This is because the companies which recondition gearboxes buy in components at trade price, and because they are able to 'even out' their prices. They will work on some gearboxes which require few parts as well as those which require substantial rebuilding – the price they charge will on average probably be that for a gearbox which requires the 'average' amount of work.

If you intend to strip a gearbox merely to cure a noise in one gear then think again. A noisy gearbox cannot be dealt with merely by exchanging the one gear in which the noise is apparent, because the teeth will have worn or be chipped (which causes the noise) in concert with the teeth to which the gear meshes. The mainshaft gears mesh with the laygear, so that this too should be replaced. The new laygear would present a different bearing profile to the other mainshaft gears, necessitating their replacement, and on it goes. If you were to merely exchange the faulty gear, then you might 'cure' a noisy third gear and in doing so create lesser noises in all of the other gears! If gearbox noise can be tolerated then the gearbox may last for many years without giving any problems other than the noise. Otherwise, obtaining an exchange reconditioned unit is recommended.

Those who have early gearboxes which have synchromesh cones rather than baulk rings are especially recommended to opt for an exchange gearbox, because working with the cones can present special problems to the DIY restorer. If any of the synchronising cones are worn or damaged, then new cones have to be shrunk onto their gears, then machined to size. In such instances, it is better to purchase either new gears with the cones already in situ and machined, or to opt for an exchange mainshaft complete – better still, exchange the gearbox for a reconditioned one.

The instructions which follow describe a gearbox overhaul; that is, the replacement of worn bearings, layshaft, thrust washers etc, rather than the complete

The gearbox as it comes out of the car. The large crack around the top of the clutch bell housing was caused by the gearbox being allowed to strike the heater platform assembly whilst being removed or re-fitted – so take extra care during these operations. Luckily, Bromsgrove MG Spares Centre were able to furnish the author with a (now rare) replacement, although it would have been possible to have had this one welded. It is a good idea at this stage to give the entire gearbox housing a good clean.

reconditioning of the gearbox, which should, if found necessary, be left to professionals.

All models except 1500cc

The gearboxes fitted to 948cc, 1098cc and 1275cc models offer four forward gears with synchromesh on second, third and fourth. Although there are detail differences between early and late examples, the procedure for primary stripping is the same.

It is vital that the insides of the gearbox are scrupulously clean, and so the first part of the job is to thoroughly clean off the outside of the casing, in order to minimise the chances of dirt getting into the unit when it is rebuilt. Many people favour the use of specialised products such as 'Gunk', which are painted on then brushed into the caked-on mixture of mud and oil before being washed off. Alternatively, you can scrape away the thick layer of oil-soaked muck which will usually cover the underside of the unit, then finish the cleaning with a toothbrush and neat petrol (taking suitable safety precautions) or paraffin. Also in the interests of cleanliness, do not carry out this work in the same building in which you have just flatted down body filler or wire-brushed a rusted component, because the atmosphere will be full of particles which will get into the workings of the gearbox. Find somewhere dust-free for this work. If you have not already done so, drain the gearbox oil.

If you choose to work with a workshop manual for cross-reference when stripping the gearbox, you may (depending on the manual you use) notice that the order of work recommended by the manual and by this book differs. You may also notice that some of the instructions differ considerably. The following is based on notes taken during an actual gearbox overhaul undertaken by the author, and they accurately describe the process.

Remove the nuts which retain the reverse light switch wire clamps (where fitted). Remove the eight nuts which retain the remote control housing, and lift off the housing. Stand the gearbox upright on supports (to allow clearance for the input shaft) on the bell housing and remove the nine nuts which hold the rear extension. Lift this a little then turn it anti-clockwise to disengage the control rod from the selector rod ends, then lift it clear.

Prise off the two springs which retain the clutch release bearing and remove this from the clutch lever fork. Unto the nut and spring washer from the clutch lever bolt, then knock back the lock tab on the bolt and unscrew this. Remove the lever.

Remove the nuts or bolts which retain the side cover, then lift away the cover and its gasket. Two springs will be seen protruding from the casing, having previously been compressed by the side cover lip. These place pressure on the selector rod plungers. Remove them, and try to shake the plungers from the casing. If they do not emerge, do not worry but leave their removal until later. Ensure that the gearbox is in neutral by lining up the three selector forks. Undo the locknuts, bolts and washers from the first/second gear selector fork and the third/fourth gear fork.

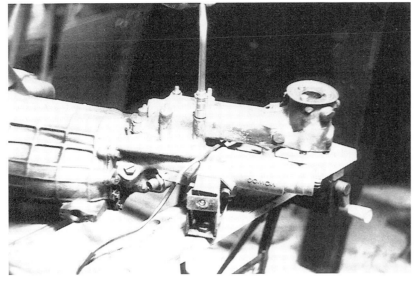

Undo the bolts holding the remote control housing in position.

The remote control housing may now be lifted away.

Remove the rear extension securing nuts then, with some gentle manoeuvring (lift a little, then twist anti-clockwise) lift away the extension.

89

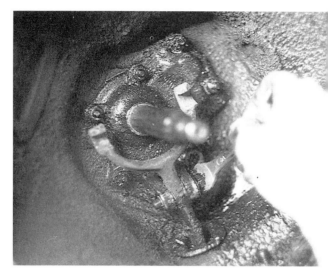

ABOVE RIGHT *The clutch release forks must be unbolted.*

ABOVE *Then remove the front cover.*

RIGHT *Turn the engine onto its front end, then remove the nuts which secure the side casing and remove this, taking care to catch the two springs which may fly out.*

ABOVE LEFT *Undoing the reverse selector fork bolt.*

LEFT *Although the author chose to keep each fork stored on its appropriate rod, in practice it is easy to work out which goes with which when you come to reassemble the gearbox.*

ABOVE *To provide positive locations for the selector rods and in order to prevent the driver from selecting two gears simultaneously, the selector rods have shallows machined into them into which locate and interlock the spring-loaded plungers. One rod can only be moved when the interlock plunger concerned has located in the machined shallow on another rod. Remove the plug shown in the photograph, the spring and the plunger (although this may not shake free at this stage and can easily be removed later).*

Turn the gearbox onto its side so that the base is facing you. Remove the lower of the two plugs towards the front of the unit, along with its spring and plunger (if the plunger cannot be shaken out, leave it until later), then remove the other plug. Using a thin-walled $\frac{7}{16}$" socket passed through the drain plug hole, undo the reverse fork locating bolt locknut, and when it reaches the head of its bolt it will turn the bolt so that the two can be removed, along with their washer.

Remove the selector rods in the following sequence; third/fourth, first/second, reverse. Lift out the selector forks and re-attach them to the relevant rods to keep everything together! The interlock balls can now be removed.

Measure the laygear endfloat; if this is greater than .003" (Midget Mk.1 & 2, Sprite Mk.2 & 3), or .005" (Midget Mk.3 and Sprite Mk. 4), make a note of the excess and obtain the correct sized thrust washer (the smaller rear thrust washer) to compensate.

Using a fairly soft metal rod, drift the layshaft forwards into the bell housing. The laygear and thrust washers will drop slightly into the bottom of the gearbox as the drift is withdrawn.

Remove the reverse gear set bolt (adjacent to the drain plug hole) and, using a large screwdriver, turn the reverse gear shaft whilst moving it forwards until the gear drops free.

The mainshaft (also known as the 'third motion' shaft) can now be removed. Use a soft-faced drift and gently tap alternate sides of the bearing housing, because the mainshaft, its bearing and the bearing housing come out together as an assembly. As soon as the assembly has emerged sufficiently from the rear of the gearbox for a pair of screwdriver blades or a puller to be placed underneath the bearing housing lip, lever the assembly the rest of the way, taking care not to damage the casing. The mainshaft can now be lifted complete from the casing. The roller bearing at the front of the mainshaft may come out (from inside the end of the first motion shaft) with it; take care to note whether any rollers have dropped out of the cage and look for these in the bottom of the gearbox where they will have fallen!

The first motion shaft can now be removed. Use a metal rod to drift it forwards towards the bell housing just enough to expose the circlip on the roller bearing within the bell housing. Remove the circlip, then gently drift the first motion shaft backwards into the casing until it is free to be lifted out. Note that the first motion shaft does not, as the author has seen implied

in one workshop manual, drift out into the bell housing!

If the various plungers did not come out of the casing earlier, use a gently curving length of stiff wire to poke them out. Make notes of where the various plungers and ball bearings fit.

The gearbox is now stripped. Clean all parts in neat petrol prior to reassembly.

Examination

Examine the gear teeth for chips and wear. Also examine the teeth of the laygear and reverse gear; if a number of teeth are damaged or badly worn, it is advised that the gearbox is rebuilt and swapped for a reconditioned one. Bear in mind that a new laygear alone will cost between 35% and 40% of the price of a reconditioned gearbox.

If the laygear is serviceable, examine its roller bearings and replace if necessary. These are retained by spring clips which can be prised out, after which, simply insert a finger into each bearing and pull it out.

Examine the mainshaft and first motion shaft bearings. If the inner race feels loose then replace the bearing in question. In order to remove the mainshaft bearing, firstly knock back the tab washer on the speedometer gear retaining nut, then remove the nut, gear, washers and distance tube. To remove the first motion shaft bearing, firstly remove its retaining nut and washer.

Examine the roller bearing from inside the rear end of the first motion shaft, and replace if necessary (later cars). The bush (earlier cars) should have a .002" to .003" clearance with the mainshaft and if this proves excessive, then the bush should be replaced. It is possible that a new bush will still have too much clearance, in which case the mainshaft end is worn and it will have to be replaced.

In order to examine the various gear roller bearings and the synchronisers, it is necessary to strip the mainshaft. This is not recommended: it is a difficult task to strip the mainshaft and an even more difficult (and frustrating) one to rebuild it. If any of the gears show signs of wear or damage or if the cone synchromesh of an early 'box is suspect, it is far better to exchange the mainshaft for a reconditioned one. If the gears are in good order but their bearings show signs of wear, then it becomes slightly more practical to opt for a DIY overhaul of the mainshaft.

ABOVE LEFT *The double-ended interlock plunger, which fits into the hole thoughtfully covered by the author's little finger in this photograph.*

ABOVE *Sliding out the layshaft.*

LEFT *Removing the mainshaft.*

First gear synchro hub stripped. Note that this example, from a 1974 gearbox, has a plunger to complicate the already frustrating reassembly of the hub. The gear and hub should be assembled so that the plunger (seen here front middle of hub) locates into the cutaway indicated by the author's outstretched digit.

The synchromesh assemblies include hubs into each of which are fitted three springs with ball bearings. The ball bearings are retained by the sliding sleeve. When the synchromesh hubs are stripped, the springs shoot the ball bearings out at considerable velocity, certainly enough to travel six to nine feet, and so you can easily lose the bearings in the typical junk of a workshop unless you take suitable precautions. When stripping the synchromesh hubs, hold the assembly in a piece of cloth so that the bearings and their springs do not disappear at high velocity. When reassembling, the author recommends that you work with the hub held inside an open topped cardboard box, so that the bearings cannot fly out into the dim recesses of your workshop.

The recommended first step is to take close-up photographs of the assembled mainshaft, to remind you on reassembly where everything goes!

Remove the speedometer drive nut (tab washer first), the drivegear and distance piece from the rear end of the mainshaft, then pull the bearing housing and the bearing from the shaft. A long three legged puller makes this task easier.

Remove the third/fourth gear synchromesh assembly from the front end of the mainshaft. Remove third gear by pressing a thin rod onto the plunger in the synchro cone, turning the gear on the mainshaft so that the plunger is held by a spline, then

pull the locking ring away and remove the plunger and spring. Third gear may now be removed, taking care not to lose the needle roller bearings. Remove first gear and the second gear synchromesh assembly, then, using a very small screwdriver or similar, press down on the spring loaded plunger and turn the locking ring so that the plunger is held by one of the splines. The plunger, second gear and its half washers and roller bearing may now be removed.

If the mainshaft or any of the gears show signs of damage then a reconditioned exchange gearbox is recommended. If the gears are all in good condition, then replace the bearings and reassemble the mainshaft.

REBUILDING THE GEARBOX

It is essential that the gearbox is rebuilt in the correct sequence.

Firstly, carefully drift the first motion shaft into position from within the casing, fit the circlip from with the bell chamber, then gently drift the assembly backwards until the circlip rests against the front face. Assemble the laygear and its bearings into position within the casing, and hold them in place with a thin rod rather than the layshaft at this stage.

Place reverse gear in the casing, and slide its

The baulk ring locates on this taper which, as can be seen, is not very good. Add to this the fact that most of the gears of this gearbox have chipped teeth, and the hard truth emerges that no less than a full rebuild is needed. Hence the advice to opt for an exchange unit.

shaft into position. Turn the shaft using a screwdriver until the hole in the shaft lines up with the hole in the casing, then screw in the locking nut.

Replace the roller bearing within the hollow end of the first motion shaft, then offer the assembled mainshaft into position, ensuring that the cutaway of the bearing housing is positioned correctly so that it cannot foul the reverse gear, and gently drift the bearing housing into the gearbox casing.

From the bell housing end, feed the layshaft into position, taking care to line up the laygear bearings correctly.

Re-fit the selector forks. Slide the reverse selector fork rod into position, and secure it with its bolt and lock nut. Re-fit the double-ended interlock plunger into the hole at the rear of the side flange, then fit the 1st/2nd rod. Push the 3rd/4th rod partially home. Push one ball bearing into the hole at the front of the side flange and locate it against the cutaway in the 3rd/4th rod. Push the other ball bearing into the hole in the underside of the casing, and push it firmly against the cutaway in the 1st/2nd rod. The 3rd/4th rod may now be pushed fully home.

Re-fit the reverse plunger, then the remaining two plungers and their springs. If you have difficulty in re-assembling the gearbox, do not force any of these components, but partially strip the gearbox and try again. Although a gearbox

represents something of a 3-D mental puzzle, with a little thought you will find that it becomes obvious what goes where.

CLUTCH

Although the clutches fitted to the 998cc, 1098cc, 1275cc and 1500cc engines all differ, they all operate in much the same manner.

The clutch disengages drive from the crankshaft to the gearbox input shaft. It consists of the flywheel, which rotates with the crankshaft, a pressure plate which is contained within a steel cover bolted to the flywheel, and the friction (driven) plate. The driven plate is normally clamped tightly between the flywheel and the pressure plate, so that it rotates with the flywheel. The driven plate fits onto splines and passes drive to the gearbox input shaft.

When the clutch pedal is depressed, a piston within the master cylinder pushes non-compressible hydraulic fluid along the piping to the slave cylinder, where it bears against a second piston which moves and operates the clutch lever. This moves the release bearing, which in turn pushes against the diaphragm or coil springs which pulls the pressure plate away from the driven plate, releasing it from the sandwich between the pressure plate and the flywheel. Drive to

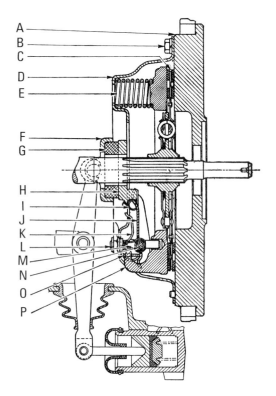

LEFT *A section through the coil spring clutch. Note the 'sandwich' of the flywheel, driven plate and pressure plate. (Courtesy Autodata)*

BELOW *A section through the diaphragm spring clutch. The principle of operation is the same as the coil spring clutch. (Courtesy Autodata)*

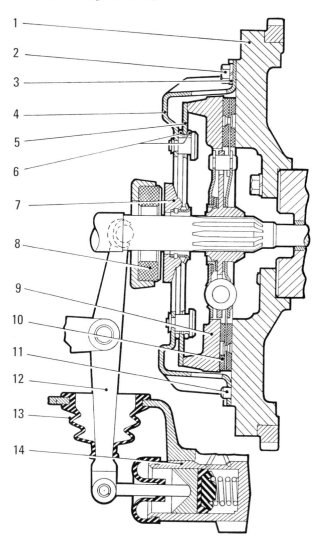

A. *Flywheel*	L. *Lever retainer spring*
B. *Securing bolt*	J. *Release lever*
C. *Driven plate*	K. *Anti-rattle spring*
D. *Clutch cover*	L. *Adjusting nut*
E. *Thrust coil spring*	M. *Eyebolt*
F. *Release bearing cup*	N. *Floating pin (release lever)*
G. *Graphite release bearing*	O. *Strut*
H. *Release plate*	P. *Pressure plate*

the gearbox input shaft is then disconnected, allowing the gears to be shifted.

In order to replace the clutch of Spridgets it is necessary to firstly remove the engine from the car (See Engine Removal).

During the course of a part or full restoration when the engine and gearbox are removed it is worth replacing the clutch and the release bearing as a matter of course. If a partially worn clutch mechanism were to be refitted into the car, then the engine would have to be removed as it wore out, with attendant dangers of scratching or denting the new paintwork. Whenever the clutch is replaced, the release bearing should be replaced, preferably along with the clutch release lever bearing.

All of the clutches fitted to Spridgets possess reference marks on the clutch covers and the flywheels, which are intended to allow the two units to be reassembled in the same relative positions. The actual marks vary according to the car in question.

1. *Flywheel*	8. *Release bearing*
2. *Clutch securing bolt*	9. *Pressure plate*
3. *Spring washer*	10. *Driven plate*
4. *Cover*	11. *Dowel*
5. *Diaphragm/spring*	12. *Release lever*
6. *Annular rings*	13. *Rubber boot*
7. *Release plate*	14. *Slave cylinder*

Make a note of the marks to aid reassembly.

It is necessary to release the pressure from the pressure plate springs gently and evenly, by undoing the clutch cover bolts in a diagonal sequence, turning each by a half turn at a time. When the bolts have been removed, the clutch cover can be lifted off its locating dowels. The driven plate is now free.

Examine the flywheel face where it comes into contact with the driven plate. It should be smooth, free from excessive heat marks (blueing is acceptable, but colours denoting higher temperatures are not) and, if not, it should either be machined or replaced.

The clutch cover and associated components can be stripped and reassembled by the DIY enthusiast but this is not recommended, because the assembly should ideally be balanced. Opt instead for a replacement, also replacing the driven plate and release bearing.

When replacing the clutch mechanism, it is necessary to correctly align the driven plate before it becomes firmly clamped by the pressure plate when the cover is bolted tight. If the clutch were to be reassembled with the driven plate out of alignment, then the gearbox input shaft would not align. There are special tools for centring the driven plate; most garages keep an old gearbox input shaft for the purpose. The cover assembly is loosely bolted into position with the driven plate inside, and the input shaft or special tool is passed through the driven plate into the hole in the crankshaft end which holds the input shaft bearing bush. The driven plate is correctly aligned when it is centralised, then the pressure plate bolts can be retightened slowly in a diagonal sequence.

THE FUEL SYSTEM

Petrol is drawn from the fuel tank by an electric pump. The fuel reaches the carburettors, where a partial vacuum created in the carburettor throat by the air being sucked in by the engine draws the fuel upwards through the main jet so that it mixes thoroughly with the air before being drawn into the combustion chambers, forming the fine mist which is burnt to power the engine.

The fuel tank

The fuel tank is situated under the boot floor. Before carrying out any operations to or in the vicinity of the fuel tank, disconnect and remove the battery.

It is usually necessary to drain fuel from the tank prior to its removal. If you are syphoning fuel into a metal container then it is wise to run a length of wire which will earth both the container and the car, to prevent static electricity from jumping from the car to the container, which could ignite the fuel.

Alternatively, you could pump the fuel out by disconnecting the carburettor fuel line and joining this to a pipe leading to a petrol container. Switch on the ignition, and the pump will empty the tank for you. When the fuel has been drained, the outlet pipe may be disconnected and plugged or sealed with plastic tape.

Remove the filler cap, the filler pipe and the wires from the fuel gauge sender unit. If you have not already done so, slacken the screw clamp on

To remove the fuel tank, firstly drain it then disconnect the fuel line and fuel gauge sender wire. Remove the filler pipe and stuff a rag into the hole in the tank to prevent fumes from escaping. Use a trolley jack to support the tank whilst you undo its securing nuts if working alone, and get the tank out of the workshop immediately; store it safely in a building which does not have an electricity supply if you intend to re-use it. If the tank is to be scrapped then fill it with water and ask your local garage to dispose of it for you.

the fuel line connection, then pull the line from the tank outlet. The author prefers to place a trolley jack under the fuel tank before undoing the retaining nuts. The tank may now be lowered from under the boot.

Examine the tank for rot and, if any is discovered, replace it. It is possible to repair fuel tanks, although this is a job which is strictly the province of the experienced professional, because trying to weld any sort of container which has held fuel could prove a highly explosive and terminal experience! Various types of repair kit are available for fuel tanks (but are not recommended), as are chemical solutions which are placed in the tank and swilled around, and which are supposed to seal pin holes. However, if a tank has rust holes then it will have tiny flakes of rust inside which, sooner or later, will cause a blockage somewhere within the fuel system. Even though Spridget fuel tanks are not particularly cheap, replacement is advised rather than repair.

The fuel gauge sender unit may be removed from the tank by gently tapping the retaining ring until its lugs are free and the unit may be lifted out. When refitting the unit, use a new seal. If the tank is to be scrapped then it is a good idea to immediately fill it with water until it can be safely disposed of. If it is to be re-used then stuff rags in the filler and gauge sender unit holes, and preferably store the tank in a separate building for safety's sake.

Examine the metal and rubber sections of the fuel line, and replace any sections which show signs of corrosion or, in the case of the rubber sections, perishing or cracking.

Carburettor

The SU HS2 and HS4 carburettors fitted across the Spridget range are simple, robust and extremely reliable units. They differ mainly in their size, the HS4 being a rather larger unit than the HS2.

Refer to the illustration to identify the components mentioned in the following description. Fuel is fed under pressure by the pump into the separate float chamber half of the carburettor (20). When the fuel rises to a set level, the float arm pushes a needle (32) into a jet to cut off the supply until the level again drops. This prevents the carburettor from flooding.

From just above the bottom of the float chamber (where sediment can settle out safely), the fuel is piped off to the carburettor main jet (13). A needle (19) slides up and down in this jet to vary the size of the hole through which fuel is able to pass, so enriching and weakening the mixture. The needle is attached to a piston (6) situated within the top bell chamber, and the piston rises as the speed of the air passing through the carburettor throat rises, and vice versa, to allow the fuel mixture to remain stable irrespective of the amount of air being sucked in by the engine. A small hole between the throat and bell chamber allows air to be sucked out of the bell chamber, creating a vacuum which causes the piston to rise.

At the top of the carburettor is a damper piston rod (8), which passes into a small cylinder at the top of the main piston. This cylinder is filled with oil to dampen the action of the piston and prevent 'flutter'. The piston itself also has a return spring (10), to ensure that it drops back promptly to reduce the fuel supply when the amount of air passing through the throat drops.

Two cables control the actions of the carburettors. The throttle cable is attached to the throttle disc (37), which rotates to vary the effective internal size of the throat and hence the volume of air/fuel mixture which the engine can draw. As the accelerator pedal is depressed the valve rotates to increase this size and the amount of mixture reaching the engine to increase its revolutions, and vice versa. The choke is a device for enriching the fuel content of the air/fuel mixture, to assist starting the engine in cold conditions. The choke cable is connected by a lever to the main jet (13), and because the choke is engaged the jet is pulled downwards to allow more fuel to be drawn into the air mixture.

A rubber pipe connects to the upper face of one carburettor. This is the vacuum advance pipe. As the throttle is depressed and the engine revolutions begin to pick up, air passes more rapidly through the carburettor throat, causing a slight vacuum. The vacuum extends up into the

RIGHT *All Spridgets were fitted with twin SU HS2 carburettors except the 1500cc, which had twin HS4 carbs. The two are extremely similar, and differ mainly in choke diameter. This illustration shows the 1098/1275 set-up. (Courtesy Autodata)*

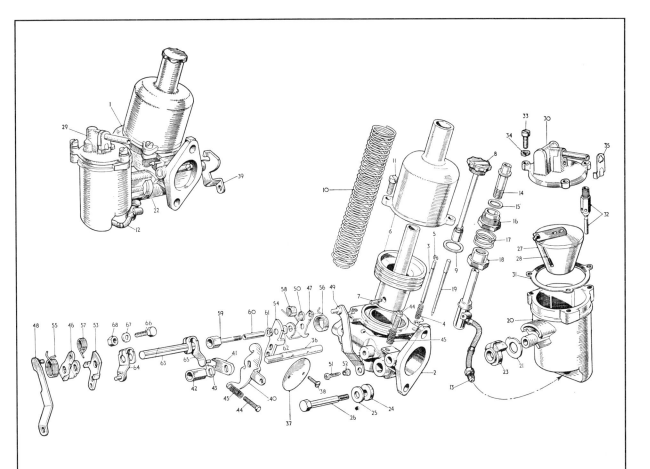

1. Carburettor body (left)
2. Carburettor body (right)
3. Piston lifting pin
4. Spring
5. Circlip
6. Piston chamber assembly
7. Screw
8. Cap and damper assembly
9. Fibre washer
10. Piston spring
11. Screw
12. Jet assembly (left carb.)
13. Jet assembly (right carb.)
14. Bearing
15. Washer
16. Screw
17. Spring
18. Screw
19. Needle
20. Float-chamber
21. Support washer
22. Rubber grommet (left carb.)
23. Rubber grommet (right carb.)

24. Rubber washer
25. Steel washer
26. Bolt
27. Float assembly
28. Lever pin
29. Float-chamber lid (left-carb.)
30. Float-chamber lid (right-carb.)
31. Washer
32. Needle and seat assembly
33. Screw
34. Spring washer
35. Baffle plate
36. Throttle spindle
37. Throttle disc
38. Screw
39. Throttle return lever (left-carb.)
40. Throttle return lever (right-carb.)
41. Lost motion lever
42. Nut
43. Tab washer
44. Throttle screw stop
45. Spring
46. Pick-up lever (left-carb.)

47. Pick-up lever (right-carb.)
48. Link (left- carb.)
49. Link (right-carb.)
50. Washer
51. Screw
52. Bush
53. Cam lever (left carb.)
54. Cam lever (right carb.)
55. Pick-up lever spring (left-carb.)
56. Pick-up lever spring (right-carb.)
57. Cam lever spring (left-carb.)
58. Cam lever spring (right-carb.)
59. Bolt
60. Tube
61. Spring washer
62. Distance piece
63. Jet rod
64. Lever and pin assembly (left-carb.)
65. Lever and pin assembly (right-carb.)
66. Bolt
67. Washer
68. Nut

vacuum advance pipe, which leads to the distributor and causes it to advance the ignition slightly to enhance performance. This pipe must be in good condition and its end connections must be airtight. If the vacuum advance pipe leaks at either end or if it is perished then the timing will not be advanced, and neat air will be drawn back into the carburettor throat, slightly weakening the mixture. The combination of retarded ignition timing and a weak mixture will have a serious effect on performance.

Carburettor removal

Disconnect the battery. Remove the air filters. Disconnect the throttle and choke cables, the return springs and the vacuum advance pipe. Slacken the clip which fastens the fuel pipe to the top of the float chamber, and pull the pipe away, taking care not to spill fuel.

The carburettors are secured to the inlet manifold by two nuts on threaded studs which are screwed into the inlet manifold. Remove the nuts, then withdraw the carburettors and their linkage as a single unit. Take care not to hold the carburettors at an angle, but keep them upright at all times to prevent sediments in the fuel bowl from getting into the jet pipe. On models fitted with emission control equipment, there will be a varying number of extra pipes to remove. Make a note of where each pipe resides before removal!

Carburettor overhaul

It is not too difficult to overhaul an SU HS series carburettor whilst it is attached to the cylinder head, although it is made much easier by improved access if the work is carried out whilst the unit is removed from the car during the restoration.

Clean the outside of the unit. This makes it far easier to work with but also reduces the chances of dirt being allowed to enter the carburettor, where it could clog up the main jet. The author prefers to use an old toothbrush and neat petrol for this. Allowing the petrol to soak well into the mixture of dirt and oil typically found on a carburettor quickly loosens it, so that it may be easily washed and brushed away.

Lift the piston manually and allow it to fall, noting whether there is any roughness (caused by the piston fouling the bell housing or dirt thereon). The piston should drop to the jet bridge with a soft 'click'; if it does not then the jet will have to be centred.

Remove the three screws from the top of the float chamber, then lift off the top and the float/needle and jet assembly. Empty the float chamber. Disconnect the fuel outlet pipe and clean the sediment from the bottom of the float chamber. Remove the fuel inlet needle (32) and examine it for a ridge which indicates that it is worn and should be replaced, along with its jet. Examine the float for damage.

Remove the three screws (11) from the bell housing, then lift the bell housing and the piston return spring (10) from the carburettor. Carefully lift the piston (6) from the main body, taking care not to place any stresses on the needle. Examine the needle for ridges and, if the slightest ridge is found, replace both the needle and the jet. Undo the screw which retains the jet and withdraw this from the carburettor body. Examine the jet for ovalness, and, if it is the slightest out of true, replace both it and the needle.

There are a range of needles, jets and piston return springs available for all SU carburettors to suit varying conditions. In order to fully assess which combination is required for your engine really demands that the car is properly set up on a rolling road, with exhaust emission equipment. However, for most purposes, you could select the standard option and tune the engine yourself.

If roughness could be felt when the piston was lifted, clean it and the inside of the bell housing and then examine both for signs of contact wear. This may be very gently removed using metal polish. If this fails to prevent the piston from sticking then both the piston and the bell housing should be renewed as a set. Both are manufactured to very close tolerances and should only ever be used in the set.

Examine the throttle spindle (36) for looseness within its bushes. If wear is apparent (this will allow air into the system and weaken the mixture) then the spindle and throttle disc may be exchanged, although wear in the bushes can be treated successfully only by replacement (not a DIY job) or replacement of the carburettor body. The best option may be to obtain a replacement carburettor from a breaker's yard. The SU HS2 and HS4 were used on such a wide range of cars

ABOVE LEFT *To strip the carburettor, firstly undo the fuel pipe at the fuel bowl end, then unscrew the jet retaining screw.*

ABOVE *The jet may now be removed.*

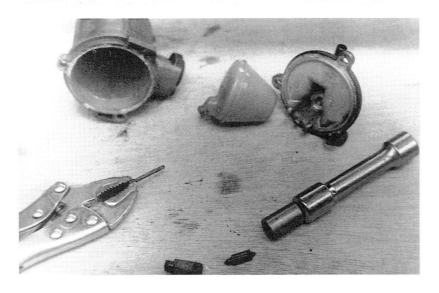

CENTRE AND LEFT *Remove the bowl fixing screw, then the top of the bowl. The inside of the bowl can then be cleaned using neat petrol and the float tested for height (any workshop manual will describe this process in full). Replace the needle and valve.*

that obtaining one should be easy.

Finally, examine the float body for damage. Holes will already have been made apparent because the carburettor will have regularly flooded, although small cracks should be dealt with by replacement. Lubricate all external moving parts using a light oil (engine oil will suffice).

If the carburettors on your car are well worn, have scoring in the bell or are allowing air to leak past the throttle spindle, it is worth taking them to an SU specialist rather than trying to repair them at home. This will usually pay dividents in performance, smooth running and economy.

Centring the jet

If removed, refit the jet bearing (14), jet bearing nut (16) and the jet adjusting nut (18) to finger tightness, but do not fit the spring (17). Fit the main jet assembly (13) into the base of the unit. Fit the needle into the piston.

The jet has to be centred so that the needle is positioned concentric with it, otherwise the needle and jet will rapidly wear. Refit the piston

Three screws secure the bell housing; remove these, and the housing, spring, piston and needle can be lifted from the carburettor body. The needle and jet should be replaced together. If the inside of the bell housing is scored or has gone oval, replace both it and the piston together.

and dashpot, then tighten the jet bearing nut whilst holding the piston down (this can be achieved by pushing a length of rod down through the dashpot bell housing). Lift the piston then allow it to fall onto the jet bridge. It should land with a soft 'click'. Lower the jet adjusting nut, then let the piston fall again. If it does not still land with a click then repeat the whole procedure.

Slide out the jet assembly, then refit the spring (17), adjusting nut and choke lever. Connect the uel pipe to the float chamber. Fit the float chamber needle and float, then refit the unit to the float chamber body with the three securing screws.

Screw the main jet upwards until it is level with the bridge, then turn it back by two complete turns (twelve flats). The carburettor may now be refitted.

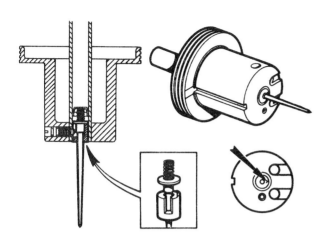

When you have rebuilt the carburettor, the jet has to be centred (unless the carburettor has the later, spring-loaded needle). Remove the jet and its adjusting screw and spring, then refit the adjusting screw and screw it home fully. Refit the jet, slacken the locking nut. Remove the piston damper from the bellhousing, then push a thin rod down to hold the piston fully down, and push the jet fully up whilst you tighten the jet locking ring. The jet should now be centred, and this can be checked by lifting the piston and letting it fall. It should land on the bridge with a click: if not, repeat the centring process. When the carburettor has been fully rebuilt, set the mixture initially by screwing the jet adjusting nut fully home, then back by two full turns. (Courtesy Autodata)

Setting the carburation

It is firstly necessary to synchronise the carburettors. Slacken the pinch bolts on the throttle and choke linkage spindles to allow the carburettors to operate independently. With the engine at idle speed, use a length of rubber hose held against the ear and in the throat of each carburettor in turn to gauge the volume of air being taken by each carburettor. Adjust each throttle stop screw in turn using the throttle adjusting screw until an even rush of air through each carburettor is detected. Tighten the pinch bolts on the throttle linkage, making sure that the two lost motion levers are pressed downwards against their respective pins so that the carburettors operate simultaneously. Then adjust each throttle stop screw by an equal amount until the correct idle speed is obtained. Low cost

vacuum gauge carburettor setting kits are available, and are very worthwhile.

Re-tighten the choke clamp bolts, ensuring that the pegs are similarly positioned relative to their respective forks.

Ideally, the air/fuel mixture should be set with the assistance of emission measuring equipment or, in the case of fast road or competition cars, with a rolling road. It is possible, however, for the amateur working alone at home to achieve reasonably accurate results with care.

Before attempting to set the mixture, all elements of the ignition system should be checked and the timing set. The engine should firstly be warmed to normal operating temperature, and the air filter covers should be removed.

Some SU carburettors (sealed type) have covers over the throttle adjusting screw and mixture adjusting nut, and these should be removed. Set the idle revolutions using the throttle adjusting screw. If the carburettor has a lifting pin, use it to lift the piston and listen to the engine revolutions as you do so. If they rise noticeably and remain higher, then weaken the mixture by screwing the jet adjusting nut upwards. If the revolutions die away when the piston is lifted then enrich the mixture by screwing the jet adjusting nut

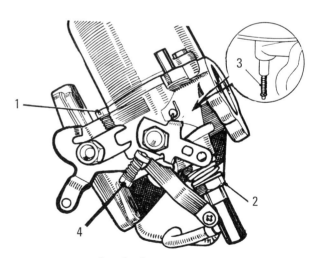

1. *Throttle adjusting screw*
2. *Jet adjusting nut*
3. *Piston lifting pin*
4. *Fast idle screw*

The adjustment points for the SU HS2 carburettor. The larger HS4 unit is very similar.
(Courtesy Autodata)

103

downwards. When the mixture is correctly set and the piston lifted, the engine revolutions should rise momentarily, then settle back to where they were. On carburettors without lifting pins, raise the piston by hand through about $\frac{1}{16}''$. Setting the mixture will probably have an effect upon the idle revolutions, so readjust using the throttle adjusting screw. Work firstly on the rear carburettor, then the front, and repeat until raising the piston of either carburettor produces the appropriate result.

After setting the carburation, take the car out on to the road, and accelerate hard from about 30 mph in fourth gear. If the engine pinks, enrich the mixture slightly by unscrewing the jet adjusting nut by one flat. If the engine still pinks, then check for air induction leaks to the carburettor or inlet manifold, then re-examine the ignition timing (it may be too far advanced). 'Pinking' sounds harmless, but it is the noise made by the pistons tipping in the bore due to pre-ignition, and in the long term it can wreck an engine.

Some cars are fitted with emission control equipment, consisting basically of an air pump which supplies air to the exhaust manifold to help burn off gases and to the inlet manifold via a gulp valve to weaken the mixture during deceleration and on the overrun. The same cars have an evaporative loss system, consisting of a charcoal canister which essentially absorbs fuel vapours and feeds them into the engine via the rocker cover. This equipment requires special tools and knowledge for testing and repair, and so work should only be carried out by an accredited dealer.

Fuel pump

To remove the electrical fuel pump, raise the rear of the car and support it on axle stands (the battery MUST be disconnected and preferably removed). Remove the electricity feed and earth wires from their terminals. Using a brake hose clamp or a small pair of mole grips with heavily padded jaws, clamp the rubber pipe which runs from the fuel tank to the pump to prevent fuel loss, then remove the pump inlet and outlet pipes. It is as well to have a large, shallow container under the pump to catch any fuel which does

escape. Undo the fuel tank pipe immediately. Remove the bolts which secure the pump to the heelboard panel, and the pump may then be removed from the car.

Remove the end cover and inspect the contact points. Following any period of inactivity (i.e. a restoration) the points are susceptible to surface corrosion which may be gently cleaned off. If the points are burned or have pitting then they and the rocker assembly and spring blade should be replaced. Check that the gap between the outer rocker and the main coil housing is 0.07", and adjust the spring blade until this is achieved.

To gain access to the diaphragm, mark the relative positions of the main pump body and the coil housing (also noting to which fixing screw the earth wire is attached), then undo the screws and separate the two halves of the pump unit. If the diaphragm requires replacement then it should be replaced along with its spindle.

A faulty fuel pump prevents the engine from running and could leave you stranded at any time, so it is always recommended that during a restoration, a reconditioned pump is fitted as a matter of course.

When restoring a car, it is advisable to fit a reconditioned fuel pump. If the existing pump is in reasonable condition, it is worth cleaning the contacts, which will corrode whilst idle during the restoration.

Mechanical Fuel Pumps

Some 1098cc cars and 1500cc Midgets were fitted with a mechanical fuel pump, attached to the engine block. These are best dealt with by straight replacement during a restoration.

HYDRAULICS

From the restoration viewpoint, the best option is to renew the entire hydraulic system of pipes, slave and master cylinders. Kits which enable the DIY enthusiast to recondition the master and slave cylinders are available, although the cost of reconditioned units is not too high bearing in mind the extra peace of mind their use brings.

All hydraulic pipes and hoses – within the braking as well as the clutch system – should be inspected regularly as a part of maintenance procedures. If a pipe is found to be defective or damaged, then drain the system by bleeding the slave cylinder, remove the offending section, take this to any service station and have a length made up or – alternatively – the sections may be purchased ready-made at Spridget specialist spares businesses.

Bleeding the system

Hydraulic systems are usually bled for two reasons; either air has entered the system accidentally, and the system is bled so that air bubbles within the fluid are ejected, or the system is bled completely so that components may be removed without hydraulic fluid (which is an excellent paint remover) being splashed onto paintwork.

Bleeding the system entails connecting a short length of rubber tubing to the bleed nipple on the slave cylinder, immersing the other end in a container of clean hydraulic fluid, then opening the bleed valve as the clutch pedal is depressed by an assistant. If the system is being bled dry, then just keep pumping the pedal until no more fluid emerges. If the system is being bled to remove air, then the bleed nipple must be tightened at the end of every pedal down stroke, and kept closed during the reverse stroke. Keep a close check on the fluid level within the master cylinder during this process, top it up regularly and do not allow the level to drop

appreciably, because to do so allows air to enter the system via the master cylinder – the worst possible point!

THE REAR AXLE AND PROPELLER SHAFT

When a car is being driven around a corner, the wheel at the outside of the circle has to travel further than the wheel on the inside. If the wheels are not to fight each other for road traction they must be able to rotate at different speeds, and so a unit called the 'differential' is built into the axle to achieve this.

Drive from the gearbox is taken through the propeller shaft to the differential, where a system of gears pass drive through the two 'half shafts' to the wheels. The gearbox is mounted onto the bodywork, but the axle is not (it is mounted on the rear springs) and the height above it of the body varies as the suspension moves. Two universal joints are incorporated into the propeller shaft to allow for this movement.

Axle removal – Half Elliptic Springs

The axle and propeller shaft can be removed from the car in conjunction with or independently of the rear springs. It is usual to take the easier course of removing the two together, although there are occasions when it is better to remove the axle and propeller shaft whilst leaving the spring front mountings in place. In the case of a full body restoration, if the spring box mounting assembly and adjacent metalwork is really rotten, then it can be better to remove just the axle, because with this removed, the improved access to the spring front mountings can help you to remove them without distorting the bodywork. It does not matter HOW weak the rusted remains of the surrounding metalwork are, if they exist then they give you valuable points from which to take measurements when you come to restore the bodywork.

Disconnect the battery. Chock the front wheels very securely, then raise the rear of the car and support it on axle stands. If the bodyshell is really weak then support the car with axle stands and wooden chocks or solid supports either side of the rear of the transmission tunnel and place a length of

The rear spring hanger assembly on this car is so weak that trying to remove the axle and springs at the same time could easily pull the spring hanger assemblies out of true, or even rip them away from the car. In this instance, it is wise to remove the axle (with or without the prop shaft) firstly, and to attend to the springs separately.

timber on top of the supports to spread the load as much as possible.

It is not necessary to split the propeller shaft and axle if both are to be removed along with the springs. If you wish to just disconnect the propeller shaft, make a mark across the two flanges so that they can be reassembled in the same relative positions. With the car out of gear and the handbrake off, rotate the propeller shaft by turning one rear wheel to bring each nut and bolt in turn into view. When all four nuts and bolts are removed, pull the propeller shaft down and backwards to free it from the gearbox. If just the axle is to be removed and the springs left in situ for the reasons described above, then it will be necessary to part the propeller shaft and the axle.

Remove the cap from the brake master cylinder, place a piece of plastic sheet over the opening and re-

fit the cap. This will reduce the amount of brake fluid which will be lost. Undo the end fitting from the main brake pipe where it joins onto the union fixed to the axle, and plug the pipe end to minimise fluid loss. Disconnect the handbrake cable end from the compensator assembly and the brake cable outer from the compensator bracket. (See: Brakes). Place a trolley jack underneath the differential housing and raise it very slightly.

The dampers have to be removed, parted at their articulated joint or disconnected from the spring bottom plate, but on a rotten car, this can result in the distortion of whatever metal remains around the spring mounting box assemblies. In such cases it is better to leave the dampers attached and to gently pull the spring bottom plate downwards and out of the way at a later stage. If the bodywork is sound then it is best to disconnect the articulated centre joint in the damper arms, because access to the inner damper mounting bolt is very awkward with the axle in situ.

Remove the nuts which hold either end of the rebound straps and pull the strap sideways off its spigot. Again, this operation can require the use of force and, if the shell is weak then it is better to merely cut through the straps rather than risk distorting the shell.

There are now two alternative methods of working. The axle can be removed still attached to the springs, or it can be separated from them and then removed. The latter is recommended on cars with weak spring front mounting points for the reasons already given.

To remove both the axle and the springs, undo the rear nuts from the spring rear shackle pins, then push these out to free the spring rear ends. Lower the assembly on the trolley jack. Then remove the four bolts from the spring front securing brackets, and balancing the entire assembly on the lowered trolley jack, pull it gently from underneath the car.

To remove the axle alone, mark the prop shaft and pinnion flanges so that they can be reassembled correctly, then remove the four fixing nuts and bolts and part the flanges. Undo the four nuts per side from the axle 'U' bolts, then disconnect the rear ends of the springs as already described and lower the assembly.

Rather than mess around trying to undo seized nuts and bolts, the author believes in taking shortcuts such as cutting through the rebound straps.

The axle can now be lifted clear by two people and removed from the car.

With quarter elliptic cars, the procedure is essentially the same, although the dampers must be disconnected. The radius arms must also be disconnected. (See Suspension and Steering.)

Rear Axle

Remove the brake fitments as described in the appropriate section of this chapter. Remove the ends of the rebound straps if still in place. Drain the oil into a container.

If you intend to increase the power of your engine or to fit a larger unit, it is worth replacing the half shafts with sturdier ones from the appropriate Spridget. To remove a half shaft, undo the single cross head fixing set screw. The half shaft should now pull free, although it may prove necessary to 'encourage' it. With wire wheel cars, firstly remove the screws which secure the hub extension. To remove the hub, bend back the tab which secures the large nut, then undo the nut. This requires a $1\frac{7}{8}''$ socket or ring spanner – if you don't have access to one, then take

The author gently tapping free the half shaft. If it proves reluctant to move, don't use excessive force but try to borrow a hub puller.

the axle unit to your nearest service centre and ask them to remove the nuts. You will need a hub puller to remove the hub, bearing and oil seal – if you don't possess one of these then you might as well get the service centre staff to renew the wheel bearings at the same time. . . .

It is not really recommended that you work on the differential at home. If the differential is giving problems, then obtain an exchange reconditioned axle or differential assembly.

The Propeller Shaft

The propeller shaft (universally referred to as the 'prop' shaft) is finely balanced because it rotates at quite high speed and any imbalance will set up unwanted vibrations when the car is on the move. Before parting the drive flanges, make marks which will enable you to reassemble and replace it exactly as it was previously.

As already stated, there is a universal joint at either end of the prop shaft. In the fullness of time,

wear in these joints will be apparent as clonks as drive is taken up. This is more marked in the lower gears where acceleration and deceleration both produce loud clonks from under the car. If the joints are not replaced then it is not unusual for the bearings within them to break up, resulting in even higher noise levels.

To remove the prop shaft, firstly disconnect the battery and chock the front wheels. Place the car in neutral and release the handbrake. Raise the rear of the car and support it on axle stands.

Make a mark across the prop shaft drive flange and axle drive flange so that they can be reassembled in the same way. Undo the four nuts and bolts which secure the two flanges, turning the prop shaft as necessary by turning a rear wheel. Lower the rear end of the prop shaft and withdraw it from the gearbox by pulling it rearwards. Make another mark across the two flanges at the front end of the prop shaft, then split these if the front universal joint is to be dealt with. Make a mark on the flange and one leg of the yoke before working on a universal joint, so that the joint can be reassembled correctly.

To dissemble the joint, firstly clean the ends of the spiders, then remove the four circlips. The four ends of the spider each have a bearing cup fitted with roller bearings within. To dissemble the joint, hold

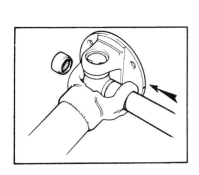
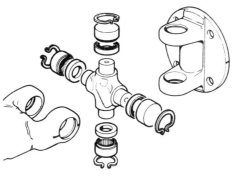
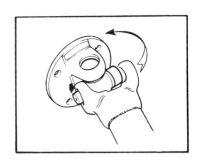

the prop shaft in the palm of your hand and sharply tap the yoke ends in turn using a soft-faced mallet. This usually encourages the bearing caps to emerge to the point at which they can be fully pulled out using a self gripping wrench. If the bearing caps will not move then try holding the assembly in a vice and tapping the bearing cap out from the inside using a long and thin drift. If this fails, hold the prop shaft in a vice and use a socket which has a large enough internal diameter to fit around the bearing cup to drift the yoke downwards and expose the cup.

Remove the opposite bearing cap, then remove the yoke. Repeat the exercise to remove the other two bearing caps. Clean the yokes and especially their bearing journals.

The universal joint kit will contain a new spider, bearing caps and needle roller bearings plus oil seals. Fit a new oil seal to each leg of the spider. The assemble the needle roller bearings into one bearing cap, holding them in position with grease. Fill the bottom of the bearing cap with grease to a depth of ⅛", then fill the reservoirs on the spider legs with grease. Assemble the spider into a yoke, then offer the first bearing cap into position, taking care not to displace any of the needle rollers. Use a suitably sized socket and a vice to push this fully home. Repeat for the opposite spider legs, then place the assembly into position in the other yoke, and repeat for the other two spider legs. The joint should move easily and freely.

SUSPENSION AND STEERING

The suspension and steering of all Spridgets is simple and quite robust and, given a little maintenance, capable of lasting many years without giving trouble. Failure to adhere to correct maintenance of the front kingpins, however, can cause premature wear. It is

Overhauling the propeller shaft universal joints. (Courtesy Autodata)

strongly recommended that a good workshop manual is used in conjunction with this book when dealing with any aspect of the steering and suspension.

Front suspension strip and overhaul

Disconnect the battery. Place chocks on the rear wheels, raise the front of the car and support it on axle stands. Remove the wheels.

Remove the brake shoes and calipers (disc brakes), and support the calipers on suitable supports to prevent strain being placed on the flexible hose. With early cars, remove the brake drum, hub and brake assembly. Disconnect the steering arm ball joint or, if this will not split, the steering arm, and the drop link from the anti roll bar.

The spring has to be compressed in some way before the suspension can be stripped, and it is important that the compression method used allows the pressure in the spring to be released in a slow and controlled manner. If the compressed coil spring is allowed to release its energy quickly, it could cause damage to the car or yourself. Firstly, raise the spring pan by placing a trolley jack underneath, then place a block of wood between the damper arm and the rubber stop to keep the damper arm in a raised position.

The spring may be compressed for stripping using a trolley jack placed under the spring pan as described, by proprietory spring compressors (tool 18G 153), or by the following method. Obtain two lengths of threaded rod and four nuts to suit, remove two of the four nuts and bolts (diagonally opposed) securing the spring pan, replace them with the lengths of threaded rods. The nuts can be run onto

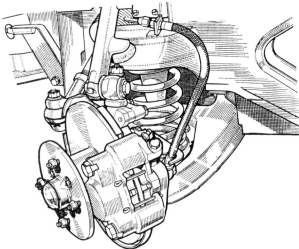

1. Brake disc
2. Caliper assembly
3. Bleeder screw
4. Caliper fluid connector
5. Steering lever
6. Suspension trunnion link
7. Rebound buffer
8. Retaining cap
9. Brake disc to hub securing bolts

ABOVE *For stripping the front suspension, you really need one of these, a wedge-type ball joint splitter – not only to split the steering lever ball joints but also (often) to remove the inner fulcrum pins, which tend to seize fully into their bushes. Begin the front suspension strip down by soaking all nuts, bolts and exposed threads in releasing fluid.*

RIGHT *The simple front suspension assembly. (Courtesy Autodata)*

the threaded rods, the other two nuts and bolts removed, and spring pressure released by undoing, in unison, the nuts on the threaded rods.

For speed, the trolley jack method wins. Compress the suspension with the trolley jack, place a wood block on the rubber stop as already described to keep the damper arm raised, then undo the top trunnion bolt. The suspension may now be lowered and the spring pulled free.

Some authorities recommend that it is not always necessary to use a spring compressive device, but for the sake of safety the author favours the use of one.

With the pressure from the springs dissipated, slacken the damper arm pinch bolt, the split pin and castellated nut from the trunnion pin, and drift the top trunnion pin out to release the damper arm from the kingpin assembly. The damper may be unbolted if desired. During a restoration, it is as well to replace the dampers as a matter of course.

Although it is possible to recondition the assembly at home, it is recommended that the spring pan and kingpin assembly is exchanged as a unit for a reconditioned one.

Steering Rack

The steering rack may be serviced at home, but it is recommended that an exchange reconditioned unit is obtained in preferance. If you wish to recondition or to remedy excess play in the steering rack, consult a good workshop manual before starting work.

Removal of the steering rack present no problems. Disconnect the ball joint ends or the steering arms if the ball joints refuse to separate. Slacken the steering column lower pinch bolt and separate the column and rack. The rack is held by two brackets; mark the relative positions of the rack and brackets to aid accurate reassembly then remove the bolts from the brackets and lift the rack clear. Note whether any shims are fitted under either bracket, and retain these for replacement when the new rack is fitted.

To fit a new rack, loosely fasten it into position, but do not tighten the bracket nuts until the steering assembly as a whole is rebuilt. Ensure that the flat on the pinnion shaft, and that the steering column pinch clamp slot are facing upwards. Connect the steering column, and connect the track rod end ball joints to the steering arms. Place the roadwheels in the straight ahead position.

Tighten the rack fixing bracket bolts, then slacken each back a fraction to allor the rack to move

LEFT *If the steering lever end will not part company with the track rod end, simply disconnect the arm at the other end. It will prove far easier to break that joint with the track rod off the car later on.*

BELOW LEFT *Disconnect the anti-roll bar.*

BELOW *Although not necessary, the author prefers to take the strain of the coil spring using a trolley jack before undoing the top trunnion nut.*

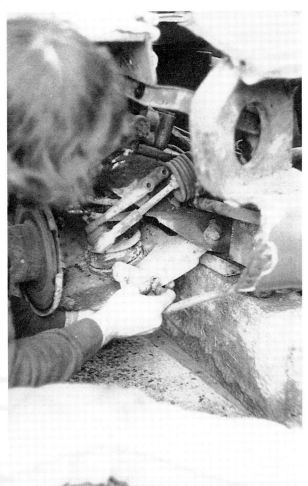

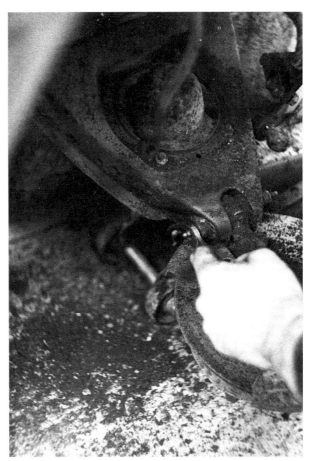

ABOVE *The entire assembly can then be lowered.*

RIGHT *You can remove the wishbone pan/kingpin assembly complete if desired, or remove firstly the outer fulcrum pin and split the kingpin assembly from the wishbone.*

sideways if pressure is placed upon it. Turn the steering wheel one turn to the left and back, then one turn to the right and back, then the other. This process will move the rack; repeat it until the rack shows no movement and is correctly aligned. Measure any gap between the mounting brackets and the crossmember, and fit the appropriate shims before tightening the bracket bolts.

Rear Suspension

Within a restoration it would be usual to replace the rear springs, their axle fittings and the dampers as a matter of course.

To strip the rear suspension, disconnect the battery, chock the front wheels, raise the rear of the car and support it on axle stands, then support the axle in a raised position using a trolley jack.

Semi-elliptic springs

You can remove the axle, prop shaft and springs together if desired, or remove just the springs if it is a case of straight renewal. To remove the springs alone, support the axle on a trolley jack, remove the front fixing bolts from inside the car, then the other two from under the car. Undo the axle U bolts, remove the base plate, then lower the spring to the ground. Remove the nuts and bolts from the rear shackle, and then pull the spring clear.

To remove the springs along with the axle and prop shaft, either remove the axle check strap bolts or cut through the strap if the bolts are seized, remove the brake hoses and handbrake cable (see Brakes), and the dampers. Remove the exhaust or the rear section if a two piece exhaust is fitted.

With the axle supported by a trolley jack, remove the various fixing bolts as already outlined, then lower the entire assembly and withdraw from the rear of the car, keeping the axle balanced on the trolley jack.

Quarter eliptic cars

Raise the rear of the car as already described, support on axle stands and raise the axle with a trolley jack until no pressure is exerted on the rear springs.

Remove the spring/axle casing shackle pin, the two spring securing bolts then the U bolt nuts. The spring may now be removed.

THE BRAKING SYSTEM

All but those Spridgets manufactured prior to 1962 were fitted with disc brakes at the front and drums at the rear, earlier cars having drum brakes both front and rear. Disc brakes are generally far more effective than drum brakes.

The main braking system is operated

1. *Spring securing bolts*
2. *Damper nuts*
3. *Spring 'U' bolt nuts*

The quarter elliptic spring of early cars.
(Courtesy Autodata)

hydraulically, with the handbrake being mechanically connected only to the rear brakes by a cable and a series of levers. The disc brakes are self-adjusting and require little in the way of routine maintenance; drum brakes have to be adjusted periodically.

Pressure on the brake pedal causes a piston to move within a cylinder (the 'Master' cylinder) which is filled with brake fluid. This fluid can not be compressed, and so it is pushed along the brake pipes which run to each wheel.

Further description of the operation of the brakes will be found in the following sections which deal with the front and rear brakes separately.

Drum Brakes

The rear brakes each contain a cylinder called the 'Wheel' cylinder, which is attached to the brake backplate. The wheel cylinders join on to the brake pipes which run from the master cylinder, and pressure from the brake fluid causes two pistons contained within each cylinder to move outwards, pushing against the shoes and pushing them apart until they meet the inside of the brake drum. Frictional material on each brake shoe is pressed against the drum and the resultant friction causes the wheel rotation to slow and stop.

The handbrake operates independently of the hydraulic system. The handbrake lever is connected to a cable which, in turn, is connected to a compensating mechanism. This is no more than a simple lever which is attached to two steel rods, and pressure on the handbrake cable is used to pull the two rods inwards. The rods are connected to levers which cause the brake shoes to expand and contact the brake drum.

Unlike disc brakes, drum brakes are not self-adjusting and require fairly frequent maintenance and adjustment. As the frictional material on the brake shoes wears, the distance between the surface of the frictional material and the brake drum wall increases to the point at which the efficiency of the brakes is affected. A simple screw-in device uses a conical spreader to push the lower ends of the brake shoes apart and so reduce the necessary travel of the shoes. See: Maintenance.

The front drum brakes fitted to early cars are very similar to the rear drum brakes, but have two master cylinders and two adjusters – one for each shoe.

Slacken off the brake adjuster on the back of the back plate, then ease the ends of the rear brake shoe out of the tappet and piston slots against the pressure of the springs. If the adjuster is seized, this may require rather a lot of effort. The two shoes and springs may then be removed complete; note where the springs locate into the shoes.

Stripping the Rear Brakes

Chock the front wheels. Disconnect the battery, loosen the roadwheel nuts or wheel spinners, raise the rear of the car and support the axle on axle stands. Remove the roadwheels.

Slacken off the brake adjuster, using the correct square 'ring spanner' tool. If maintenance has been lacking, the adjusters may be found to be seized solid, and the use of outright force in any attempt to move them will quickly damage the adjuster studs. Clean all dirt from the area and soak the exposed section of the threads in releasing fluid before attempting to slacken them again. If this fails to move the adjusters, then you could use heat but for the nearby fuel tank and brake fluid (which is VERY inflammable) pipes, both of which would make the use of heat very dangerous. It is best in such circumstances to dispense with this part of the operation and to try to free the adjusters at a far later stage.

If the adjusters can be slackened then the brake drum should slide easily off the wheel studs after the two cross-head set screws have been removed; if not, try tapping the outside of the drum with a leather-faced mallet while pulling the drum. If the adjusters were seized solid then the shoes may be in contact with the brake drum and there is often no alternative to using brute force to remove the brake drum. The author had to resort to using large screwdrivers as levers, because the adjusters on the project car (which had been standing in an orchard for over two years) were seized solid.

The inside of the drum and the brake assembly underneath may well be covered with a layer of thin dust which must NOT be breathed in, because it is asbestos dust. Gently clean this off (DO NOT try to blow it away with the compressor, although using a cylinder vacuum cleaner to suck in the dust is perfectly acceptable) while wearing a dust mask.

The brake shoes are held in position at the top by the wheel cylinder piston jaws, and at the bottoms by a similar but fixed bifurcation in the adjuster mounting bracket. Prise the top of one shoe, then the other, from the wheel cylinder piston jaws. Then prise the bottoms of the shoes from the adjuster mounting bracket jaws. The shoes have to be eased away from the handbrake operating lever ends. Note the positions of the two connecting springs before removing them and lifting the shoes away from the backplate.

Undo the brake pipe end fitting from the wheel cylinder. Two problems can at this stage manifest themselves. Firstly, the fitting can be seized and very difficult to move without distortion. Secondly, it can be seized on to the brake pipe, so that even if it will turn, it will twist and kink the brake pipe. With care and patience, it is usually possible to overcome these little difficulties, although on the project car every component was in such poor condition that the decision to replace them was taken. The system was of course completely bled first. If this work is being carried out as normal maintenance/repair operations, be prepared to plug the pipe end fitting to prevent fluid loss. Old brake pipes should be replaced as a matter of course during a restoration. Keep the originals as intact as possible, and most garages will be able to make up replacements to the same length, which you can then bend so that they follow the lines of the originals.

The wheel cylinder is retained by a circlip and washer. The circlip locates in a groove and very often seizes into it, so that its removal demands the use of force.

Remove the rubber boots and the pistons from the wheel cylinders. If the bores of the cylinders are in poor condition, replace the cylinders. If they are in generally good condition then replace the piston seals and rubber boots.

Sometimes the bleed nipple will shear off as you try to undo it; when this happens it is probably best to replace the wheel cylinder complete.

In order to remove the brake backplate (so that heat can be safely applied to a seized brake adjuster) you will have to remove firstly the halfshaft and then the hub assembly. See: Axle. If the brakes are being attended to as part of a restoration then the backplate should be removed anyway for cleaning and painting.

Handbrake

To strip the handbrake mechanism further, remove the split pin from the compensator assembly cleavis pin, then withdraw the cleavis pin to free the cable end. The cable outer is held on to the compensator bracket by two adjusting nuts, slacken these and remove the cable. Two nuts and bolts hold the compensator bracket to the axle bracket. Remove these, then move the entire assembly to one side and free the first handbrake end lever, then to the other side to free the second.

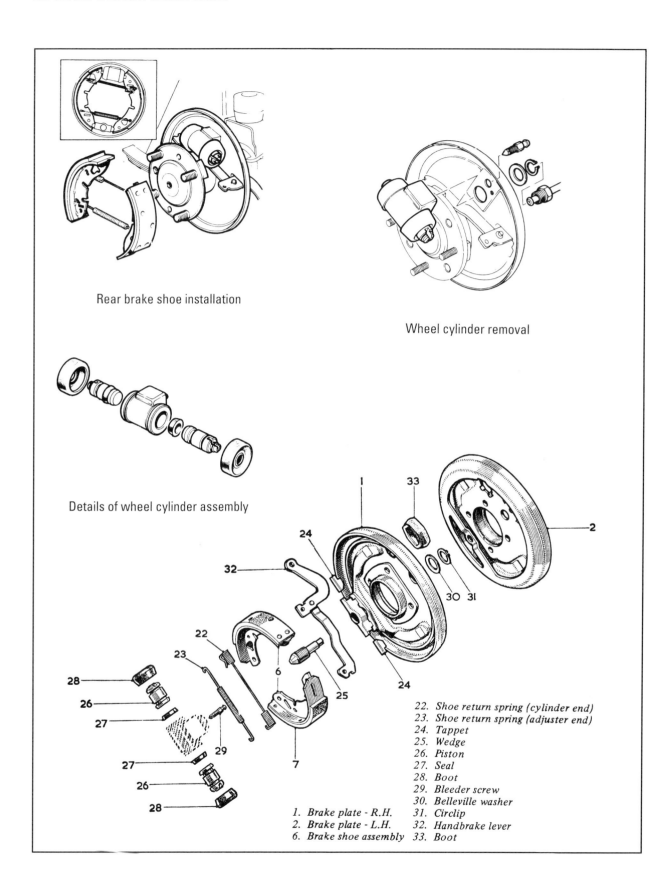

Rear brake shoe installation

Wheel cylinder removal

Details of wheel cylinder assembly

22. Shoe return spring (cylinder end)
23. Shoe return spring (adjuster end)
24. Tappet
25. Wedge
26. Piston
27. Seal
28. Boot
29. Bleeder screw
30. Belleville washer
31. Circlip
32. Handbrake lever
33. Boot

1. Brake plate - R.H.
2. Brake plate - L.H.
6. Brake shoe assembly

LEFT *The rear brake assembly stripped. (Courtesy Autodata)*

ABOVE *This is typical of what happens to a car after it has spent three years out of doors in an orchard. The brake pipe is hopelessly seized into the union, and will buckle as the union is undone from the wheel cylinder. The bleed nipple is also seized and the back plate has rusted thin, so that 'restoration' of the rear brakes becomes renewal of all of the components.*

If the handbrake operating lever has to be removed, firstly remove the nearside seat to improve access. If the car has a handbrake warning light, be sure to disconnect the battery (although you should do this as a matter of course before starting almost any type of work on the car), then remove the wires from the operating switch. Remove the set screws which fasten the lever assembly to its mounting plate or, if these have previously been mangled, remove the bolts which secure the mounting plate to the transmission tunnel. The cable end is held by a cleavis pin; remove its split pin and free the lever assembly from the cable.

Front Drum Brakes

These are similar in operation to the rear drum brakes, with the exception that there are two wheel cylinders (one for each shoe) and two adjusters. The adjusters are operated by a screwdriver which is inserted through a hole in the backplate after removal of the rubber dust cover. Stripping the brakes is essentially the same as stripping the rear drum brakes with the exceptions of the dual wheel cylinders and their connecting pipe and the two adjusters.

Front Disc Brakes

The disc brake assembly is contained within a casting which is called the caliper, and consists of two large pistons which move towards each other when the hydraulic fluid is pressurised. A frictional brake pad is held in front of each piston, one either side of the disc. Pressure on the brake pedal therefore forces the pads onto the disc, slowing it.

Disc brakes do not need adjustment. They only

117

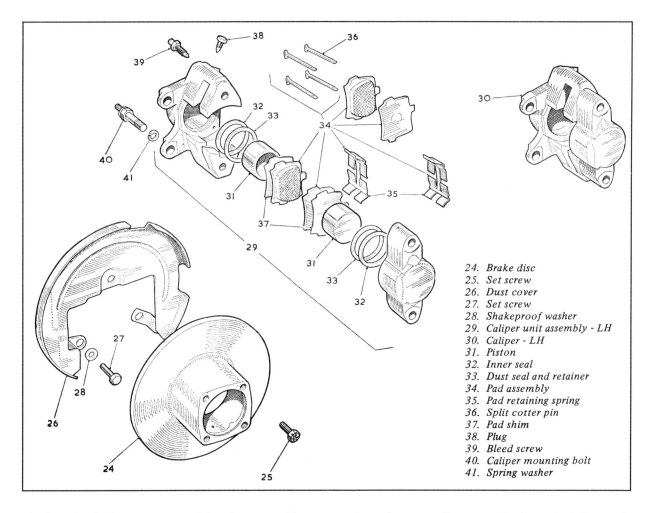

24. Brake disc
25. Set screw
26. Dust cover
27. Set screw
28. Shakeproof washer
29. Caliper unit assembly - LH
30. Caliper - LH
31. Piston
32. Inner seal
33. Dust seal and retainer
34. Pad assembly
35. Pad retaining spring
36. Split cotter pin
37. Pad shim
38. Plug
39. Bleed screw
40. Caliper mounting bolt
41. Spring washer

The front disc brake components. Although it is possible to replace the pistons and seals at home, it is not an easy nor a pleasant task; exchange reconditioned units are advised. (Courtesy Autodata)

generally require attention when the frictional material on the pads wears down so that replacement becomes necessary, or following the discovery of a brake fluid leak. However, the disc will often be scored or possess too much run-out (meaning that it is distorted) and the operating pistons will often be found to have rusted badly on restoration project cars. A lightly rusted disc can be cleaned up if not deeply scored or distorted (in which case it should ideally be replaced). Rusted pistons are another matter entirely.

Although it is now usually possible to acquire stainless steel caliper pistons, the originals were chrome plated. As the frictional material of the pads wears, the pistons emerge further from the caliper,

and it is this exposed section which, in the fullness of time, deteriorates as the chrome flakes off and the underlying steel rusts. When the pads are replaced, the pistons have to be pushed back into the calipers and, if the pistons have rusted, this would mean pushing rusted and flaky chrome and steel back past the two caliper/piston rubber seals, which naturally must not happen.

In such cases the pistons must be replaced, along with the dust and sealing rings. Stainless pistons are recommended although the price difference between these and ordinary chrome plated ones can be substantial.

Some Spridget spares suppliers will happily provide you with a reconditioned caliper assembly on an exchange basis, and most have seal kits in stock. Not all, however, bother to keep stocks of caliper pistons, and you may have to shop around in order to locate these.

At the time of writing, the price difference

between new pistons and seals and exchange calipers was not too great (the exchange calipers cost around 25% more), so that the latter has some attraction.

Stripping Disc Brakes

Disconnect the battery, slacken the roadwheel nuts or wheel spinners, chock the rear wheels, raise the front of the car and support it on axle stands. Remove the road wheels.

The disc pad retaining springs are held in position by two large split pins. Remove these, then the retaining springs and pads. Knock back the locking tabs on the two large bolts which secure the caliper to the axle assembly, then remove the bolts, taking care to support the caliper so that no weight falls on the length of flexible brake hose.

There are now two alternative methods of working on the caliper. The first (which is used during general maintenance/repair) is to leave it attached to the brake hose so that each piston can in turn be pushed out using the foot brake. The second (which is used during a restoration) is to remove the caliper from the system entirely. In either case, begin by thoroughly cleaning off the caliper, so that there is no dust and rust to find its way into the unit as it is stripped.

If the unit is to be left attached to the brake hose, support it in some way (a large tin or similar is ideal) so that no weight can fall on the brake hose, and preferably place absorbent material underneath to catch the small amount of fluid which will be lost. Otherwise, follow the instructions given for the second working method.

If the unit is to be removed from the car, begin by placing a proper hose clamp (or a mole grip with padded jaws) on the brake hose to prevent fluid loss. If the unit is being removed as part of a complete restoration strip-down, begin by bleeding the brake until no fluid remains in the master cylinder or the pipes leading to the caliper.

Clamp one of the pistons using a lightweight 'G' clamp, then remove the other by pressing the brake pedal gently (caliper still attached to brake hose) or by air pressure. If the unit is removed from the car then use a foot pump to pump the caliper out. DO NOT use a compressor unless the air pressure output from it can be 'turned down' to around 10psi. If you applied high air pressure to the caliper then it would come out with amazing (and dangerous) velocity.

Using a thin-bladed screwdriver, prise the dust seal metal cover out from the caliper cylinder, followed by the rubber dust seal and the rubber fluid seal. Clean the cylinder and especially the seal grooves before replacing the old fluid seal with a new one. Do not fit the dust seal and outer metal ring at this stage, because it makes fitting the piston far more difficult. Lubricate the seal and piston with clean brake fluid, then offer the piston into position and press it into the cylinder until 6mm or so protrudes, ensuring that it remains square to the bore and that the cutaway section is pointing in the correct direction (towards the hub). The author usually uses a 'G' clamp with a flat section for this purpose. Assemble the dust seal and its retaining ring onto the piston, then press these firmly home into the caliper.

Clamp the new piston into position and repeat the process for the other piston.

Master Cylinder

The brake master cylinder sits alongside the clutch master cylinder in an steel fabrication on the driver's side footwell top panel. The brake and clutch pedals pivot on a bolt which passes through two lugs at the bottom of the fabrication, and they are connected to the cylinders' bifurcated pushrods by cleavis pins. Before stripping the system disconnect the battery. Take care not to spill brake fluid on to surrounding paintwork, because it is a very effective paint remover!

Before the master cylinder can be removed it must be bled (keep bleeding one brake until the master cylinder is empty), the brake pedal must be disconnected, and the brake pipe end fitting must also be disconnected. The two nuts and bolts which hold the cylinder can then be undone, and the cylinder removed. Alternatively, during a restoration it is usual to remove the entire brake and clutch master cylinder assembly in one go, and to work on the individual items after they have been removed from the car. In this case, the nut and bolt holding the brake and clutch pedals are removed in addition to the work already listed, then the fabrication can be unbolted from the footwell top panel and lifted away in one piece. This makes access to the nuts and bolts which hold the two master cylinders far easier.

To strip the master cylinder, lift away the rubber boot and remove the circlip which retains the pushrod assembly, then withdraw the pushrod and

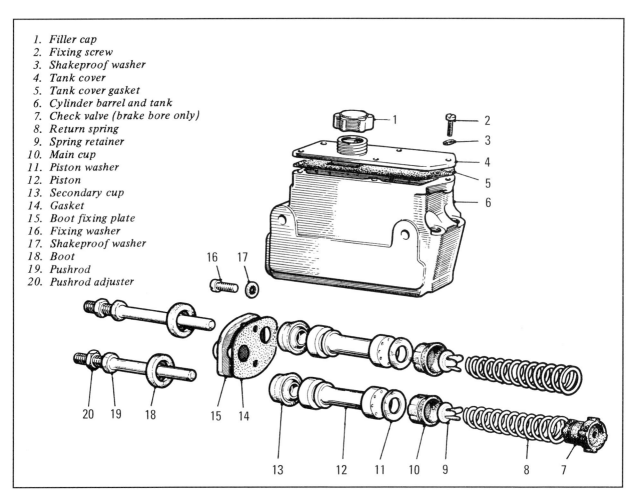

1. Filler cap
2. Fixing screw
3. Shakeproof washer
4. Tank cover
5. Tank cover gasket
6. Cylinder barrel and tank
7. Check valve (brake bore only)
8. Return spring
9. Spring retainer
10. Main cup
11. Piston washer
12. Piston
13. Secondary cup
14. Gasket
15. Boot fixing plate
16. Fixing washer
17. Shakeproof washer
18. Boot
19. Pushrod
20. Pushrod adjuster

ABOVE Early brake/clutch master cylinder. Repair kits for these should contain full instructions. (Courtesy Autodata)

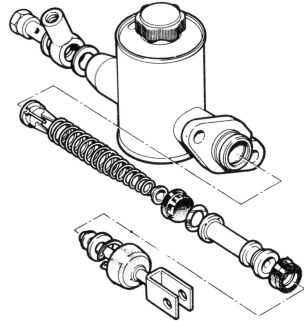

RIGHT Later type master cylinder components. Repair kits for these should contain full instructions. (Courtesy Autodata)

the piston/spring assembly. Three different types of master cylinder were fitted to Spridgets; these are, single line with integral reservoir, single line with separate reservoir, and dual line. The former two types are very simple to dismantle and repair with widely available kits containing new seals and a spring. The dual line system is rather more complex, and it is recommended that instructions on stripping and servicing these are sought in a good workshop manual.

THE ELECTRICAL SYSTEM

There is a fundamental difference between mechanical and electrical components; before mechanical components fail, they almost invariably give warning signs such as an unfamiliar noise, a drop in oil pressure or a rise in temperature to tell the owner that failure is looming or sometimes imminent – when electrical components fail it is usually without any warning.

The consequences of sudden failure of an electrical component can be severe, jeopardising the vehicle and its occupants. A lighting or ignition system breakdown on a crowded motorway at night presents immediate and obvious dangers. An insulation breakdown in the permanent-live circuits can cause a fire, perhaps in an inaccessible area such as behind the dashboard, which can fill the car with choking fumes in seconds or ignite upholstery, sound-proofing materials or petrol.

It is essential, therefore, that the electrical circuits and components are checked quite regularly for adequate standards of insulation. Wires should be checked for insulation damage including cuts, crushing or abrasions; terminals and in-line connections should be regularly checked to ensure that they are not vibrating or being pulled apart. A set of spare light bulbs and fuses should always be carried.

The following notes on safety are written for those with little or no understanding of electrics. Many of the car's electrical circuits are fused. A fuse is a thin strand of wire or strip of metal which has no insulation and which is of a specific thickness and consistency to melt (and hence break the circuit to which it is fitted) if the electrical energy which passes through it exceeds a pre-determined level.

Fuses are rated according to the current which they can carry, and their job is to protect wiring and electrical components from damage due to too-high electrical energy. If a fuse 'blows' then there will be a reason, and on no account should the blown fuse be replaced until the fault has been found and rectified. A blown fuse should NEVER be replaced with one of higher rating, with strips of metal foil, etc.

When a wire shorts to earth (a short-circuit is a direct connection which has no resistive load and hence allows maximum current flow), the battery discharges at its maximum amperage (current) rate through the wire. The resultant wattage (energy) passing through the wire is far higher than it is able to tolerate. On those circuits not fitted with a fuse, the wire quickly becomes red-hot. This firstly melts and then often ignites the insulation, causing a fire.

An electrical fire can start just about anywhere on the car. If it starts near a fuel line or the petrol tank then the results can be explosive. If an electrical fire begins behind the dashboard then the car will be full of choking fumes within a very short time.

No matter how collectable and original a car, there is a strong case for fitting a battery isolation switch, which may be reached from the driver's seat and which immediately disconnects the battery should there be any sign of an electrical fire starting. Such switches are widely available and cannot be accidentally operated because they must be both lifted and twisted in order to disconnect the battery.

A battery isolation switch should in most cases come complete with suitable wiring and fitting instructions; if not, it is as well to buy from a company which can carry out the fitting or at the very least make up suitable lengths of wiring and advise on the fitting.

Electrical Components: repair and replacement

The Lucas components used across the entire Spridget range and including the dynamo/alternator, switches and relays, the ignition system, may all still be obtained either brand-new or, in the case of larger items such as the starter motor and generator, on an exchange basis as fully reconditioned and guaranteed units. There can not, therefore, be any legitimate reason for attempting DIY repairs to any of these components, bearing in mind that a poor DIY repair to an electrical component can fail and at best leave car and driver stranded and at worst cause an electrical fire which could be terminal for both car and driver.

ELECTRICAL SYSTEM OVERVIEW

Electrical power is generated by either a dynamo (positive earth cars) or an alternator (negative earth cars), and stored in the battery for use in starting the car and in making up any shortfall when demand outstrips supply (if almost all devices are simultaneously switched on). The dynamo wires run to the control box (voltage regulator) and then to the starter solenoid; the alternator wires run directly to the starter solenoid (the solenoid is a kind of electrically operated switch which is operated by a small current from the ignition switch and which completes a circuit with a much higher current which is sufficient to turn the starter motor).

Battery

The battery must be firmly clamped into position; any potential for movement is an MOT failure point. Also, battery acid which spills from an insecure battery will quickly destroy paintwork and corrode metal.

    The battery is situated under the bonnet on the heater assembly platform and usually requires little in the way of maintenance. The level of the electrolyte (fluid) should be periodically checked and maintained (using only distiled water) at a height of ¼″ above the lead plates. Every three to six months the battery may be removed, disconnecting firstly the earthed then the live side, and the specific gravity (SG) of the electrolyte checked using a hydrometer. This should range between 1.210 and 1.290 for a fully charged battery and 1.050 and 1.130 for a fully discharged one. In temperatures over 27 degrees celsius the readings should be at the lower and of these ranges and at temperatures under 27 degrees celcius they should be towards the upper end.

    If the SG of different cells shows variation then either a plate will have buckled and the battery will soon fail, or the electrolyte in the low reading cells contains too high a concentration of distiled water. In this case, some may be siphoned off and replaced with fresh electrolyte, which is readily obtainable from garages.

    If the car is used only for short trips or under conditions of high current drain then the battery may need recharging from time to time. It is recommended that the battery is charged at the lowest possible rate of amperage (current) and that 'boost' chargers are not used, as frequent use of too rapid a charge rate can cause damage to the battery.

When the battery is removed from the car, clean the terminals and cover with a thin layer of petroleum jelly; also, inspect the battery for cracks or leakage and the battery compartment for corrosion.

    One terminal of the battery is earthed (connected to the car's bodyshell) and the other is connected by a thick wire to the starter solenoid. Early cars had a positive earth, which can complicate the fitting of certain electrical accessories.

The Loom

The wires which carry electrical energy via fuses and switches to the majority of electrical components are contained tightly-bound within the loom. The wires are colour-coded so that they may be traced easily and compared to wiring diagrams, and some colours are used by manufacturers to denote certain functions. Brown, for instance, often signifies that a wire is permanently live and that the circuit may well be independent of any fuse. Black wires usually all run to earth and red wires are usually found in circuits which operate independently of the ignition switch, such as parking light circuits. Not all manufacturers conform to the same conventions.

    In many examples of the Spridget it may be discovered that previous owners have run wires of inappropriate colour, sometimes to bypass a length of damaged wire and sometimes when fitting an electrical accessory. Such wires should be replaced with others of the appropriate colour, so that future problems can be traced more easily.

    If a car has too many lengths of inappropriate wire or if the loom itself shows signs of damage, then it will be worth replacing the loom. These are widely available for all years and models of the Spridget.

Dealing with electrical faults

Electrical faults never 'cure' themselves, and intermittent faults which can appear to correct themselves are bound to re-emerge, possibly at such a time that they present a danger ie., lights going off at night. Even more importantly, an apparently inconsequential intermittent fault can in fact be a symptom of a far more serious fault, such as a loose spade connector on a permanent-live and non-fused brown wire which, if allowed to fall away and come into contact with the bodywork (earth) will cause a fire within seconds.

ALWAYS trace and rectify electrical faults as soon as they become apparent. If for any reason you are unable to immediately tend to an apparent fault then at the very least you should note down the exact nature of the fault and the circumstances in which it occurred (ie., which devices were in use at the time, whether it was raining etc.).

THINK SAFETY. Always begin by disconnecting the battery. Check the relevant fuse to see whether it is either blown or heat-discoloured, in which case too high a current has passed through it. Remember at this stage that a blown fuse is not a fault but a symptom of one; do not merely replace a blown fuse without locating the real fault.

You will require a circuit testing device, which could range from a Multi-meter down to a small battery, bulb and crocodile clip tester.

The first step is to identify the components associated with the fault, which in addition to the component in which the fault is apparent (ie, wiper motor, light bulb etc.) might include a switch or switches, fuse, relay and wires, and which may be traced via the circuit diagram. Locate each component in turn and ensure that it is the correct one for your particular car, as a previous owner may well have substituted an almost identical alternative which may have different connectors.

On the wiring diagram, back-trace the wires which lead from the faulty unit through any switches or relays to the power source. It is often helpful at this stage to make a small simplified sketch of the circuit, clearly marked with relevant details, such as wire colours, terminal numbers and so on. This will be far easier to work with than a full wiring diagram. Check that the correct colour wires are actually fitted to the power source, switch, earth, etc.

Remember that one side of the battery is earthed, that is, it is connected to the bodyshell of the car. One side of any electrical unit can also be earthed, so that the bodyshell acts in effect as a length of wire between the two. This reduces the amount of cabling in comparison with that needed in GRP-bodied cars, but it also increases the chances of a short-to-earth fault occurring, as any live wire or connector which comes into contact with any part of the bodywork will cause a short-circuit which allows the battery to discharge at its maximum rate (until the wire actually melts). In order to stress the dangers of accidentally shorting a live wire to earth it only needs to be stated that maximum battery discharge involves more than sufficient power to turn the starter motor

with the car in gear; in other words, enough power to move the car.

Think logically. If a unit fails to operate and a fuse is not blown somewhere within its operating circuit, then either there is a disconnect in the power feed or the earth connection is suspect. Check the earth first, and if this proves sound then use the circuit tester to check continuity between the various elements in the circuit back to the main power feed. Check also that the relevant switch is operating properly, using the circuit tester. If no faults in the circuit are apparent then the unit is faulty.

If a unit fails to operate and an in-line fuse is found to have blown, then there will be a short to earth somewhere in the wiring or the unit itself. Isolate each section of wiring and each electrical component in turn and use the circuit tester, with one terminal earthed, to check for a short circuit. If none is found then the fault could lie with the component itself, or there could be an intermittent earth problem somewhere within the circuit. If in doubt, always consult an auto-electrician.

Fitting a Loom

This can be a tricky and sometimes frustrating job with the potential – should you get your wires crossed, in a manner of speaking – for disaster if you re-connect the battery and start an electrical fire.

Before touching the existing loom, lay the new loom out along the floor or on a table surface next to the car, so that the front lights, rear lights and dashboard wires are all adjacent to their corresponding areas.

Using a wiring diagram and comparing with the wire colours of the existing loom, note and label each terminal on the new loom; a biro and masking tape are ideal for this purpose. It is a good idea to check off all of the wire terminals on the old loom by perhaps placing a tag on each. Do not proceed further until every single connector on the new loom (and preferably the old one) is thus labelled and double-checked; if you have been given an incorrect loom by mistake, then it is better to discover so before it is half fitted!

Disconnect the battery. Cut the old loom out, leaving a short length of wire on every terminal to assist in identification. Begin fitting the new loom through the bulkhead grommet to the dashboard area, then run the sections under the bonnet and under the car. Further fitting is simply a matter of disconnecting old spade and other terminals, and replacing them with the appropriate wire from the new loom.

If you decide to fit electrical accessories, then it is wise to take advice from an auto-electrician or even to undertake the physical fitting of the accessory and leave the wiring to a professional. Never fit extra units to a fused circuit without ensuring that the fuse rating is sufficient to meet all eventualities, and do not be tempted to uprate the fuse because it is matched to the existing units' safety levels.

Notes on Engine Electrical Components.

When replacing the dynamo on early cars, always polarize the unit before connecting it up and starting the engine. This entails bolting the unit into place then momentarily touching a live wire to the smaller, field terminal of the dynamo. Reconditioned dynamos from reputable sources will always come complete with fitting instructions describing how this is achieved. If you turn on the ignition and discover that the ignition light is behaving in an unusual manner, such as remaining on after the ignition has been turned off, immediately disconnect the unit and re-polarize it.

Distributor Removal

Type 25D4   Disconnect the battery. Remove the distributor cap then turn the crankshaft until the rotor arm is pointing at the number one cylinder terminal. Remove the low tension lead and the vacuum advance pipe. Undo the split housing plate screws and withdraw the distributor.

Type 45D4   Disconnect the battery and remove the distributor cap. Turn the crankshaft until the timing groove in the crankshaft pulley aligns with the static timing mark, and the rotor arm is pointing at the number one cylinder terminal. Remove the low tension lead and the vacuum advance pipe. Undo the clamp plate screws and withdraw the unit.

Restoration and Electrics

A full restoration presents the ideal opportunity to overhaul the entire electrical system and to replace tired old units before they fail. It is surprising how many 1960s Spridgets still have some of the original electrical fittings, such as the wiper motor, switches and dynamo, still fitted thirty years on. Because the car will be off the road for some considerable time during a restoration, you have the ideal opportunity as soon as the car is stripped to take larger items to a specialist for reconditioning, so that you can refit the original components (maintaining authenticity) but have the peace of mind of knowing that they are not nearing the end of their days.

When rebuilding a car with a restored bodyshell, the wiring loom will be one of the first items to be fitted, which unfortunately means that there exists ample scope for damage to occur to it during the rest of the rebuild. Always take the greatest care when fitting heavier components that you do not pinch or crush any of the wires.

TRIM AND FITTINGS

Dashboard removal

The small size of the Spridget makes any operation behind or under the dashboard rather awkward due to the cramped access. It is often better to release the dashboard and angle it forwards to that it can be accessed from the top than to grovel around underneath it! If the dashboard is being removed completely from the car during a restoration which includes the fitting of a new loom, then life is made very much easier because the wire endings can simply be cut away rather than prised from their terminals. In the cases of cars from the Midget Mk.2/Sprite Mk.3 to the 1500, the dashboard has to be removed before the screen can be removed.

All Models – Disconnect the battery.

Midget Mk.3/Sprite Mk.4

Remove the steering column cowls which house the flasher switch, then remove the flasher unit and disconnect the wires from the ignition switch. Remove the steering column complete.

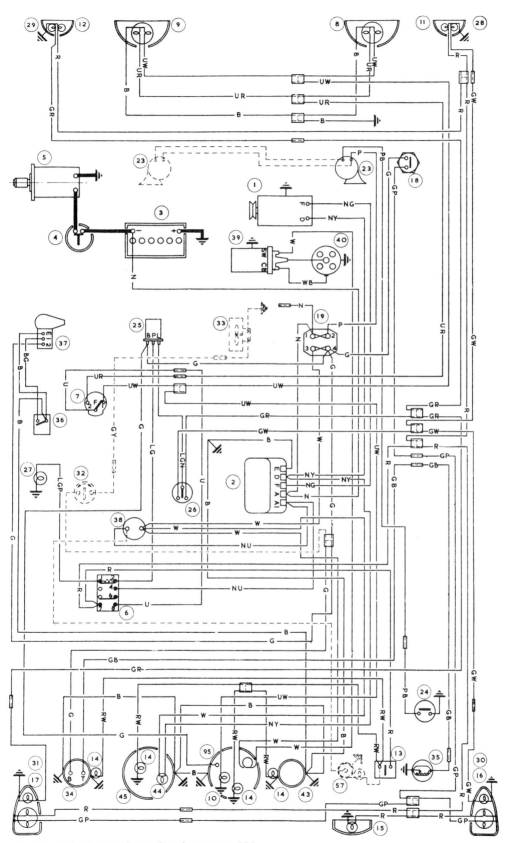

Wiring diagram for Midget Mk.1/Sprite Mk.2. Refer to key on page 132.

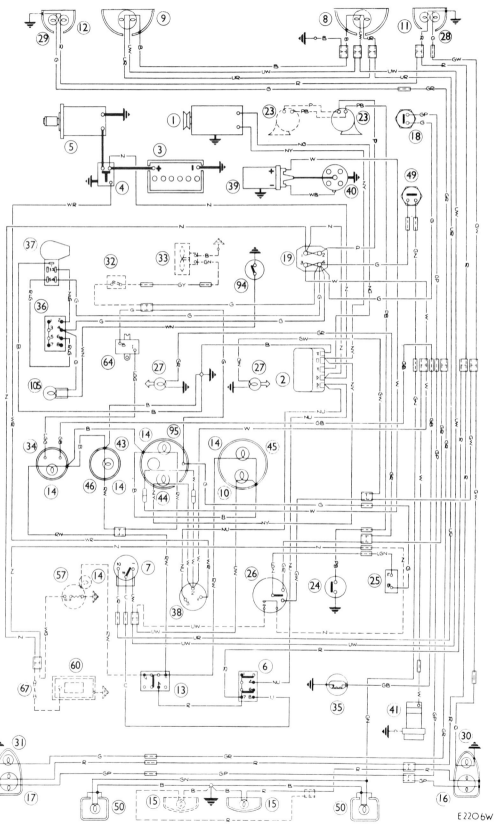

Wiring diagram for Midget Mk.3/Sprite Mk.4. – Negative earth. Refer to key on page 132.

E 2206W

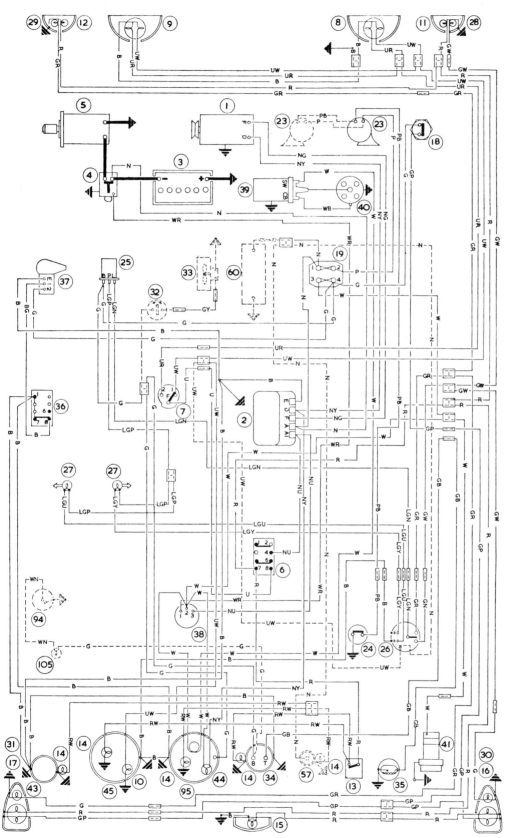

Wiring diagram for Midget Mk.2/3 and Sprite Mk.3/4. – Positive earth. Refer to key on page 132.

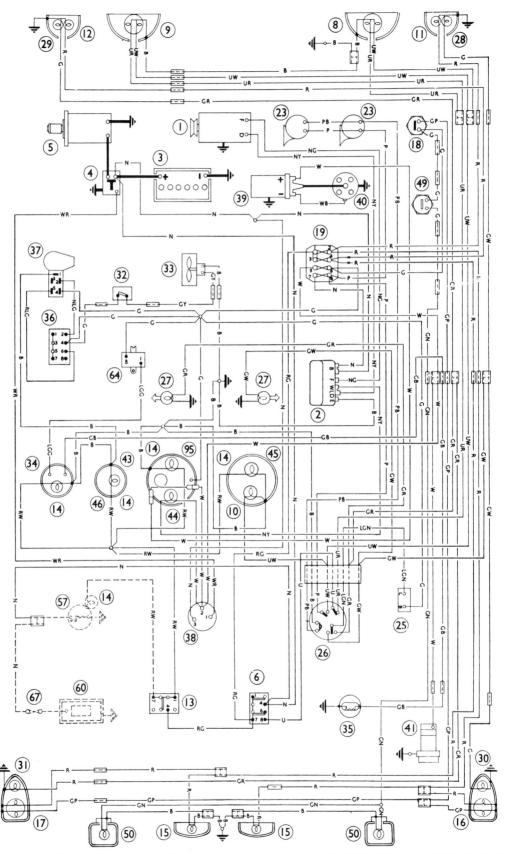

Wiring diagram for Midget Mk.3/Sprite Mk.4. – Negative earth (commencing Car No G-AN5-74886 (MG) and H-AN10-85287 (Sprite)).
Refer to key on page 132.

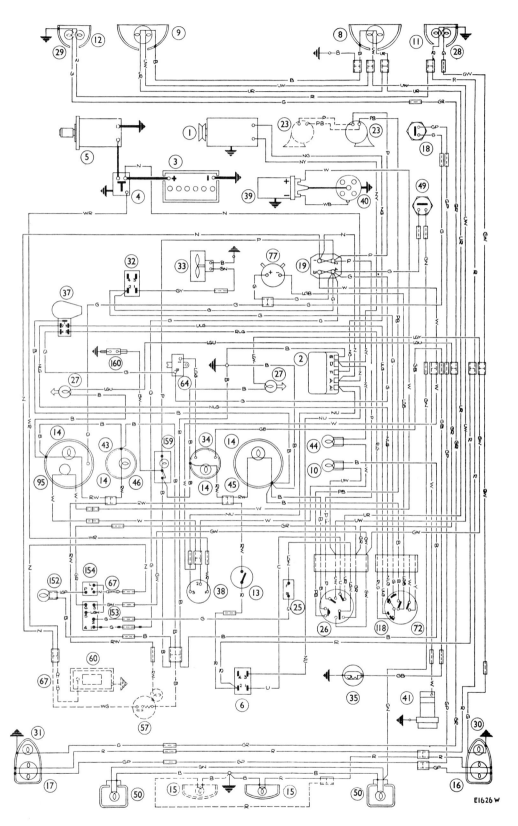

Wiring diagram for Midget Mk.3./Sprite Mk.4. (USA) – Negative earth. Refer to key on page 132.

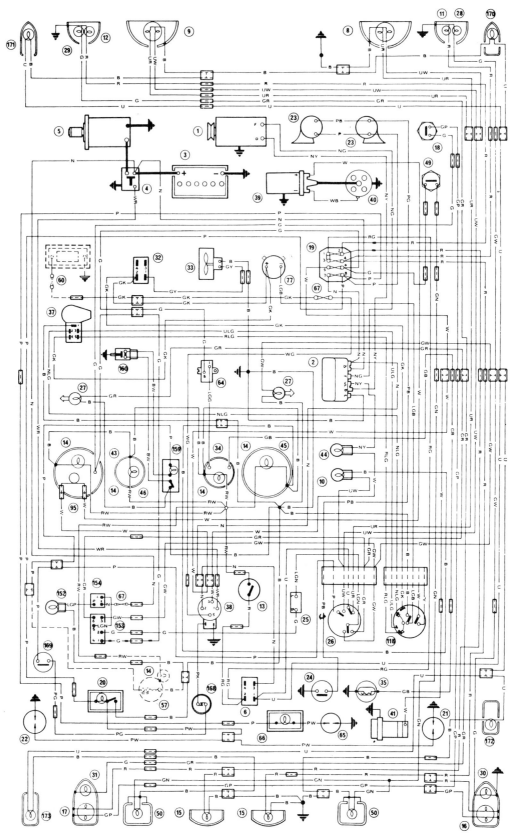

Wiring diagram for Midget Mk.3 (USA) – Negative earth (commencing Car No. G-AN5-89515). Refer to key on page 132.

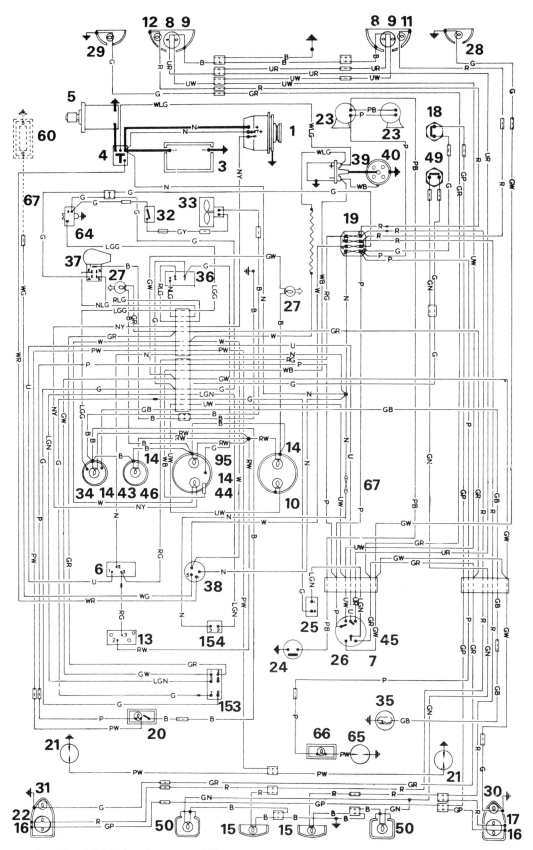

Wiring diagram for Midget 1500. Refer to key on page 132.

Key for Wiring Diagrams Pages 125–130

1.	Dynamo
2.	Control box
3.	Battery
4.	Starter solenoid
5.	Starter motor or starter switch
6.	Lighting switch
7.	Headlamp dip switch
8.	R.H. headlamp
9.	L.H. headlamp
10.	High-beam warning lamp
11.	R.H. parking lamp
12.	L.H. parking lamp
13.	Panel lamp switch
14.	Panel lamps
15.	Number-plate illumination lamp
16.	R.H. stop and tail lamp
17.	L.H. stop and tail lamp
18.	Stop lamp switch
19.	Fuse unit
20.	Interior courtesy lamp
21.	R.H. door switch
22.	L.H. door switch
23.	Horns
24.	Horn-push
25.	Flasher unit
26.	Combined direction indicator/headlamp flasher or
26.	Combined direction indicator/headlamp flasher/headlamp highglow beam/hornpush switch
26.	Combined direction indicator, headlamp flasher, headlamp high-low beam switch
27.	Direction indicator warning lamp
28.	R.H. front flasher lamp
29.	L.H. front flasher lamp
30.	R.H. rear flasher lamp
31.	L.H. rear flasher lamp

32.	Heater booster motor switch
33.	Heater booster motor
34.	Fuel gauge
35.	Fuel gauge tank unit
36.	Windscreen wiper switch
37.	Windscreen wiper motor
38.	Ignition/starter switch
39.	Ignition coil
40.	Distributor
41.	Fuel pump
43.	Oil pressure gauge
44.	Ignition warning lamp
45.	Speedometer
46.	Coolant temperature gauge
49.	Reverse lamp switch
50.	Reverse lamp
57.	Cigar-lighter – illuminated
60.	Radio
64.	Bi-metal instrument voltage stabilizer
65.	Luggage compartment lamp switch
66.	Luggage compartment lamp
67.	Line fuse
77.	Windscreen washer pump
94.	Oil filter switch
95.	Tachometer
105.	Oil filter warning lamp
118.	Combined windscreen washer and wiper switch
152.	Hazard warning lamp
153.	Hazard warning switch
154.	Hazard warning flasher unit
159.	Brake pressure warning lamp and lamp test push
160.	Brake pressure failure switch
168.	Ignition key audible warning buzzer
169.	Ignition key audible warning door switch
170.	R.H. front side-marker lamp
171.	L.H. front side-marker lamp
172.	R.H. rear side-marker lamp
173.	L.H. rear side-marker lamp

Key for Wiring Diagram Page 131

1.	Alternator
3.	Battery (12-volt)
4.	Starter solenoid
5.	Starter motor
6.	Lighting switch
7.	Headlamp dip switch
8.	Headlamp dip beam
9.	Headlamp main beam
10.	Headlamp main beam warning lamp
11.	R.H. sidelamp
12.	L.H. sidelamp
13.	Panel lamp switch
14.	Panel lamp
15.	Number-plate illumination lamp
16.	Stop lamps
17.	R.H. tail lamp
18.	Stop lamp switch
19.	Fuse unit (4-way)
20.	Interior courtesy lamp
21.	Interior lamp door switches
22.	L.H. tail lamp
23.	Horn

24.	Horn-push
25.	Flasher unit
26.	Direction indicator switch
27.	Direction indicator warning lamps
28.	R.H. front direction indicator lamp
29.	L.H. front direction indicator lamp
30.	R.H. rear direction indicator lamp
31.	L.H. rear direction indicator lamp
32.	Heater or fresh-air motor switch
33.	Heater or fresh-air motor
34.	Fuel gauge
35.	Fuel gauge tank unit
36.	Windscreen wiper switch
37.	Windscreen wiper motor
38.	Ignition/starter switch
39.	Ignition coil
40.	Distributor
43.	Oil pressure gauge
44.	Ignition warning lamp
45.	Headlamp flasher switch
46.	Coolant temperature gauge
49.	Reverse lamp switch

50.	Reverse lamps
60.	Radio (if fitted)*
64.	Instrument voltage stabilizer
65.	Luggage compartment switc.
66.	Luggage compartment lamp
67.	Line fuse for radio*
95.	Tachometer
153.	Hazard warning switch
154.	Hazard warning flasher unit.

*Optional fitment circuits shown do⸱

CABLE COLOUR CODE

N	Brown	LG	Light Green
U	Blue	W	White
R	Red	Y	Yellow
P	Purple	B	Black
G	Green		

When a cable has two colour code letters the first denotes the main colour and the second denotes the tracer colour

Disconnect the choke cable end from the carburettor and the cable from the tie at the heater unit. Disconnect the heater control by pushing in the small plunger which allows the control knob to be removed, then undo the lock ring and withdraw from the rear of the dashboard. Remove the lock ring from the windscreen washer control, and withdraw this.

Partially drain the coolant and remove the bulb-type temperature sender (where applicable). Support the dashboard and remove the fixing screws. Tilt the dashboard to improve access, then place a rag under the oil pressure sender pipe and remove this from the gauge. Remove the various wires.

Midget Mk.2/Sprite Mk.3

Rather than remove the steering wheel, the steering column is lowered. Pull the horn wire from its terminal under the dashboard. Remove the column surround then remove the bolts which hold the column bracket.

Remove the setscrews which hold the dashboard, then angle the dashboard to allow access for the various wires and cables to be disconnected.

Frogeye, Midget Mk.1/Sprite Mk.2

Remove the steering wheel by prising out the boss centre cap then undoing the large nut and pulling the steering wheel from its splines. The dashboard is held by a number of nuts, bolts and crosshead screws. Remove these, then undo the speedometer and tachometer drive cables, the oil pressure pipe, the starter and choke cables and the water temperature gauge sender (from the radiator). Pull the dashboard into the cab slightly and angle it to improve access to the back. The various wires can be cut or disconnected as appropriate.

DASHBOARD RESTORATION

Reconditioned dashboards are available for all years of Spridget. Many owners, however, will prefer to restore their own, which is a straightforward business. Simply remove the dashboard as already described, then remove from it all switches and dials. The dashboard can then be cleaned back to bare metal and re-sprayed using crackle black paint which is widely available from Spridget and MG specialists. Undertaking this work at home allows you to correct any non-standard features, such as a superfluous and non-original switch or gauge which may have previousy been fitted. If a non-standard gauge or switch is removed, simply butt weld steel into the hole whilst the dashboard is at the bare metal stage.

The switches and gauges fitted across the Spridget range should all be available from specialists. It is worth checking the switches fitted to your car for originality, and replacing as necessary, at this stage, whilst the dashboard is back to bare metal.

Crash rail

Atop the dashboard later Spridgets are fitted with a padded 'crash' rail. This should be removed during a body restoration to prevent damage from occurring to it, and it may prove necessary to recover it if it is torn or badly stained.

The rail is held by eight nuts which run onto semi-captive threaded rods held within the rail. Undo the nuts – taking care not to loose the plain split washer on each rod – and lift the rail away.

To recover the rail, obtain suitable material from a Spridget or MG speciatist. If you can, remove the old covering and use this as a template; otherwise, cut the material rather over size to begin with and then tailor it down until it fits. The author has found that the trade prefers spray-on 'contact' type adhesive for this, although the first-timer might be better advised to use an adhesive which allows the cover to be adjusted for a short period before it cures.

WINDSCREEN ASSEMBLY REMOVAL

Disconnect the battery and remove the windscreen wiper blades and arms.

Early cars

On early cars, the windscreen is held between two support pillars. Support the windscreen assembly and undo the five crosshead screws which pass through each support pillar. The windscreen assembly may now be lifted clear.

Sprite Mk.3/4, Midget Mk.2/3

Remove the dashboard as already described. Support the windscreen assembly then undo the centre and A post set screws. The windscreen assembly can now be lifted clear.

Later cars

Loosen the windscreen wiper wheelbox nuts. Remove the rear view mirror and sun visors (if fitted), and move the dashboard far enough to gain access to the A post set screws. Support the screen assembly, then undo the A post setscrews and the centre stay bolts. The windscreen assembly may now be lifted clear. The seal may partially stick to the frame and partially to the bodywork, and tear as the assembly is lifted, and if it shows signs of doing so, then it is best to replace the seal as a matter of course.

CARPETS AND INTERIOR PANELS

It is possible to replace Spridget carpets with carpet cut from the roll and stitched by hand. However, complete sets of properly fashioned carpets are available for Spridgets, and these will usually give a far better result at not too much extra cost. The edges of such carpet sets should be bound to prevent fraying. Furthermore, properly tailored carpets should include a heel pad, without which, a plain carpet will wear very quickly indeed. Be warned, however, that some of the very low cost carpet sets which are offered might not be of very high quality. If you can, try to find a set which includes a moulded carpet for the transmission tunnel, rather than one which has cuts and tucks in it.

Carpets which become wet should ideally be removed from the car and not re-fitted until both they and the underlying painted surfaces have been thoroughly dried. Unfortunately, in common with many cars, the section of carpeting which is underneath the seats may not be removed unless the seats are firstly removed. The author always takes every opportunity to give the upper surface of the floor extra paint protection followed up by liberal amounts of waxoyl, to help keep rust at bay in those instances when it is not possible to immediately remove the carpets following a soaking.

All interior panels for all years of Spridget are now available in the original colours. As old panels become tatty the hardboard underneath slowly breaks up, so that removing the material and recovering is not a practical option. It is worth replacing all the interior panels at the same time as seat covers, so that the two colour-match. Old seat covers and panels fade especially quickly in an open car during the summer months, and to replace one without the other will usually mean that the car interior does not look very smart.

Fitting seat covers is not too difficult, especially if you drape a plastic bag or a sheet of curtain material over the seat back before pulling on the new cover. Always replace seat foams at the same time as covers. The difference between the price of a set of covers and having new covers actually fitted to your existing seats should not be too great, and it is worth considering having the work carried out professionally.

Old leather seats can sometimes be rejuvenated, and more modern vinyl seats can be treated by Vinylcote or a similar product, which can be mixed to the appropriate colour.

HOOD

Little looks worse on a nicely prepared Spridget than a tatty hood. It is possible to repair a torn hood in a variety of ways, depending on the hood material, although anyone restoring a Spridget will usually opt for replacement. A surprisingly wide variety of hoods are available for later Spridgets, Midget Mk2/Sprite Mk3. These come essentially in two forms; with or without the header rail fitted.

The header rail is the rail which clips onto the windscreen surround top. The general idea is that you can buy the more expensive hood with the header rail or save money and buy the hood without, then cut the header rail out of your own hood and fit this to the new.

Various materials and weights of hood are available. The author recommends that you buy the best which you can afford if the car is to be used in the rain, because the long-term consequences of water ingress around a cheap hood will be a rotten floor! The author prefers double duck material to synthetic alternatives.

To fit the hood which is supplied without a

header rail, firstly remove the rail from the old hood. Pull the front rubber seal out, then drill out the pop rivets from its fixing channel, then clean the rail and key it ready for glueing. Mark the centre of the front edge of the new hood using chalk. Refit the header rail onto the windscreen surround, then fit new fasteners (where appropriate) to the new hood, and fit it along its rear edge, ensuring that it is symetrical. Erect the frame. Pull the hood over the frame to the header rail – not too tight – and position it so that the chalk centre mark lies directly over the windscreen centre rod. Hold the hood in this position (keep it reasonably taut, but do not over stretch it, because it may later shrink) whilst an assistant makes a chalk mark on the inside of the hood material to show where the material reaches the header rail.

Apply preferably a slow glue to both the header rail and the appropriate section of the hood, and pull the hood into position and hold it until the glue sets. Reassemble the rubber channel and the rubber.

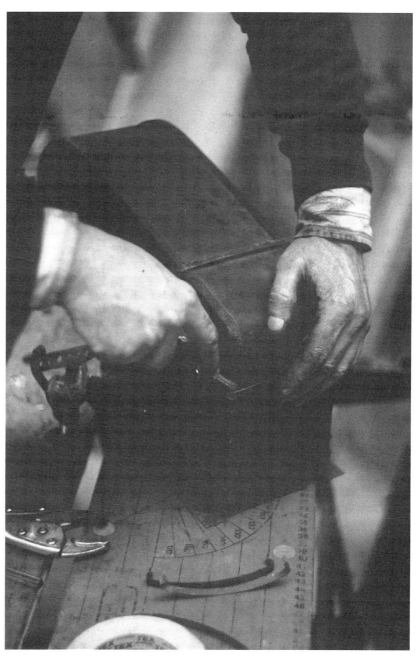

The heater unit is held together with spring clips. Clean the radiator fins, check it for leaks – flush it through if you like- and reassemble.

5 · BODYWORK REPAIR AND RESTORATION

Professional restoration businesses which deal with Spridgets usually also restore MGBs, as well as other classic sports cars. If you ask whether a professional restorer would rather restore an MGB or the smaller Spridget, most of them would reply that they would far rather work on the MGB. A small car is by no means necessarily easier to restore than a larger one, and Spridget repairs are especially difficult in the area of the heelboard and the rear chassis rails/boot area.

Before plunging head first into a DIY Spridget bodyshell restoration, readers are advised to study this chapter in its entirety and then consider whether their own skills and facilities are good enough for the task, or whether commissioning a professional restoration or buying in a new Heritage bodyshell might be a better option. If you do decide to carry out a DIY restoration, but discover part-way through the job that it is really beyond your abilities, then bring in a professional mobile welder to finish off, and get him to go over your existing work, just to be sure that the welds are strong enough.

Another matter for consideration is whether the costs of new and repair body panels needed for a full restoration, plus the costs of consumables such as welding wire, primer paint and so on, approach the cost of a new Heritage bodyshell. Before starting a restoration, add up these and any other costs which you can think of and, if the final body restoration cost is close to that of a new shell, decide whether the small cost saving to be made after many months of hard labour is really justified, or whether a new shell might be a better proposition.

Classic car restoration is often depicted in the many books and magazines on the subject to consist largely of cutting away rotten old panels and grafting in new, like a great surgeon heroically performing a life-saving operation. This is actually an important but nevertheless relatively small part of the work encountered in car bodywork restoration. In fact, the bulk of the work of restoration is actually concerned with the far more humdrum business of cleaning. For every minute spent welding, there will usually be an hour or several of cleaning, ranging from scraping away underseal, mud, tar and rust from the underside of the car to cleaning burnt oil deposits and sundry dirt from engine and transmission components.

A large percentage of the restorer's time will also be spent in trying to establish and maintain a coherent and workable 'filing system' for the various components of the car. This is essential if you are not to later waste countless hours in trying to find the right nut, bracket or set screw for a particular component. If your workplace does not offer sufficient dry storage (shelves or drawers) then it is advisable to build some before starting to strip the car.

This chapter will deal with both body repair and restoration, but will as far as possible present the various tasks in the order in which a complete body restoration might typically progress. This approach is intended to save a lot of duplication. However, because many people who start to replace just the sills of their Spridget will discover that far more than just a sill or two actually needs replacing on their car (and many 'sill replacements' can end up as full body restorations), many readers who set out on such a single task might have reason to be grateful for the layout of this chapter!

Unfortunately, because there are so many possible permutations of panels which may require either repair, replacement, or even someone else's bodges to be put right, and because the order of work can vary according to which panels require attention, a single book cannot possibly cover all eventualities. As already stated, the text broadly describes jobs as they crop up in a full body restoration. If you discover that the work which your car requires does not appear to slot into the given work sequence, then think out the job carefully before hacking away at rotten panels. Remember to leave in place any panels which can act as datum points for the fitting of others, before they too are replaced. Do not strip out a complete assembly of several panels and leave yourself with no datum points or guides to show you where to fit the new metal. It is also vital, of course, to leave sufficient panels in place at any given time to give the bodyshell sufficient strength and rigidity to prevent it from becoming distorted.

The only part of the text which is given separate coverage is sill replacement, because it is quite common to find that an otherwise sound car has rotten sills.

More so than during mechanical repair work, a good workshop is highly recommended for body repair and restoration work. A damp work place will be a constant source of frustration, because new panels will begin to rust as soon as (if not before) they are fitted. Good all-round lighting which illuminates the sides and underside of the car is essential, and a solid, level, crumble-proof concrete floor is absolutely vital. You will require plenty of dry storage for components. If you merely pile them up in a corner then rebuilding the car will be a nightmare because you will waste hours finding parts and many more hours cleaning rust from them if the area in which they have been stored is damp. You will doubtless be surprised after stripping the car to a shell that so many components could possibly fit into such a small car!

Some specialised tools and equipment are essential for restoration. Some form of welding equipment, if only a cheap MIG, is recommended even if you intend to bring in an outside welder to carry out the bulk of the work, in order to allow you to tack panels into position for final welding up by the professional.

WELDING EQUIPMENT

There are four types of welding equipment which the DIY restorer might typically consider. These are Arc, Mig, Gas and Spot welding equipment. Arc welding equipment is comparatively cheap to buy but has severe limitations regarding the thickness of metal it can be successfully used on. If the metal is less than ⅛″ thick (ie. all body panels) the fierce arc welder will quickly burn right through the metal which it is supposed to be joining! Arc welders are better suited to use on heavy section agricultural vehicle metal and are useless for the vast majority of car restoration work. An accessory called the Kel Arc Body Welder is available, however, which is claimed to cut the hot amps from the arc welder and to have a stitching motion which lifts the rod on and off the metal, allowing it to cool and preventing the rod from either sticking to or burning through the metal. The author has not had the opportunity to test this equipment. The costs of the Kel Arc attachment and an arc welder will still be slightly under the purchase price of a MIG welder.

The MIG welder surrounds its electrode (in wire form) in an inert gas, so helping to prevent the metal from burning through. It may therefore be used on the thin metal of car body panels. Two types are available. The more traditional MIG welder uses gas from either a small cylinder strapped to the unit or from a larger, remote cylinder, and different gasses are required for different metals. The newer type of MIG (the 'gasless' MIG which can only be used on steel) substitutes a substance contained as a core within the wire for the gas. Because large gas cylinders are expensive to buy, hire and fill and because small gas cylinders have to be replaced frequently at high cost, this newer type of welder appears to offer advantages. The main advantage of the gasless MIG is that it possesses only one consumable (the cored wire) to run out of! The MIG welder is probably the best type for a newcomer.

The majority of the welding covered within this book was carried out using a SIP 'Handymig' Gasless MIG welder; a unit which proved quite easy to use and which is capable of first-class results. The cored wire needed for a gasless welder is more expensive than that for a gas MIG, although as no gas need be purchased for the former, the running costs of the two will not differ greatly. The fact that there is only the one consumable (the cored wire) to run out is very much in the gasless MIGs' favour, although the author has on occasions experienced difficulties in obtaining the specialised cored (often referred to by shop assistants as flux-cored) wire locally. Make absolutely certain that any wire you buy for a gasless MIG is the correct type, because mistakes do happen.

Gas welding is arguably the most versatile of all, and can produce excellent results in the hands of a skilled person. Arc, MIG and spot welders all use electricity to heat a very small area, whereas in gas welding a gas torch is used to heat both metal and welding rod, and a larger area of metal tends to become very hot during gas welding. The greatest drawback is that the heat which is necessary tends to warp body panels and can easily give a new panel a corrugated finish! Gas welding equipment can also be used for brazing and for heating stubborn nuts and bolts which refuse to move otherwise.

Spot welders are the easiest in use, although they are limited insofar as they can only be used (unless a range of very expensive special arms and tips are also available) for joining together the edges of two metal 'lips'. For such joins they give an unbeatable combination of ease of use, strength and neatness. No wire nor welding rod is required, because the spot welder uses electricity to heat and fuse two panels together. Few DIY restorers would go to the expense of buying a spot welder because of their limited applications, and most opt to hire them as and when necessary from a DIY store or tool hire business. If you do use a spot welder then it is vital that the metal to be joined is truly spotless. The slightest traces of corrosion or other contamination will result in very weak welds.

Another accessory which has been available for the Arc welder for some time is claimed to allow users to spot weld two sheets of steel with access from one side alone, whereas the spot welder requires that one electrode is placed either side of the join. The Arc welder accessory has not been tested by the author, and while he cannot vouch for them he cannot see any reason why they should not work. It would be vital that the panels being joined were firmly gripped in some way immediately either side of the single electrode, however, because the heat generated in the outer panel would be greater than that generated in the inner one, and because the two panels would therefore expand at different rates it could prove difficult to hold them firmly together whilst the weld was made. Still on the subject of Arc welder accessories, kits are available which enable it to be used for brazing. Whilst the author has heard no

comment detrimental to any of these Arc welder accessories, he has yet to find an experienced professional restorer who champions them.

Most welding equipment can only produce neat and strong results if the operator possesses the appropriate skill. The quickest way to acquire such skills is to enroll on a short welding course, perhaps an evening class at a college. Whilst it is true to say that you can teach yourself to weld, it is not recommended that you do so (especially using your own car as a guinea pig). Because the MIG seems to be the type of welding equipment most commonly owned by the DIY restorer, an introduction to its use follows. If you wish to find out more then there are several excellent books available on the subject.

Using a MIG Welder

The MIG is (apart from the spot welder) arguably the easiest of welding devices for the beginner to use for general bodywork repairs. This does not, however, mean that it is an easy matter to produce clean and strong welds on typically thin body panels for, unless conditions and the user's skills are both excellent, there are many obstacles to good welding.

The worst problem to beset the novice is that of 'burning through', when the electric current melts straight through the metal which it is supposed to be joining. This can occur if the wire feed speed is too slow (or intermittent, which can indicate a fault in the welder), if the gun is moved across the metal too slowly, if the current is set too high or if the shielding gas/core fails to do its job.

When the metal to be welded has become thin through rusting then the chances of burning through are greatly increased, and hence the advice to always cut back to not only clean but also to strong and thick metal before attempting to weld.

The correct preparation of the metal which is to be welded is important. All traces of rust, of paint, oil, grease and any other contaminant must be cleaned from the surface to avoid poor adhesion and spitting. ANY impurities which find their way into the welded joint will substantially weaken it.

When a joint is being welded, both surfaces should be thoroughly cleaned and then clamped in some way so firmly that the heat of the welding process does not distort either. Small sections may be clamped, although longer runs are usually affixed using self-tapping screws or alternatively pop rivets.

First Steps with a MIG

Always practice on scrap metal and do not attempt any welding to the bodywork of your car until you are capable of producing consistently good results.

Safety is the most important consideration. Never weld in the vicinity of a petrol tank nor any other container which holds or has held combustible fluids especially if the container is now empty or near-empty (an empty petrol tank contains more explosive fumes than a full one). Also, before welding any part of the car bodywork, disconnect the alternator or dynamo and the battery.

Always use a proper welding mask. If you view the electric arc with the naked eye then you will later suffer an immensely painful phenomenon called arc eye. Arc eye is painful enough to drive most sufferers to seek hospital attention. The radiation given off by the MIG is not just harmful to eyes, but to skin as well, so always ensure that you are well protected.

Always wear protective clothing, especially strong leather gloves, and a hat (to prevent your hair from catching fire as the sparks shower) is a good idea. It is as well to wear old, thick items of clothing, as you will inevitably burn holes in most of them.

Never take liberties with the electric current, which is of a low voltage but quite powerful enough to kill some people. Ensure that you weld only in dry conditions, and keep trailing leads off damp floors.

When firstly attempting to weld, try to run a bead onto a flat sheet of 16g-20g steel rather than attempting a joint between two pieces. Begin by cleaning the metal thoroughly of all rust, paint and grease. Trim the wire protruding from the MIG nozzle to around 10 mm. Place the earth clamp on the steel, put on all protective clothing then switch on the machine. Place the wire against the steel, pull the face visor in front of your eyes then press the trigger and begin to push or drag the gun along the surface of the steel, keeping the gun at an angle of around 70 degrees from the horizontal. Do not allow the mask to get too close to the weld, because sparks will quickly ruin it. Wrap-around face masks, particularly those which attach to the user's head, are recommended,

Some of the main types of welded joint. The arrows show the angle at which the MiG gun should be held for best results. The gap in the butt joint should be roughly equal to the thickness of the metal in question. The lap joint is useful because pop rivets or self-tapping screws can be used to pull the two pieces of metal tightly together, not only to obtain a stronger weld but also to help line the two pieces up correctly. The joddled joint has the advantages of the lap joint but places the surfaces of the two sheets level. With both the lap and joddled joint, one of the two welds shown will usually be sufficient, and the lower weld is optional. Do not be tempted to over-weld joints, because the welded joint is far more brittle than steel sheet – in an accident it will tend to break open rather than help absorb energy. The corner joint is the most difficult to do, and you may find it far easier to form a folded lip on one of the panels to turn it into a lap joint.

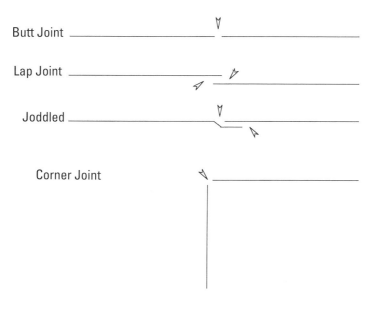

Butt Joint

Lap Joint

Joddled

Corner Joint

because the alternative flat masks can allow in extraneous light from the top and sides which dilate the pupils and make the viewed image of the welding process appear very dim.

When you first attempt to weld it will appear that everything happens at once, sometimes too quickly for you to establish gun movement before burning through begins on thinner metal. The solution is to keep on practicing and adjusting the settings on the MIG to suit the steel you are welding until you master the art. The author is not possessed of particularly steady hands, and he has never found achieving good welds with the MIG an easy matter. The greatest problem is that of running the weld away from the intended join. He overcomes this problem to a great extent by resting the side of the MIG pistol grip against a solid object such as a length of scrap box section steel which is arranged so that it is in line with the intended join. Many people use proper head-mounted welding visors rather than the 'lollipop' type of mask typically supplied with cheaper welders, and this allows them to use their 'spare' (and heavily gloved) hand to help guide the MIG. Basically, the visor is tilted upwards so that the person can place the pistol grip onto the metal and support it using both hands (do not allow your hand too close to the 'business' end), then a flick of the head moves the visor downwards over the eyes, and welding can begin. Do not blame the author if you crick your neck trying this, though!

If, after giving it your best shot, you discover that you are not really cut out for welding then bring in a skilled welder. The author can weld well enough for smaller tasks, but when seam welding a large job – such as a floor pan – he always gets an expert to do the work.

MIG 'plug' welding is an easy method of producing neat and strong joints. This simulates a spot weld, and is achieved by drilling holes in the uppermost of two panels which are to be joined, then clamping the panels tightly together and filling the holes with weld. The weld fuses to the bottom panel and to the side of the hole in the top panel. After surplus weld has been ground down, the results can be very neat and strong.

There are various types of joint which you will have to deal with. The butt joint is, as the name suggests, a join between two sheets of metal which butt against each other. A small gap should be left in between the two so that the weld can properly penetrate the joint, and the ideal tool for achieving this is the 'Inter-Grip'. This small device (sold in packs of five) can hold flat or curved panels tightly together for butt welding equally well. They are available from Frost Auto Restoration Techniques (see address in rear of book). Other joints include right angles (which can be difficult) and stepped joints (detailed in the following paragraph). Practice all types of joint because they will all be needed during a typical restoration.

A joddler (variously referred to as a 'joggler' 'jodder' and, more properly, as an edge setter) is a great aid. This tool places a step into the edge of a panel to allow it to overlap yet remain at the same level as the panel to which it is to be joined. The better joddlers incorporate a ⅛″ punch, for punching holes in steel through you can produce neat plug welds.

Two types of joddler are commonly commercially available. The less expensive is the scissors type, which can incorporate a plug weld hole punch. The more expensive alternative works rather like a can opener and utilises two stepped wheels which are pressed either side of the steel and then turned using a ½″ ratchet drive as a winder. The author uses the scissors type, but found that the effort needed to step an edge into steel of greater thickness than 20g was too high. He made up a cheap alternative using a large mole wrench, with two stepped blocks welded into the jaws (see photograph and illustration). The mole wrench allows pressure to be built up as two or more passes are made over thick steel with the tool.

The joddled joint has a great advantage over the butt joint. Because the two halves of a joddled joint can be pulled tightly together and because the stepped edge of the joddled panel is parallel with the rest of the panel, the two panels naturally tend to be flat when they have been welded together. With the butt joint, it is easy to inadvertently weld the panels up so that they are not quite in line with each other. This becomes important when one of the two panels being joined is under any sort of stress. One instance which springs readily to mind is when a repair lower quarter panel is being welded on to the front end of a rear wing. The cutting process which removed the unwanted metal can easily have distorted the remaining metal. A joddled repair panel pulls this back into correct alignment when the panels are temporarily clamped with pop rivets or self tapping screws prior to welding.

The alternative to welding is to bring in a skilled welder as and when required. There are many self-

This is a commercially made joddler, and very good it is too, although stepping a long edge, or stepping an edge in thicker sheet really makes the forearms ache. Note the hole punch, which produces burr-free holes for MiG plug welding.

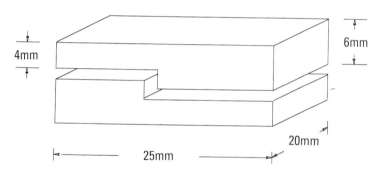

4mm

6mm

20mm

25mm

The author made up his own joddler by carefully filing two steelbocks to the dimensions shown here. In practice, the corners were not absolutely square, which is probably a good thing, because if they had been then they would have cut into the metal. Grip the blocks (separated by a piece of 20g steel, to give the blocks the correct final alignment) in the jaws of an old pair of mole grips, then MiG them into place.

The author's home-made joddler offers one big advantage over commercially available alternatives (in addition to being cheaper), which is that pressure may be applied progressively by winding up the mole grips and making two or more passes over the edge to be stepped.

These handy fellows are the Frost Intergrips, which can be used to hold together two sheets of curved steel ready for butt welding.

And this is how they work. Simply pass the leg through the gap, push in the locking bar and then tighten up.

On this demo piece, the author made the mistake of tacking the two pieces of metal too closely to the Intergrips. Weld shrinks as it cools, tending to draw butt welds together and tighten the grip on the Intergrip legs. Tack weld at least 10mm away from the Intergrip legs, and you'll have no problems.

employed and mobile MIG and gas welders who may be hired by the hour, and they are usually listed in the telephone directory. Those welders who mainly work on cars will usually also be quite skilled fabricators, able to quickly make up repair sections.

When hiring a skilled welder it is as well to prepare as much work per visit as possible, otherwise the travelling expenses could eclipse the actual welding charges! For most DIY restorers, hiring a skilled welder is probably a better solution than learning to weld, because you will get better results and be able to drive your car safe in the knowledge that the sill welds will not spring open the first time you drive over a pothole!

Sykes Pickavant produce a wide range of body repair tools, some of which are a luxury and others which are essential for the DIY restorer. At the very least, try to obtain a small selection of hammers and dollys, because they will be needed time and time again.

OTHER TOOLS AND EQUIPMENT

A means of raising the shell to a comfortable working height and keeping it there are needed. Strong steel trestles can easily be constructed and if two steel box sections are laid across these, you will have a solid and level platform onto which a few strong adults should be able to manhandle the bare shell. The Spridget shell is not very heavy – the author can comfortably roll it onto its side unassisted. An angle grinder with cutting and grinding wheels plus a sanding/linishing wheel and perhaps a cup brush will save hours of very hard work when you have to clean old paint, underseal or rust from metal. You will need a selection of tools for cutting sheet metal, such as aviation shears (straight and curved), a Monodex cutter, hacksaw, sharp bolster chisel and lump hammer. Pneumatic chisels which work from compressors are marvellous if your pocket runs to a large enough compressor to power one, because they allow you to cut body panels without the distortions which a bolster chisel produces. The twin problems

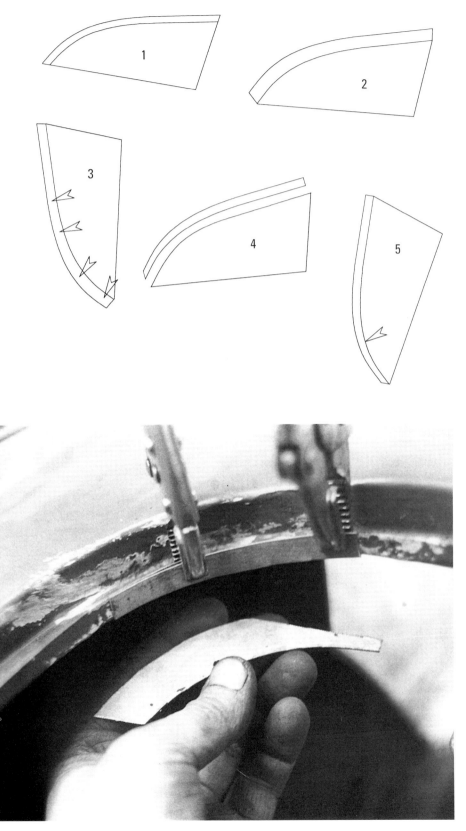

LEFT AND BELOW *Panel beating is one skill which the DIY restorer would do well to master. When fabricating your own repair panels, it is often necessary to create a lip of concave or convex form, and there are two ways of achieving this – panel beating or construction through welding. Cut out the repair panel, leaving sufficient metal at the edge to form the lip, and scribe on the line for the fold (1). The author then starts the fold using mole grips with smoothed jaw faces (2), and increases the fold in this manner until the main part of the panel just starts to buckle. At this stage, he thickens the metal of the lip by heating one small area at a time and beating it as shown on page 146 (3). The alternative method is to cut out the base and the lip separately (4), then to weld the two together along their seam (5). In making a small repair section for the boot aperture corner, the author cut and clamped into position the new lip, and then scribed the shape of the base onto sheet steel and cut this out.*

The base and lip were then clamped into position and tacked together using the MiG.

The two pieces were then removed as one, and seam welded.

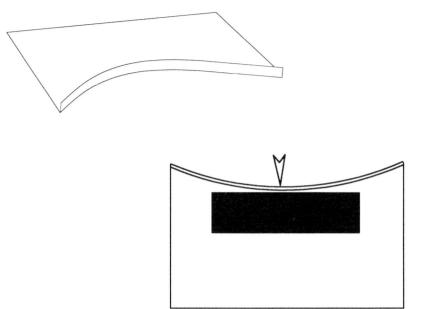

Forming a concave lip requires that the metal of the lip is stretched. Proceed by starting the fold as described in the text, heat one small area at a time and then hold it over a dolly as illustrated, beating in the direction of the arrow to thin and hence stretch the metal. It is advisable to practise your 'tin-bashing' skills on scrap sheet steel before trying to make repair panels for your own car.

with the tool are its noise level (guaranteed to annoy neighbours) and its appetite for air, which can easily outstrip the capacity of smaller compressors.

Another very useful but incredibly noisy air tool is the descaler. This tools uses air power to hammer a number of pins down onto a rusted surface, and can quickly remove all traces of rust and leave a surface ready for degreasing prior to welding or spraying. The noise level generated by working on a large, resonant panel with either this tool or the air chisel, however, is so great that the user must wear some form of hearing protection. In some countries, laws will allow neighbours the legal means to curtail such noisy activities. In the UK, noise is now treated as a form of pollution, and the Authorities could be brought in by a neighbour if you were to make too much noise.

Speaking of compressors, these are incredibly useful, not merely for spraying, but for blowing rust and dust out of nooks and crannies. They are also useful to have to hand for blowing out minor welding fires which can start when paint, underseal or trim in the vicinity of the area being welded suddenly catches fire. Buy the largest compressor which you can afford, because very small units are quickly drained of air by certain attachments, and the motors have a short 'duty cycle' which causes them to shut off automatically to prevent them from overheating. This sometimes happens just as you really NEED them!

The author has also found that an old cylinder-type vacuum cleaner is one of the most useful tools in

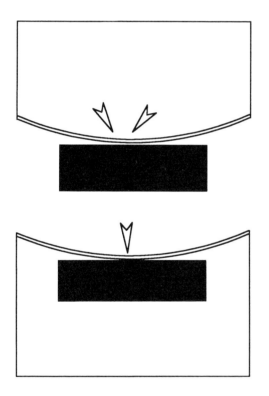

The basic skills for stretching and shrinking metal. For a convex lip (top) the metal must be shrunk rather than stretched. This is accomplished by heating one small area, holding it over a dolly as illustrated, and then beating in the directions of the arrows to bunch up the metal and hence thicken it. For a concave lip (below), the metal must be stretched as already described.

the workshop. Cleaning off an old bodyshell generates a tremendous amount of dust which, if you try to clear it with a broom, will mainly escape into the atmosphere only to re-settle elsewhere. If you are spraying then such dust will ruin the finish; if you are rebuilding a mechanical component then the dust will enter the 'works' and cause accelerated wear. The vacuum cleaner deals with this problem and is also useful for cleaning loose paint and rust flakes off the bodyshell, and for clearing dust from nooks and crannies before painting.

A pop-riveter is essential for fixing some items of trim but also very useful for positioning some panels prior to welding. Hand-powered pop rivet pliers are cheap to buy, and you should always look for a set which has long handles, because using them for any length of time can really make your hand ache! Air-powered alternatives are available, but it is up to the individual to decide whether the amount of pop rivetting to be done justifies the extra cost of these. The more ambitious restorer who wishes to fabricate some of the repair panels will benefit from a full set of panel beater's tools, although a rubber faced mallet, a selection of hammers and dollies can be substituted with some success.

Adrian Wadley (Ace Welder) kindly loaned the author this set of three panel beating hammers and four dollys; add a butane blowtorch for heating metal, a pair of aviation cutters and good old shears, and you have a junior panel beaters' kit with which you can fabricate remarkably complex repair panels yourself once you have the experience.

USE AND ABUSE OF BODYFILLER

Whilst the appearance of panels which will ultimately be hidden underneath carpets or underseal is not important, it is obviously important that external panels are not only strongly fitted but also that they look good. Unfortunately, many of the operations during a restoration create welded seams which will show up through paintwork and which consequently need to be hidden before painting. Shallow dents in external panels, which can easily be accidentally caused during the mechanical build-up, also have to be hidden, along with rivelling caused by welding heat. The materials for achieving a smooth surface and the correct lines in such cases are either body filler or lead (or a combination of these).

Many classic enthusiasts abhor body filler despite the fact that, if properly used, this material can give perfectly acceptable results. Unfortunately, body filler has suffered from a 'bad press' because the number of cases of filler misuse easily outnumber cases of proper use.

Body filler is intended and perfectly acceptable for filling shallow dents in external and non-structural car body panels, provided that the metal has been cleaned bright and degreased thoroughly prior to the application of the filler. It is not intended to be used to bridge holes, nor to fill deep dents or cover up areas of bodyrot. Yet those looking for an elderly example of the Spridget will doubtless encounter many cars in which quite large holes and deep dents have been filled with a lump of bodyfiller, in which structurally essential panels have been 'repaired' with a mixture of GRP and bodyfiller, and in which filler has been applied over rust (in which case it soon drops out again). Little wonder that the stuff has such a poor reputation.

Bodyfiller should only be used to obtain a smooth surface on metal which has shallow dents, such as might result from heat distortion during welding operations, from minor parking bumps, or on a seam produced following the fitting of a repair part-panel. The filler is the modern equivalent of lead, because bodyshops and car manufacturers for many years treated small undulations in external car body panels by firstly painting on a lead 'paint', melting this to 'tin' (coat) the area in question and to form a strongly-bonded layer to which the lead can adhere, then melting on and spreading with a spatula further lead to build up to the required height. This process is known as 'lead loading' or 'body soldering'. Bodyfiller is far easier to use than near-molten lead, as well as being inherently safer! Lead loading kits and associated equipment are available and widely advertised.

Lead loading offers one great advantage over body filler because the lead fully seals the surface over which it is applied, and in doing so it prevents future rusting (as long as the metal underneath is bright when coated with lead). In the author's experience, many professional restorers use lead loading for this reason, although obtaining a final smooth finish with lead is not an easy process, and many of these restorers use body filler on top of the lead to obtain the best of both worlds!

A combination of lead loading and the use of body filler is especially useful when dealing with welded seams. Clean then degrease all the area in question (the metal must be perfectly clean), then paint on solder paint, which is obtainable from companies such as Frost Auto Restoration Techniques (address at the back of the book). Apply heat to the solder paint until it melts and coats the metal, then wipe away any flux from the surface using a damp rag. The metal is now sealed, and may be built up using either lead or body filler.

It must be pointed out that lead is highly toxic, so if you do decide to work with it, treat it with the caution you would if dealing with any other toxic chemical. Never try to work lead using any sort of sanding device, because this would create a health hazard were you to breathe in lead dust. Use only body files to shape lead.

Using Bodyfiller

In order to use body filler successfully, it is vital that all traces of rusting, paint (including primers), oils and other contaminants are removed from the surface to be treated. Filler cannot adhere strongly to painted metal, because the join can only be as strong as that between the paint and the metal! If you apply filler over the slightest amount of rust then you can expect it to literally drop out at a later date when the rusting spreads sufficiently underneath. If you apply filler over contaminants then you may find that poor adhesion results, or the filler could chemically react with certain contaminants.

If cleaning the metal renders it very thin then you should not use bodyfiller because it will offer very little strength and furthermore, most types of filler are quite rigid and will be very inclined to loose adhesion to a thin and hence very flexible panel, or even to break up as the panel flexes. The only safe option in this situation is to weld in new metal.

Check the surface carefully for high spots. Whilst you can fill and smooth down low areas, high spots cannot be linished out and must be beaten out before the filling process begins. If there are any deep holes, beat these out as shallow as possible, where access permits. Equipment is available for pulling out dents, and consists of sliding hammer rod to which a number of attachments may be affixed. The attachments can fit through a small hole in the surface of the metal, and the sliding hammer is then used to knock out the dent. If the surface can be made clean and yet remain sound, 'key' the surface with a

36 grit disc, then use spirit wipe to remove any grease or oil contaminants.

Most fillers consist of a thick paste and a separate hardener; a chemical catalyst which accelerates the hardening of the filler. The filler itself usually comprises a polyester resin with a mineral-based powder, which forms a thick paste. Alternatives with tiny metal particles instead of the mineral powder can be obtained today. These offer the advantage of not being porous but might not give such good adhesion as the mineral products, which have far smaller particles. Mineral body fillers are porous.

Mix up the smallest quantity of bodyfiller which you feel you can get away with, and always follow the manufacturer's instructions relating to the relative amounts of filler and hardener. Ensure that the filler and hardener are properly mixed and of a uniform colour. Cleanliness is vital, because any foreign bodies in the filler will simply 'drag' as you try to smooth off the surface.

Apply bodyfiller in very thin layers, allowing each to fully harden before adding the next, and gradually build up the repair to the required level. Do not be tempted to apply one thick layer of filler, because this may have small air bubbles trapped within it which will only become apparent when you begin to sand down the surface. Also, some resins and hardeners generate heat as they cure, and, if you apply too thick a layer, the extra heat generated by the greater mass might over-accelerate the curing process.

Build up the surface until it is slightly proud of the required level and leave it to fully cure before sanding it down. If sanding by hand, then use a sanding block; electric random orbital sanders and air-powered dual action sanders really come into their own when working with bodyfiller, and can both save much hard work and help to gain better results. The author has found the random orbital electric sander which takes $\frac{1}{3}$rd of a sheet of paper, gives the best results, because it offers a large contact area and so helps to avoid sanding the filler into a concave section. However you sand down the filler, always wear a dust mask, because the tiny particles of filler in the air can cause respiratory problems if you inhale enough of them. Before you begin sanding down body filler, ensure that no engine or transmission components are lying out in the open workshop, as the filler dust really does manage to get everywhere!

Most body filler is porous; that is, it can absorb moisture. If the filler is allowed to become wet before it is primed, then the moisture can remain in contact with the surface of the metal underneath, and all of your hard work will have been to no avail! Therefore, it pays to spray primer over a filled area as soon as the sanding is completed. Do not try to sand down filler using wet 'n dry paper with water!

MAKING A START

Take several colour photographs of your car from various angles, have these blown up to 10′ x 8′ and hang them on your workshop wall. These will serve in moments of despair as the best possible inspiration, giving you the motivation to carry on when every fibre of your body is screaming to be let out of the workshop, never to return!

Before embarking on bodywork repair or restoration, it is necessary to properly establish the full extent of rusted or rotted metal on the car. If you omit this stage then you could easily find that you are carrying out jobs in a sequence which makes the tasks more difficult than could be the case. Even worse, you could discover that the sequence in which you were carrying out the work allowed you to inadvertently build in body distortion (which very nearly happened during the work on the project car, as you will learn shortly), so that the very last panel of the sequence to be welded on simply would not fit! You could even strip off a sill, intending to carry out a fairly straightforwards replacement, only to discover that there was no clean and sound metal to which you could weld the replacement if the edges of the floor, footwell side panel and heelboard assembly, plus the bottom of the A post were all rotten – a not uncommon scenario.

The easiest way to discover all rot in a car is to strip it to a bare shell and send it or take it away for dipping in an acid bath. This process strips all paint, underseal and rotten metal from the shell, leaving some surfaces which can be immediately primed and others clean enough to begin welding to. Before considering the use of an acid bath, ensure that the bodyshell is not too extensively rotten, because some really rotten examples of the Spridget could emerge from an acid bath in a very weak state. Moving such a bodyshell afterwards without distorting it could prove almost impossible.

Irrespective of whether the shell is dipped in an

acid bath or not, begin by probing every panel of the car vigourously with a sharp metal implement (an old screwdriver is ideal) to find all rust and rot. What you discover in this way will have a great bearing on how work on the car can subsequently proceed.

Underseal presents problems to the restorer. No matter how unblemished the surface of underseal, it can hide serious and spreading rot. It has to come off, and this can be accomplished in a variety of ways.

Underseal clogs abrasive papers and cloths very quickly, rendering them useless. Ordinary wire brushes will have no effect on underseal, and high-speed cup brushes used in angle grinders merely rip away filaments of underseal which stick to whatever they hit. Large flat areas of underseal can be dealt with initially using a blowtorch to soften the material and a wallpaper scraper to remove the bulk of it. Have a fire extinguisher handy before trying this! Alternatively, underseal can be scraped away using an old wood chisel. Both of these methods will remove much of the underseal, but leave enough of it on the surface to still clog abrasive papers. Use paraffin to soften the remaining traces of underseal, then wipe it clean with a rag.

If not only the sills (you can expect the sills of most Spridgets to need replacement if any other aspect of the bodywork needs attention) but also the footwell sides and front, heelboard and rear side chassis strengtheners, perhaps the floor pans and A post bottoms have all rotted (not untypical) then you are looking at a complete engine-out restoration or a re-shell. This work could alternatively be undertaken by raising and working on one side of the car at a time, but the chances of your building in body distortion would be great. In such instances it is advisable to remove all possible stresses from the bodyshell by stripping out every mechanical, electrical and trim component, so starting off with a bare shell. If you decide to work on the car one side at a time without firstly stripping it then be very careful

RIGHT *Before embarking on a full body restoration, add up the costs of repair and replacement panels, then add on the costs of welding consumables, abrasive papers, primer paint, labour etc. Subtract this from the cost of a new Heritage shell and only then reach a decision on whether to restore or re-shell. In the background are both square and round rear wheel arch shells, and the attractiveness of the latter might well result in some pre-1972 RWA Midgets or even RWA Sprites appearing on the roads!*

that, when raised to the working position, every heavy component (engine, gearbox, axle and suspension member) is fully supported so that no weight whatever from them can distort the shell. In practice, with a rotten shell this is so difficult that it is not recommended.

Stripping components from the body shell is covered in the relevant sections of this book. However, when the components are being stripped from a car with a rotten body, there are a few points worthy of consideration.

Rotten cars invariable have rusted and seized fastenings. The usual methods of removing these (large levers, impact wrenches and hammers to hit these with) will very often bend or even rip out the part of the body to which they are fastened. Exerting great force on, for instance, a spring hanger box bolt, can move the box assembly or even rip it away from really badly rotted floor, damper and heelboard panels, leaving the restorer a real mess to sort out. Hammering away at a suspension bolt which has seized into a rubber bush or metal sleeve can pull the chassis member to which it is attached out of line, and the repair might then warrant the use of a jig in order to ensure straightness.

When dealing with a rotten body shell, always drill or grind away any fastenings which do not move under reasonable force. Drill out self-tapping screws rather than use an impact wrench. Cut rebound straps rather than wrestle with their mounting bolts.

Before you start to strip the car, take the precaution of removing the battery, then remove the fuel tank and, where applicable, the electric fuel pump. These precautions will make the rest of the task safer. Begin stripping the interior of the car by removing the seats. The bolts used to fasten the runners will usually be seized and worse, it is very difficult to get either an electric drill or an angle grinder to them. It is recommended that the seats (followed by the carpets, footwell and sill trim) are amongst the first components to be removed because this will enable you to lift the carpets and fully investigate the floor, heel board and sills, and therefore to decide on the true extent of the required work.

Then remove the windscreen to avoid any possibility of damaging it when removing the engine. Also, strip out the dashboard (necessary to remove the windscreen) and any other trim which requires you to step into the cockpit, while the car is still on its roadwheels, because at this stage, your weight will still be evenly distributed at the rear between the four spring mounting points. (Not strictly applicable to the Frogeye and Mark 2 Sprite/Mark 1 Midget, although the springing between the car and the floor will lessen the chances of your weight and movements in the car causing distortion).

The author would recommend that the front wings are removed next, followed by the radiator and then its surround. This improves access, gives far greater space in which to manoeuvre the engine and gearbox from the car, and it reduces the chances of damage occurring to the bodywork during this operation.

Next remove the engine and gearbox. If the body shell is really rotten then gain access to the propeller shaft/differential flanges by raising one side of the car using a trolley jack and a length of box section steel or a sturdy length of timber to distribute the load from the main cross member to the heel board. Be very careful when raising and lowering such a car, because a sudden movement caused by a slipping jack can result in body distortion occurring.

Remove each door in turn and remove the trim, windows, quarterlights and regulators before re-fitting the doors into position (they do help to stiffen the shell a little). Strip any remaining trim, carpet or sound deadening material from inside the car. Bleed the hydraulics, then remove the brake and clutch master cylinders and all brake pipes (remembering that brake fluid is highly flammable) and the fuel line.

After the engine has been removed, support the front chassis rail/cross member assembly on sturdy runners and strip the front suspension, remembering to use cutting equipment rather than brute force to deal with hopelessly seized components. Then raise the rear of the car and remove the axle, again, cutting, drilling or grinding rather than hammering! Support the rear of the car at the transmission tunnel rear end and under the wing to boot floor reinforcers.

The supports placed underneath the front 'chassis' assembly, the main cross member and the transmission tunnel should all be at the same height, so that the assembly is solid and level. The supports at the back of the car can then be 'adjusted' on the most rotten examples if necessary to give the correct door gaps, because such adjustments on a rotten car will move the entire rear end of the car up and down, causing alterations to the gap between the B post and the door. The author then recommends placing a straight edge (box section steel or similar) with a spirit level on top across the tops of the doors, inner front wings, front chassis legs and rear wing top fillets in turn. This will highlight any twisting of the bodyshell, and adjustments can be made to the car's supports to counteract this.

On many cars, the sills will both be rotten as will the metalwork which adjoins them, so that the only real strength in the centre section of the car remains the transmission tunnel. This rarely rots to any great extent and is all that prevents such cars from folding up in the middle! The join between the transmission tunnel and the centre section of the heel board is usually quite sound, but the ends of the heel board assembly (which join onto the rear side chassis rails) are usually rotten, and hence the need to align the rear of the car after supporting the front end.

By supporting the car on building blocks topped with wood, the author hoped to avoid body distortion from occurring during the restoration. This was not to be, as the text will reveal. If you support the shell in this manner, place some of the blocks at ninety degrees to others, so that the shell cannot topple.

Supporting the car for sill only replacement

Whilst it is by no means unknown for a Spridget to possess rotten sills but sound adjacent metal, it must be stated that it is an unusual scenario. Before embarking on a sill-only replacement, double-check the condition of all adjacent panels, because the job will almost invariably entail more work than you might be bargaining for! Check the condition of the A and B post lower ends, the footwell side panels and the floor edges.

If you have only to replace the sills on a Spridget, then it is possible to work with the car on its roadwheels. The problem with this is that the work can be back-breaking, because you will be working so close to the ground, and many of the operations will have to be carried out whilst you are lying on your side. A professional bodyshop charged with replacing Spridget sills would normally work with the car on its roadwheels, but with the car placed on a lift which raised the sill to a comfortable working height. In fact, for a straight sill replacement (given that all other bodywork is sound enough to weld to) it may pay to consider having it carried out professionally,

LEFT AND BELOW *The ladder chassis and strong central cross member of the Spridget make distortion unlikely, but it is essential that the rear end is supported at the correct height to give proper door gaps. Here, the author is measuring the door apertures top and bottom, to check one side of the car against the other.*

ABOVE RIGHT *Twisting of the body is to be avoided at all costs, but it is easy to build it in unless careful checks are made throughout the restoration. The spirit level is placed across the front ends of the ladder chassis legs, and the position of the bubble noted.*

RIGHT *Place a sturdy straight edge across the car as shown, and compare the position of the spirit level bubble with that when it is placed on the ladder chassis legs. If it differs, the body supports can by adjusted to compensate. Do this before you remove the sills, so that the maximum body stiffness is retained.*

The author also checked the diagonals from the dashboard side area (photographed) back to the opposite side heelboard top corner.

because the work is so simple with the car on a lift that time required and hence the charges should not be too great. If you do commission a professional sill replacement, incidentally, always make it clear to the restorer that you want even gaps between the sills and the front wings – with a 'quickie' sill replacement, you could otherwise end up with uneven gaps.

There are various see-saw and other devices available for the home restorer which can raise the entire car on its wheels to a more comfortable working height for sill replacement. These devices, however, are quite expensive and take up rather a lot of workshop space when not in use. For the average home restorer, access will be improved by raising one side of the car at a time, the other side remaining on its road wheels. Because the engine and gearbox will in most cases be left in situ and placing heavy loadings on the front 'chassis' assembly, it is essential that you give full support to this structure. Support the axle on an axle stand.

The author would recommend that the car is raised initially using a trolley jack and a length of sturdy timber or box section steel which extended from the centre cross member back to the heel board, and placed roughly half way between the transmission tunnel and the sill area. Then place supports underneath the appropriate side of the front side chassis rail in such a position that they are able to take the combined weight of the engine and gearbox. Place sturdy supports under either end of the length of box section which you used to raise the car. Check carefully for any evidence of twisting and rectify this if necessary before you begin to cut out the old sills. Also check that the door gaps are even front and back. Very often, the greatest give-away of rotten sills will have been the discovery that the tops of the door gaps were smaller than those at the lower edges (vice versa on cars with quarter elliptic rear springs) because the car has sagged.

Whilst the car is being supported prior to specific work or to a full restoration, it is vital that the doors are left in position, because they can help to prevent the car from sagging as it is moved. It is not unknown for people to cut an old pair of doors in two and then weld the top halves into position when repairing a really rotten open-topped car; others simply weld steel rods across the door aperture to maintain the car's shape.

Many people add internal bracing to the external means of support for the shell in order to prevent the car from moving. A stout piece of wood is placed between the heel board and the bulkhead panel, then slight pressure is added using wooden wedges. Whatever means you employ to keep the body shell straight during restoration, check regularly as the work progresses that the shell is maintaining that shape by trial fitting the doors, checking the gaps and the alignment of the top edge.

Raising and supporting the car for more extensive work

If extensive work is envisaged on the car then it is highly recommended that the car is stripped to a bare shell. Because by definition a shell which requires a lot of work will be weak, it must be raised and supported in such a way that it can easily be checked for body distortion, which could occur either when the car is raised or when rusted metal is cut away during the restoration. The author believes that the best way to achieve this is to keep the shell level to the ground.

The last items to be removed when stripping the shell should be the front and rear suspension and roadwheels. This means that as the car is raised from the ground, the minimum number of heavy components which could possibly distort the shell remain attached. On the project car, the author used building blocks topped with lengths of wood to support the various front 'chassis' members and the rear end of the transmission tunnel. Because the blocks and wood used were of constant height and the garage floor was level, this method of supporting the shell reduced the chances of body distortion. However, it was found that the rear end of the car, aft of the transmission tunnel supports, was able to move slightly and in so doing it altered the door gaps. This movement was possible because the sills, floor and heelboard inner and outer panel ends were all rotten and weak. The rear end was thus firstly supported using a trolley jack and a length of stout timber across the boot floor. This enabled the height of the rear end to be altered sufficiently to correct the door gaps. Solid support blocks and chocks of EXACTLY the correct height should then be substituted for the

trolley jack, because hydraulic jacks cannot be relied upon to maintain a consistent height over any period of time.

It is essential to initially (and throughout the rebuild) check for and remedy any twisting of the bodyshell. This can best be achieved using lengths of straight steel (such as sturdy angle iron) and a good spirit level. Place a short length of straight steel across the two front chassis members, place the spirit level on top and note carefully the position of the bubble. Transfer the spirit level to a longer length of steel (or wood) which is placed across the door tops, the rear wing tops and/or the small 'boat tail' sections underneath the rear lights, and ensure that the bubble is at the same attitude. If not, then adjust the supports of the shell until it is true throughout its entire length. Re-check these levels and any comparative measurements which you may have taken as the job progresses, to ensure that you do not inadvertently build in body distortion.

The higher that the shell can be raised the better, although most people will settle for a height of perhaps between one and two feet above the ground. Some work will still prove awkward, but the only alternative is to construct a strong welded framework with built-in supports for the bodyshell and to try and raise the shell onto this. If you envisage replacing or repairing the floor or heelboard, however, the shell should be raised as high as possible (waist high seems ideal) to give reasonable access.

FRONT WING REMOVAL

This is normally the starting point for any bodywork restoration. The Spridget front wing is bolted into position so that (in theory) it can be removed easily; in most cases, the bolts used will have rusted solid and removal is consequently anything BUT easy!

Trace back the wires from the lights to the bullet connectors, and part these. Unless the car has at some time in the past been re-wired by an incompetent, the wires each side of a bullet connector should be of the same colour. If not, then mark where each wire goes on a masking tape tag. It is not strictly necessary to remove the lights themselves, but it is recommended because a certain amount of hammering will usually prove necessary to deal with some of the wing mounting nuts and bolts, and this will damage the bulbs and possibly the lenses as well.

Working inside the car, remove the trim cover panel from the footwell side panel. A run of three vertical bolt heads should be found on the footwell side panel. Remove these, plus the bolt which can be seen just above the line of the sill and which engages with a captive nut held in a bracket inside the wing.

Drill out the pop rivets from the grille surround trim. Where the wing joins on to the valance, there should be nuts and bolts (do not be too surprised to find that the panels have been welded together!).

Remove the nuts and bolts if possible, or use the angle grinder to cut through them if they are seized or to part the joint if it is welded. Finally, undo the bolts which run along the engine bay side channels, leaving the top one until last. The wing should be supported as the last nut is removed, and it can then be lifted away.

SILL ONLY REPLACEMENT

The sill assembly consists of an upright inner member, a pressed outer member and end fill sections. It is attached to the footwell side panel, the floor, the main cross member, the inner and outer 'A' posts, the 'B' post, the B post to wheelarch pressing, and to the inner and outer heelboard panels.

It would be most unusual to have to replace a sill without the footwell side panel also needing attention, because the inner sill and adjoining footwell side panel rust in concert! To improve access to this panel, begin by removing the front wing as already described.

Open the door and remove the trim which runs around the lip. Count the number of thicknesses of metal which can be seen in the doorway sill top; if there are more than two or if the join is anything other than spot welded, then this sill has been replaced (or bodged) at some time in the past. Examine the state of the bottom of the inner and outer 'A' post. These will have to be repaired or replaced if they have rotted along with the sill.

Remove the seat, grinding or drilling out the four bolts and nuts if they are seized (be warned, this job can be a real pain!). Remove the trim panels covering the inner sill panel and the B post to wheelarch pressing. Remove the carpet from the side edge of the inner heelboard panel. Examine the floor edges where they adjoin the inner sill, the lower end of the B post to wheelarch pressing, and the heelboard inner and outer panel edges where they all adjoin the sills. If serious rot is discovered anywhere then the panels will have to be repaired or replaced before work can proceed on the sill itself.

Check the door gaps and, if they are uneven, remedy this by careful jacking and supporting of the floor adjacent to the sill. Use a length of stout timber or preferably box section steel, supported at each end by a jack. When you are satisfied that the door gaps are correct, remove the door by undoing the three cross-head set screws which secure each hinge, whilst taking the weight of the door. The set screws are often seized into position and an impact screwdriver may well be needed.

The old sill sections have to be cut away. The method of achieving this will vary with the individual car. On some cars, the sill will all but have rotted away on its own and will part company at its welded seams under light pressure! On other cars, use either a sharp bolster chisel, air chisel or the angle grinder with a cutting wheel. Remember to wear stout leather gloves when cutting metal because some of the remaining edges can be as sharp as razors. It is best to cut out sections of the sill to improve access to the joints rather than trying to part the various joints straight away. When the bulk of the sill has been cut out, you can then drill out the spot welds along the various seams and easily part them.

Take great care when cutting around the base of the inner 'A' post and the cross member ends not to damage the lugs to which you will be welding the new sill sections.

With the inner and outer sill removed, use the angle grinder to clean up the edges to which the new sill will be welded. Any repairs to the footwell side panels, the floor edge (NOT the entire floor; if this is to be replaced then the sills will have to go on first), the heelboard end, the B post to wheelarch pressing and the jacking point should be carried out at this stage.

Offer up the new sill sections and clamp them at either end or secure them with the minimum number of pop rivets or self tapping screws, then re-fit the door and check that the door to sill gap is correct and that the door side gaps are still correct. Trial fit the front wing and adjust the outer sill if necessary to achieve a tight fit between the two, because little looks worse on a Spridget than an uneven gap between sill and wing. When you are satisfied that everything lines up properly, remove the door. Drill out the pop rivets or remove the self tapping screws

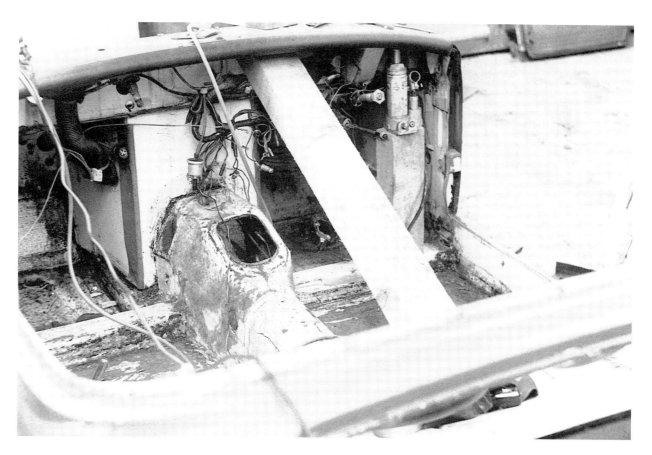

When only the sills are being replaced on an otherwise strong car, bracing usually takes the form of timber wedged in between the heelboard and dash assembly as shown.

and remove the sill panels. Clean up the edges of the inner sill where it is to be welded, and punch or drill holes if you are to fix it using plug welds. Refit only the inner sill and secure it in the same way as before using the same fixing holes so that it is in the correct position. Using more pop rivets, self tapping screws and/or clamps, ensure that all mating surfaces which are to be welded together are held tightly together. The author then likes to carry out a final trial fitting of the outer sill section, door and wing before welding up the new sill.

The lower edge and the top join within the door aperture are best spot welded if at all possible. The other edges can be joined using 1″ runs of weld along the seams or by using plug welds. Grind down any surplus weld before welding on the sill outer. Remove the temporary fixings and re-fit the outer sill. Check again the front wing to outer sill fit before clamping the outer sill into position ready for welding.

GENERAL BODY RESTORATION

Given that the project car was a complete 'basket case' more suitable for re-shelling than restoring, the majority of body restoration jobs common to all Spridgets were encountered during the restoration and are covered in this chapter.

With a car like the project car, it is vital that components are replaced in a sequence which keeps the entire shell as strong as possible at all times to help prevent distortion. It is worth re-stating that panels should be left in position for as long as possible to provide datum points for the other panels to which they will be joined. The recommended sequence for a 'basket case' is as follows. Footwell sides and front. A post inner and outer. B post to wheelarch pressing. Sill. Rear wing lower front quarter. Heelboard/spring box hanger assembly. Floor. Rear side chassis rails. Boot floor. Exterior panels.

The idea behind the above sequence is that above a certain line, sound metal will usually be found on all but the very worst examples (absolute re-shelling candidates). The restoration begins by welding new panels onto this sound metal and then progressing downwards, working in such a way that the old panels which remain help strengthen the shell as much as possible during the course of the work. Remember that even a rusty panel can help to preserve the shape of the car. Before commencing any of the following jobs, strip the car as though for a sill replacement. Remove all interior trim from the side being worked upon.

FRONT 'CHASSIS' ASSEMBLY

It would be very unusual to discover extensive serious rot within this heavy assembly and, if such rot were discovered, then re-shelling the car will in most cases offer the best solution. Problems with the ladder chassis are usually confined to specific small areas of rust or to distortion of the assembly. Distortion should be rectified only by professionals who have the use of a jig, because it is essential that the suspension mountings are true after the chassis assembly has been straightened. Do not, incidentally, panic when you notice that the two main runners are bent upwards; this is normal.

Chassis rot is usually confined to the lower closing panels, each of which can be simply ground off and replaced with heavy gauge steel sheet if necessary. It is well worth replacing the closing panel from the front cross member if (as is usual) it has been distorted through being used as a jacking point.

Footwell/Inner Front Wing Assembly

The footwell top panel is usually sound, although on the driver's side corrosion can begin if brake/clutch fluid is allowed to strip away the paintwork and expose the underlying metal. If these panels need replacing, then Heritage now produce a combined footwell top/front panel, which extends right down to the floor.

The transmission tunnel side panel of the assembly rarely rots because, like the transmission tunnel itself, it benefits from a covering of engine/transmission oil, although on examples which have been allowed to rust slowly away in the great outdoors, you could discover some rot. If so, then the chances are that the transmission tunnel will also possess rot and, in such circumstances, you are strongly advised to consider re-shelling the car, because it will probably require the attentions of

ABOVE *The author was inadvertently supplied with an inappropriate inner A post for his car. Do check that all repair panels match the originals exactly before fitting them: even if the difference is only the lack of a courtesy light switch, it is annoying.*

RIGHT *This block of wood topped with a bottle jack is intended to prevent the scuttle from twisting whilst the old A post assembly is cut away.*

professionals and the use of a jig to rebuilt it, not to mention so many body panels that the price of the repair panels alone gently nudges that of the new bodyshell.

If the top footwell panel is rotten then the front inner wheelarch assembly which adjoins it will also usually be rotten to the extent that replacement becomes necessary. The difficulties of replacing the

entire assembly may encourage the DIY restorer to consider (where practical) patching or using individual or part repair panels as opposed to full rebuilding.

If the top panel is rotten, then the outer side panel will be very likely to require replacement. The two panels could be cut out and replaced together, although the author would personally prefer to leave the side panel in situ – no matter how weak – as a datum point for the replacing of the top/front pressing. The side panel could then be tackled separately, along with the sills (which would be certain to require replacement).

The first step is to cut away part or most of the old inner wing assembly (assuming it to be rotten) by cutting close to each edge rather than by drilling out spot welds in the usual manner. The inside vertical panel is best left if at all possible, because this joins

onto the side plate assembly (the triangular assembly which joins the chassis to the footwell assembly and inner wing) to form a compound assembly with great strength. The inner wing top and outside edge are available separately. If the inner panel has rotted badly, then the entire inner wing assembly may be purchased ready built.

With the inner wing out of the way, take the opportunity to clean up components such as the side plate assembly while access is good. Drill out the spot welds from the quadrant inner wing to footwell assembly reinforcing panel and part the joins gently, because replacements do not yet appear to be available.

Before starting work on the footwell assembly, obtain the replacement/repair panel and measure both it and the existing panel to ensure that the new one is the correct size, or to find the cutting line in the case of a repair panel (remembering to leave enough for a stepped edge). Drill out the spot welds from the inner and outer top edges of the top panel. If the entire top panel is being replaced, then working from inside the car, drill out the spot welds at the rear of the panel.

If the front footwell panel is rotten, then the front end of the floor and the flat panel between the front footwell panel and the pedals will usually also have succumbed. If so, you can merely cut these away, but if the floor front end is sound, then drill out the spot welds and part the joins carefully. The same goes for the triangular stiffener between the front footwell panel and the inner wing side panel.

With the assembly removed, clean up all visible metal surfaces and treat to a good quality rust-resistant primer (except areas to be welded). The actual reassembly process will vary according to the repair or replacement panels being used, but in all cases be certain to accurately line up and clamp the panels tightly together before welding begins. Although the entire assembly was originally spot welded, few enthusiasts will have access to the extra long spot welder arms necessary to replicate the original welds. It will be necessary to resort to plug welding for much of the work, even if you possess a spot welder. The plug welds can be supplemented if desired by seam welds.

The side footwell panel is often rotted at its lower edge even when the other panels of the footwell assembly are very sound and rust-free, because it rots in concert with the inner sill to which it is attached. Repair sections comprising the lower half of this

LEFT *The author always prefers initially to cut well below the final cutting line, because this usually improves access to the job and makes it easier to achieve an accurate final cut. Note that the row of spot welds along the top of the footwell side panel has been drilled ready for separation.*

BELOW *To ensure that the top scuttle panel does not twist, frequently check the door diagonal measurement in addition to the scuttle-to-sill drop measurement.*

RIGHT *The footwell side panel cut away on the project car. The weak sills obviously provide little in the way of stiffening for this side of the body, and so it is vital that the side is supported properly.*

BELOW RIGHT *This length of heavy box section steel runs from the heelboard, under the main crossmember to the toeboard area, so supporting the length of the body. Note the use of scissors jacks to support the steel; unlike hydraulic jacks, their height should remain constant.*

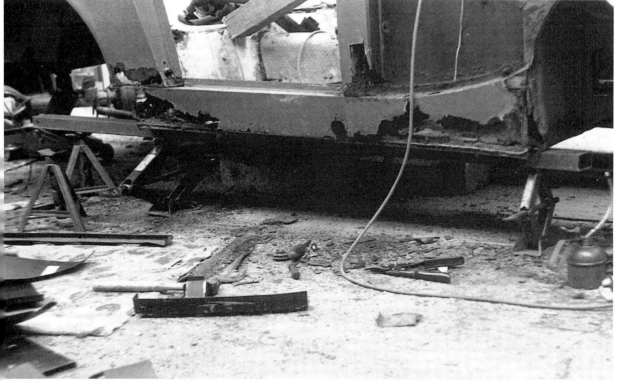

panel used to be available, although they do not appear to be available at the time of writing. Some people weld large plates over the lower half of this panel and the inner sill, as witnessed on the project car. This is not a good solution! You can quite easily make up a repair panel for yourself if you possess good sheet steel cutters and an edge setter. Make a paper or cardboard template of the area needing replacement, allowing for a stepped edge to fit over the sill at the bottom and another at the top to fit against the remains of the old panel. Do not make the repair panel too high, because if you do then you will have to accurately drill various holes for the fitting of the wing, etc.

It is unfortunate that both inner and outer A posts are attached to the footwell side panel, as is the sill structure. If the footwell side panel is rotten, then it is almost certain that both the lower end of the inner A post (containing the lower door hinge) and the tops of the inner and outer sill are also rotten. This work could be carried out with the inner and outer A posts left in situ (provided that they were both sound, which is unlikely) if the many spot welds which hold both these and the side reinforcer panels (though which the windscreen fits) to the footwell side panel could be found and drilled out. This is anything but easy. A total rebuild including the inner and outer A posts, and sill replacement is far more probable and is thus covered here.

Before cutting any metal away, firstly place a support of some kind (such as a stout length of timber) between the floor cross member (which should itself be chocked from underneath to prevent it from sagging) and a solid point under the top shroud, to preserve the correct height of the latter when supporting metalwork is cut away. Drill out the spot welds from the top and side seams of the footwell side panel. The sill seam will almost always be so rotten that it falls apart, although if not, drill out the spot welds and part the two panels carefully, so that the existing sill top can serve as a guide for the fitting of the new panels.

Measure up the outer A post repair panel then mark the existing one to find a cutting line. It is best to cut just underneath this line and then to clean it up carefully afterwards and bring it to the correct height. Cut carefully along the join with the outer sill top edge, and cut up the front side of the A post panel. The panel is folded over the rear side of the inner A post assembly, and this may be prised open so that the outer can be removed. Offer up the replacement inner A post assembly (if it is a part panel) and mark a cutting line or drill out all of the spot welds which hold it from inside the car through the footwell side panel if a full assembly has been chosen.

Repair sections for both the inner and outer A post are available in varying heights, from short to full length. These should contain the hinge plates and, where appropriate, the box for the interior light switch. The author would recommend that the full length assembly was chosen.

Fit the new footwell side panel first. Clean and dress the various flanges to which it will be welded and plug weld it, taking careful measurements to ensure that it is in the correct position. If the old inner sill remains in position then it will show you the correct position for the rear of the new panel. The author favours supplementing plug welds with seam welds.

The A post inner used on the project car was a pattern pressing. It proved to be too wide. When welded into position, everything looked perfectly OK and it was not until the new outer sill section was offered up that the author realised that the A post inner protruded almost $\frac{1}{8}$" outside the outer sill. The A post cover is supposed to be flush with the sill yet, if fitted to this infernal inner pressing it would have stuck out by almost $\frac{3}{16}$" and looked awful! To cut the offending item out at this stage would have meant wrecking the footwell side panel, so it was simply hammered inwards. A professional restorer I spoke to had also encountered this problem. Moral? Always trial assemble ALL panels together before welding any of them in. The other moral is of course to consider whether you can afford the proper Heritage items, which should fit without any problems.

With the new footwell side panel in position, bolt the new inner A post to the door hinges and fit the door into position with small wooden wedges to keep its base level with the sill and so that the catch engages (the door will be far easier to manhandle if the glass and regulator are firstly removed). If the sill has rotted away or been removed at this stage, then clamp up the replacement panels as best you can, using the jacking point, floor and front and rear adjoining metal as guides to position it. Hold the rear of the structure at the correct height on a small jack. Check that the door gaps front, rear and below are correct, then mark the position for the inner A post onto the footwell side panel. Remove the door and clean up the surface of the footwell side panel and the sides of the inner A post where you will be welding.

RIGHT *Offer the footwell side panel into position and lightly clamp it whilst you check the scuttle-to-sill measurement prior to welding.*

BELOW *Skipping forwards in time (the new outer sill is in position), just look at how the inner A post overlaps the sill: both panels from the same manufacturer! The author spoke to a professional restorer and discovered that he had encountered the same problem and had dealt with it in the same crude way as the author – knocking the inner A post inwards.*

BELOW RIGHT *At the top, the inner A post was not looking much better, being proud of its true position. Again, it was knocked inwards slightly.*

LEFT *The new footwell side panel has been welded into position and, although it provides some rigidity for the scuttle, the assembly will not be strong enough until the sill has been replaced.*

BELOW LEFT *To find the correct location for the inner A post, attach it to the door, fit the door then scribe marks on the footwell side panel. Note that the rear end of the sill has been left in situ, to give a guide to the height of the door.*

RIGHT *Clamp the A post firmly before starting to weld it into position.*

FAR RIGHT *Not exactly pretty welding, but not exactly an easy weld either. This was later tidied up by a very good welder, but for the moment, it provided enough strength for the task in hand.*

Some means of temporarily holding the inner A post in position is needed, and the author chose to leave the door attached and to tack weld it, although removing the door and fixing the A post with self tapping screws or pop rivets would be acceptable alternatives. When the A post is held reasonably securely, re-check the door gaps for a final time then, with the aid of an assistant to take the weight of the door, open it, remove the hinge set screws and lift it clear. Plug weld the top of the inner A post through the holes in the windscreen support plate, and seam weld it as much as you like elsewhere!

The outer A post panel can be butt welded at its top edge, seam or plug welded at the front edge, and have its rear edge folded over the inner panel at a later stage, after the sill has been replaced. This is to allow full access for welding the inner A post bottom flanges to the sill top, which is essential for the rigidity of the inner A post. It is a good idea to tack the outer A post into position, hang the door and ensure that it opens freely.

Footwell 'Pedal' Panel

The small panel which sits between the front footwell panel and the pedals rots out along its lower edge where it adjoins the floor. The front edge of the floor does not appear to be served with a separate repair panel at the time of writing, and although it would not be too difficult to fabricate one, in such cases the floor is usually cursed with extensive rot so that the entire floor section requires replacement. The pedal panel itself is easily fabricated, and should be plug welded into position after the fitting of the floor, which is itself the last major part of the body restoration when undertaken in this order.

On the project car, the panel was rotten only over its outer half and, rather than cut out perfectly good metal, the author simply chopped off the outer half. A repair panel was fabricated, then an edge was stepped into it to allow it to fit flush with the existing metal. This work was carried out at a later stage in the rebuild, when the old half floor had been removed.

Having rebuilt the front end of the main body of the car down to the tops of the sills, you should turn your attention to the rear end and again cut upwards to find strong metal to which you can weld. You then build downwards until you reach the rear end of the sills, and then finally fit the new sills!

On many cars, the spring box assembly will be sound, but the outer ends of the inner and outer heelboard panels (plus the rear of the floor) which enclose it will usually be thoroughly rotten. This was the case on the project car. The author decided to begin work on the area by providing locating points for the rear of the sill, so that the sill could be fitted and provide much-needed rigidity for the shell before

With the seats, carpet and inner sill trim removed, the true state of the sills and floor edge (which usually rot in concert) becomes apparent. The large hole at the base of the B post is where the seat belt mounting used to live – some safety belt.

Even though the sills and floor are scrap, it pays to take them apart as gently as possible. This avoids moving any adjacent panels which – even if rotten – act as datum points. If you part the join along the top edge of the sill, it can be pushed downwards and the bottom (floor) join will usually come apart easily.

the critical heelboard assembly was also cut away. If you cut away too much metal at one time, the chances of the entire bodyshell distorting are increased greatly.

Before work can begin on this area, it is necessary to remove whatever remains of the sill in such a way that the adjoining panels (or what remains of them) are left undisturbed in their original locations to act as datum points during the rebuild. See the earlier section dealing with sill replacement for the stripping and cutting sequence.

Access to some of the metalwork in this area is confounded by the weakness of the shell and the consequent fact that you cannot now step onto the floor without terminally distorting the entire side, and by the lower rear wing front, which is usually well rotted. There is little which can be done about the former, but because the lower rear wing is almost certain to be rotten on a car with rotten sills, a replacement repair or full panel should be obtained, offered into position to find the cutting line (leaving sufficient for a stepped edge) and cut.

B Post to Wheelarch Pressing

This panel tends to rot out in a line just above its join with the inner sill and, rather than replace the entire panel (which would *really* make the shell weak and liable to distortion if you so much as stared at it for too long), the author decided to have a go at fabricating a repair panel. This was complicated by the fact that he had to cut the old panel part-way through one of the sculpted holes in order to find clean and sound metal. Nevertheless, using a paper template, a pair of aircraft cutters, a half round Swiss file, hammer, anvil, sundry mole grips and a lot of patience, the panel was constructed.

With the sills offered into position and raised to the correct height, the panel was offered into position and the edges to which it was to be joined ground back as carefully as is possible with an angle grinder. The panel was butt welded along the top join and plug welded down each side to the remnants of original stiffeners. (See photo sequence).

With this panel in place, the sills could be welded into place. All adjoining edges on both the inner sill and the areas to which it was to be welded (not forgetting the areas for spot weld electrode contact) were cleaned up. The jacking point reinforcer on the project car was, unusually, sound, and so it was

With the outer sill out of the way, you can carefully attack the inner, taking care not to damage the lugs on the crossmember.

cleaned and treated to a few coats of Bonda Prima. The flanges at the end of the cross member were cleaned up. The inner sill was offered into position and firstly clamped whilst it was correctly aligned with regard to the door (re-fit this temporarily to check alignment), the footwell side panel and the B post to heelboard pressing. The inner sill was then temporarily fixed in position using pop rivets, and the outer sill was clamped into position over it. The door and front wing were temporarily fitted to check alignment, and the sill end fillers were also fitted (if you have the inner and outer sill components staggered then the end fillers will not fit!).

The wings and doors were removed and the sill components moved and re-clamped until the gap at

LEFT AND BELOW LEFT *At times like this a desperate sense of 'What have I let myself in for' can strike the DIY restorer. Have confidence. The front end has been rebuilt downwards from good metal, and now it's time to do the same at the B post. That floor will have to come out, but for the moment it is helping to keep everything together, so leave it where it is.*

ABOVE RIGHT *The lower end of the B post assembly inner pressing was thoroughly rotten and, by rights, the entire panel should have been replaced. The author elected to fabricate this small repair panel. Here, it is being offered into position to check for correct shape before final shaping.*

CENTRE RIGHT *Here, the repair panel is being checked with both sills offered up into position. Lines were scribed where the top edge met the original panel, and this was cut and the new panel butt welded into position.*

RIGHT *A second panel was also fabricated and butt welded behind the first, before the sills were welded on and whilst access was still fair.*

the door bottom edge was parallel and the front end of the outer sill mated correctly against the adjoining curve on the front wing. At this stage, burrs on the edge of the floor (where it had been parted from the inner wing) were pushing the inner sill outwards, and so the decision to cut away the edge of the floor was taken. This happily coincided with the author putting his hand deep into his pocket to buy an air chisel, and what a useful tool this proved to be! With the forked chisel end in position, it cuts sheet steel quickly, easily and accurately. The wing, door and outer sill were removed, and the inner sill was welded into position, starting with the jacking point reinforcer. Those edges which could be spot welded were dealt with using a borrowed spot welder after the sill had been firstly tack welded along its entire top and lower edges with the MIG welder.

With the inner sill in position, the outer sill was again offered up but this time it was held with self tapping screws whilst the door and front wing were again trial fitted. After suitable adjustment, the outer sill was firstly tack welded then spot welded along its top edge within the door frame and along its lower edge.

At this point, the shell appeared surprisingly strong, and the author decided to celebrate the purchase of his air chisel by removing the rear section of the floor so that he could gain better access to the heel board. Do not hack through the seat runner reinforcers using an angle grinder with a cutting wheel fitted unless you have previously removed the fuel pipe! The author, naturally, suddenly noticed a clear fluid bubbling up through the slot which he was grinding through the floor. . . .

The lower rear wing repair panel which was next to be fitted was (unusually?) a very good fit. It was offered into position and a fitting guide scribed in the usual manner, after which a cutting guide was scribed to allow an overlap for joddling. The front and rear corners of the overlapping area were ground away because they could not be joddled. The wing was cut away using the air chisel, and the remaining edges joddled. Self tapping screws were used to pull the joins together tightly, then the door was trial fitted to ensure that the lines were correct.

At this stage problems were experienced with the MIG welder or, more properly, with a batch of .8mm wire which dragged so much in the liner (through

LEFT *At this stage, the author decided to temporarily reconstruct the front end of the car; the sills could be clamped into position. This allows their various lines to be checked before they were welded up. Many adjustments were necessary before the author was happy with the positioning. The entire process would be repeated after the inner sill had been welded into position and before the outer was welded.*

ABOVE AND RIGHT *It is vital that metal which is to be welded is spotlessly clean, and rather than scribe around the edges of the crossmember lugs and B post inner pressing repair panel to show which areas of the inner sill to clean the author tried spraying on paint. Not one of his better ideas, because the paint all had to come off afterwards, and was more difficult to clean away than the existing black paint. Stick to scribing marks. Hold the inner sill in the correct position with self-tapping screws or pop rivets rather than clamps, just to ensure that it cannot move before you weld.*

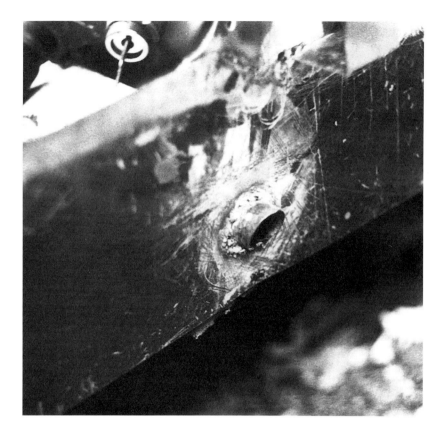

The jacking point on the project car was sound and so after being cleaned back, the inner sill was welded to it. Note the curve in the bottom of the inner sill panel, caused by the old floor edge join pressing against it. The solution is simple: cut out the floor when the inner sill is welded up and giving some rigidity to the shell.

Weld the front end of the inner sill to the footwell side panel.

The front toe board was hopelessly rotten at its base, and so the rot was cut out at this stage and new metal welded in.

After welding up the inner sill front and back, the author decided to cut out the rotted old floor which had been slightly distorting the inner sill, allowing the lower edge to be trued up.

LEFT *Now it was time to repeat the exercise but with the outer sill. This was clamped into position and initially fixed using bolts through the footwell side panel as shown.*

BELOW LEFT *Then the front wing was offered into position. It was difficult to accurately assess the closeness of the important sill end/lower wing join because of damage to the wing. However, after some dressing of the wing and repositioning of the sill, a satisfactory marriage was achieved.*

RIGHT *The Spridget looks so much better with tight wing to sill gaps, but it is by no means unusual to find Spridgets with poor gaps. It may in some instances be possible to lessen the gap by adjusting the wing, but the author believes it is better – where possible – to adjust the sill.*

BELOW *Just to be on the safe side, the author checked that the door leading edge to wing trailing edge gap was parallel and wide enough for the A post cover to be fitted. It was.*

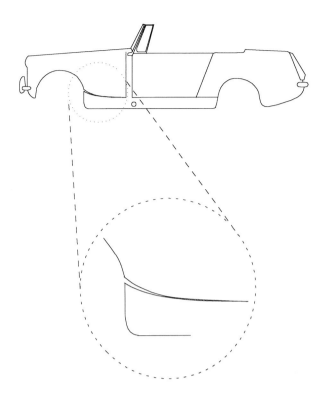

which the wire runs to the gun) that the tension on the driving wheels of the MIG had to be increased to overcome it, which caused the teeth of the driving wheel to cut into the wire, making the surface rougher so that it dragged within the liner even more and, eventually, stopped altogether. The author, blissfully unaware of the intermittent wire feed speed, suddenly started experiencing the most atrocious burning through whilst undertaking one of the most cosmetically important external welds of the entire restoration! He realised what was happening before too much damage was done, and three days later (local 'Welding Supplies Specialists' failing as usual to keep welding supplies such as MIG wire and liners in stock – thank heaven for Mail Order), the job was concluded with .9mm wire and a new liner. A tip for owners of MIG welders keep enough wire in stock to keep you occupied for at least a week, plus spare tips and a spare liner.

When you accidentally burn a hole in a panel, you can fill it with weld by welding on to the edge of the hole all the way around until it is filled. To avoid burning through during this operation, 'pulse' the weld onto the metal. Afterwards, the angle grinder can be used to take excess weld away.

Despite the problems with the MIG wire, things

were going well; too well, as it happened, because the next time the author came to work on the car he decided to firstly re-check that the bodyshell was true – and it was not. When the shell was raised and supported initially, the author had checked that the front and rear ends of the car were level. Sometime between this and the welding into position of the B post to inner wing pressing repair section, the shell had distorted, with the result that the offside rear was a full ⁵⁄₁₆″ too far above the sill. This was confirmed by measuring the height of the rear wing top front above the sill top. The distortion probably occurred from visitors to the workshop leaning on various parts of the bodyshell, so be sure to instruct all visitors to touch nothing!

Rectification entailed removing the lower rear wing repair panel (scrapping it) and cutting ⁵⁄₁₆″ out of the B post to inner wing web, closing up the gap by careful jacking of the rear nearside quarter of the car and butt welding the join using Frost intergrips to hold the two halves together. Because this was not as strong as the original joddled weld between the pressing and the sill, the author cut a reinforcing bracket from the remnants of the old lower wing repair panel and welded this to the sill top and to the inside of the web.

The simple moral of this unhappy episode is to always check and then double check for correct body alignment before welding ANY panel into place. It is also a good idea to ban visitors from touching the bodyshell!

More distortion was then discovered, although this was easily rectified. The rear of the lower portion of the rear wing (which had been cut away) had sprung outwards and away from the car. This manifested itself when the new wing repair panel was offered up as a visible angle between the existing wing and the repair section. To rectify this, the author made a simple clamp from a length of ½″ threaded rod, which passed through the top hole in the damper panel and which located onto the offending area of the wing with a large washer. At the same time, a small scissors jack was placed between the lower edge of the damper panel and the sill, to maintain the correct attitude of the latter. The lower wing repair panel was then again welded into position.

Because of the height at which the rear wing had been cut during the rectification work just described, there was insufficient metal left for a joddled join, so that the two panels had to be butt joined. Even after the careful alignment already described, the two

LEFT *With the outer sill position fixed at the front end, the height of the rear end was already determined and was fixed using a large self-tapping screw.*

RIGHT AND BELOW *One last check remained. The sill end fill pieces will not fit if the sill is too far forwards or backwards. Happily, in this case, both end fill pieces slotted neatly into place. The sill front position was then finally fixed using self-tapping screws in place of the bolts.*

LEFT *Before welding, the author took the opportunity to get as much paint as possible onto the parts of the sills which would soon be enclosed. For spot welded seams, use proper zinc welding paint for further protection against future rusting.*

BELOW FAR LEFT *The spot welder gives the neatest and strongest welds on suitable seams. If you do not possess one then it is worth hiring one for the day to do the sill centre section and bottom edge welds.*

BELOW LEFT *The final part of the job is to replace the rear wing front lower edge. If you use a joddler on the top seam, then it should automatically line up the two panels when you pull them together with self-tapping screws.*

ABOVE *Some small degree of tailoring is necessary to fit part repair panels. To get the rear corner to fit, the author clamped it then re-shaped it with a small hammer.*

LEFT *A certain amount of hammer work may prove necessary to get the curves of the rear wing and sill into line. Fix the repair panel using self-tapping screws before welding.*

panels were not perfectly aligned after they had been welded. This highlights one of the advantages of lapped joints over butt joints. With a lap (or joddled) join, the two panels concerned are inclined to automatically align as the panels are drawn together with pop rivets or self tapping screws. If plug welds are used to join the panels, then they will remain exactly as they have been welded. If panels have to be forced into position and butt welded whilst they are under any tension, then they can distort during or after welding.

HEELBOARD ASSEMBLY

This is a fairly complex structure (slightly more complex on quarter elliptic sprung cars than on half elliptic), consisting of an inner heelboard panel within the car and an outer panel visible from underneath the car, to which the damper bracket is fitted. In between these fits the triangular spring mounting box assembly, plus a triangular reinforcing pressing.

Examine the assembly closely and ascertain the extent of the rot. On all but the worst examples the spring mounting box assembly will normally possess some surface rust but may otherwise be perfectly sound. The outer ends of the heelboard panels will usually be rotten and the centre section will usually be sound except in cars which have been allowed to slowly rot away without being used. There are essentially two options open at this stage. The heelboard panels can be replaced in their entirity. Alternatively, the ends of the heelboard panels can be replaced, along with or independently of the damper brackets.

When the Spridget bodyshells were first assembled, the heelboard assembly and transmission tunnel etc. were built up independently of the floor (and then attached to it) and the resulting assembly was completed independently of the top half of the car, which was itself built up into a separate assembly. The top half of the car was then lowered

LEFT *Because of the problems detailed in the text, the author was forced to scrap the first wing repair panel and fit a second in its place, in so doing losing the stepped edge of the wing bottom and having to butt weld instead. It was necessary to tension the lower wing as shown in order to line the two up correctly.*

Removing the carpet from the rear parcel shelf and heelboard often reveals this sort of mess. Whilst the spring hanger assembly itself is made from too heavy a gauge of steel to rot, the inner and outer heelboards rot badly. When this sort of rot is apparent at the top of the heelboard assembly, you can expect to find far worse rot lower down.

onto the lower half. The restorer does not enjoy the luxury of easy access to areas such as the heelboard which the original method of manufacture (and, the author believes, the way Heritage shells are currently built) permitted.

The inner heelboard could be replaced with the floor in situ, although if this panel requires attention then in 99% of cases the outer heelboard and spring box assembly will also require attention. In order to gain access to replace the spring box assembly, it is necessary to cut away the rear section of the floor. This is no great burden, because it is highly probable

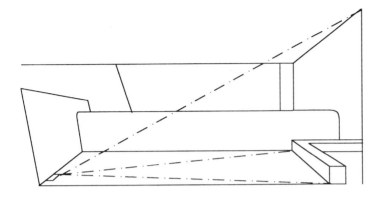

Before attacking the heelboard assembly, it is vital that you firstly establish a method of accurately positioning the replacement panels. By taking the three measurements shown here, from either end of the crossmember and from a fixed point on the top scuttle, you can fix any single point. This illustration shows how to fix the position of the inner heelboard.

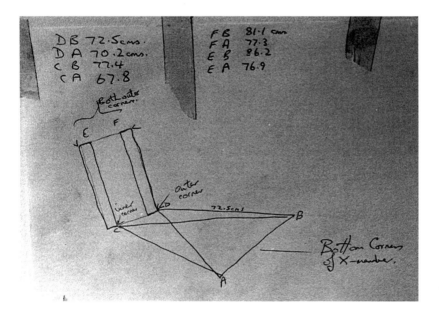

After the inner heelboard has been cut away, fix the position of the spring hanger assembly. Draw up a diagram showing all of the necessary measurements, and put it somewhere safe. This is taped to the workshop door, so that it cannot be mislaid! In addition to the measurements on this diagram, the author took drop measurements from a straight edge placed across the body of the car.

that the floor rear edge will need attention on any Spridget with heelboard rot.

Before starting work in this area you should take exhaustive measurements which will later allow you to find or confirm important datum points, using '3D' triangulation. This could mean measuring from the lower outer corner of the inner heelboard panel to the inner end of the main cross member (where it joins the transmission tunnel), to the sill end of the cross member and to perhaps the top of the A post. Taking three measurements from fixed points in this way allows you to accurately fix any point in space. You can then cut away supporting metalwork safe in the knowledge that if some part of the bodywork does distort then you can fix its position and brace or squeeze it or the panel which it is to be welded to back there! It is essential, however, that you frequently check that your fixed measuring points have not moved as work progresses.

The four vital datum points to be fixed initially are the tops and bottoms of the heelboard panels. The measurements must be recorded in a clear and concise format which you cannot later mis-read. Perhaps the following example will illustrate the best method.

Offside Inner Heelboard

Fixed point	Measurement
Opposite A post top inner corner	....
Crossmember/transmission tunnel	....
Inner heelboard/transmission tunnel	....
Offside Outer Heelboard	....

Fixed point	Measurement
Opposite A post top inner corner	....
Crossmember/transmission tunnel	....
Inner heelboard/transmission tunnel	....

(The outer heelboard measurements can only be taken after the inner heelboard has been removed).

Full Heelboard Replacement

You must have good access to the underside of the car and the higher the car is raised the better, because there is little more difficult than welding uphill whilst lying on your back in a cramped space (swathed in clothing for protection from the sparks which will be showering you!).

Increase if possible the number of supports holding the rear end of the car, because this will be very liable to distortion when the heelboards (and especially the damper brackets) are cut away. Then check that the shell is still true using the methods already outlined. Drill out the spot welds which secure the outer edges of the panel. Cut the rear edge of the floor pan away from the inside edge of the heelboard and continue to cut out the entire floor section. Cutting out the floor up to the central cross member allows you to stand inside the car and improves access for the following work. Drill out the floor seam spot welds and part this join. Mark the line where the heelboard joins the transmission tunnel and drill out the spot welds which connect the two. Cut along the remaining top seam, where the original

heelboard bends to the horizontal, leaving sufficient metal to weld the replacement panel to. The panel is now held only by the spring mounting boxes. Drill out the spot welds here then part the joins and remove the panel.

With the inner heelboard panel out of the way, fix the locations of the front corners of the spring hanger box assemblies using triangulation as already described. The best points from which to measure are probably the tops of both A posts and one corner of

Before you cut the heelboard assembly completely away it is wise to take a measurement or two from the transmission tunnel to the sill, just in case the sill moves or is accidentally knocked as the work progresses. Cutting away the heelboard/spring hanger assembly is difficult and unpleasant work, the worst part of which is trying to part the spring hanger assembly from the forward extension of the damper bracket. The author was unable to get a drill into the small area in order to drill out the spot welds here, and finally resorted to cutting the spring hanger assembly in half top to botton using a cutting disc in the angle grinder.

the transmission tunnel/cross member. The author used the ends of the cross member and combined these with a vertical measurement taken from a bar laid across the top of the car. Also fix the locations of the outer heelboard corners in the same manner. Also, measure the distance between the two damper brackets, the distance from the transmission tunnel end to the sill and the distance from the damper bracket to the sill. This is to check that the sill does not move before the heelboard repair panels are in place and that the damper bracket is in the correct position. If your car is so rotten that you suspect that some body distortion may have already taken place, try to locate a new Heritage bodyshell (you will find them at Heritage-approved dealers) and take measurements from this. All this measuring and recording might seem tedious, but any amount of trouble justifies not ending up with a 'bent' Spridget!

The outer heelboard is fixed to the floor rear edge, the transmission tunnel, the damper brackets, the (this edge will usually be rotted away) B post to wheelarch pressing and to the horizontal top face of the boot pressing. Take your measurements as outlined previously before cutting this panel away, again starting at the bottom edge, working your way up the sides (also the damper bracket) and finally the top.

Cutting out a spring box assembly is by no means an easy task.

The outer lip is spot welded to the heelboard and fully accessible from underneath the car, but the inner lip is another matter. This is but a third of a 'sandwich' comprising the lip itself, the heelboard and the damper bracket lip. Access to the spot welds from the outside is awkward, and so the author folded back the spring box assembly front lip in order to get a twist bit to the spot welds from inside the car. To make matters worse, a strong reinforcing plate for the damper is mounted both to the damper bracket and to the spring box assembly. Access with a drill to attack the various spot welds joining the plate to the spring box assembly is almost impossible. Some may feel it preferable to rip out the entire assembly, damper bracket and all, rather than to wrestle with the difficult to reach spot welds. The author persevered with the latter course and found it difficult though by no means impossible.

The outer edge of the outer heelboard on the project car was thoroughly rotten and easily removed. The author cut through the heelboard as shown in the accompanying illustration, drilled out

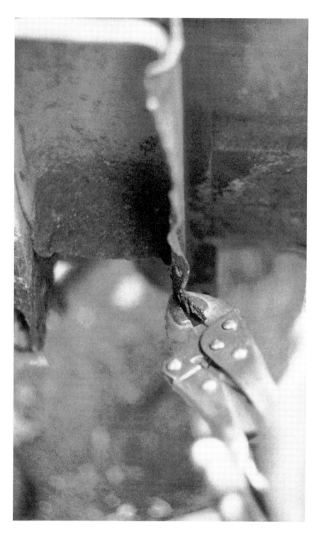

Bending back the spring hanger front lip in order to drill out the spot welds.

the spot welds then used a combination of a very sharp chisel and mallet, supplemented with the air chisel, to finally remove the old spring box assembly without damaging either the damper bracket or the reinforcing plate.

The area where the outer heelboard, transmission tunnel and floor come together is rather complicated in that there is another stiffening pressing which passes under the transmission tunnel. The author found that it was possible, with care, to open the three-layered join, cut out the old floor and later re-fit the new floor under this pressing.

Clean up and dress all areas which are to be welded, then fix the heelboard temporarily into

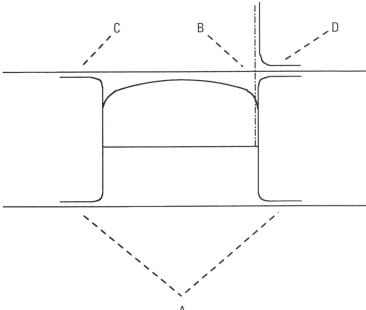

C   B   D

A

ABOVE *Skipping to the nearside of the car, this shows just how much metal has to be cut away. Because the damper brackets play the greatest part in supporting the rear of the car, it is vital that the boot area is fully supported throughout.*

A cross section of the heelboard/ spring hanger assembly. If you are replacing the heelboards in their entirety then simply drill out the spot welds (D) to free the damper bracket, and drill out the spot welds connecting the damper reinforcing plate to the spring box (not shown here), and cut out the heelboard assembly complete with the spring

box. If you are replacing just the end sections of the heelboards, firstly measure the repair panels against the old heelboards to ensure that you do not cut too much away. Then, drill out the spot welds in the inner heelboard (A), then the spot welds which hold the damper bracket to the outer heelboard (D); some of these spot welds also fasten the one spring

box lip. Then, drill out the spot welds (C) and cut the outer heelboard in a vertical line (B). Drill out the spot welds which hold the damper bracket reinforcing plate to the spring box (not shown here).
Cut away the inner and outer heelboards.

187

LEFT *The outer heelboard repair panel in position. Now the damper bracket can be welded to it.*

ABOVE *The spring hanger assembly clamped into position. At this stage, the author checked and double checked every measurement before fixing the position of the hanger by drilling two holes through its rear lips and the outer heelboard, and using bolts to maintain it in this position. Note that the rear spring has been fitted as an extra check on the positioning of the spring hanger assembly.*

RIGHT *When the bolts were in position, it became apparent that the rear lips of the spring hanger needed to be dressed so that they lay flat against the outer heelboard.*

FAR RIGHT *The spring hanger was then removed, and the edges to be welded were cleaned up. The two vertical runs of holes are for plug welding.*

position, using your previously made marks and measurements to ensure correct placement. If you can obtain access to a spot welder then this can be used extensively on the outer heelboard for the joins along the top edge, the damper bracket (it is highly recommended that this is spot welded) and the lower edge. *Do not forget* to provide a captive nut for the fuel pump fixing bracket if the panel does not have one already fitted. This can be fitted before the panel is offered up, and it can be an awkward task to fit one at a later stage. Because this assembly will be enclosed, it is a good idea to provide a second, 'back-up' captive nut adjacent to the first, just in case it should ever drop away from the panel whilst you remove the fuel pump at a future date! If you provide a second captive nut, fill the thread with paint to prevent it from

rusting, and remember to put a tap through it to clear out that paint if you ever come to use it.

The spring hanger box assemblies are welded on next, again using, if at all possible, a spot welder. It is unlikely that the average DIY restorer will possess a spot welder let alone the range of arms and electrodes necessary for a job such as this. The alternative, adopted by the author on the project car, is to use plug welds supplemented by seam welds. Use the measurements taken previously to ensure that these vital pressings are welded into the correct positions. Making a mistake in placing these assemblies may have an effect on the handling and roadholding of the completed car, so be very careful!

When the spring box assembly has been welded into place, check carefully for correct alignment; it is

by no means unknown for the welding process to distort the relatively flimsy outer heelboard panel, with the result that the spring box sits at an angle. Check that the outer heelboard and the spring box assembly are at right angles to the sills, and if not, rectify matters either using a heavy mallet or (the recommended option) by making up a 'dummy' rear floor section with folded edges and clamping this to the rear heelboard and the sill. This will keep everything aligned whilst the inner heelboard panel is welded into position.

The inner heelboard panel can then be welded into position. Drill or punch holes to enable you to plug weld the panel to the spring hanger box assembles, because there will not be sufficient room to work with a spot welder. To find the positions for

ABOVE *Several points of interest. Firstly, thanks to Ron Hopkinson for the outer heelboard repair panel. Secondly, note that the sill end fill has been used to help fix the position of the panel. Thirdly, note the heads of the bolts which are now holding the spring hanger firmly.*

RIGHT *The spring hanger assembly welded into position. The rear spring has been attached again to check that the spring hanger is correctly positioned; welding heat could have distorted the outer heelboard to which it is attached. At this stage, it is still possible to make slight adjustments to the position of the spring hanger.*

ABOVE *The inner heelboard is then plug welded to the spring hanger assembly front lips, it is seam welded along a joddled joint with the remains of the existing heelboard, and seam welded along its outer lip. The car is now strong again. The closing panel along the top edge of the heelboard is simply cut from steel sheet.*

RIGHT *The author then fabricated repair sections for the inner wheelarch front end and the wheelarch to boot floor reinforcer (rear side chassis rail). With the plug welds ground flush and a coat of primer, the job looks quite passable.*

these holes, simply place a dab of thick paint top and bottom of each of the flat surfaces of each spring hanger, then place the inner heelboard in position and press it so that the paint marks are transferred across. It may prove necessary to let in a strip of metal along the top between the inner and outer heelboard panels, particularly at the edges, where rot is common.

Heelboard Repair Panels

The author discovered that although all Midget/Sprite spares stockists which he approached stocked the repair panels for the inner heelboard, few stock the equivalent for the outer heelboard. Ron Hopkinson's MG Centre – which had recently taken over the well-known Spridget specialist 'Spridgebits' – was able to provide the necessary panels.

Proceed generally as before, taking exhaustive measurements so that everything can be welded back into its rightful position.

BELOW *On the nearside of the car, the job progressed in much the same way, except that the author fabricated a repair panel for the inner wing front end whilst access was good.*

RIGHT *The original intention had been to use a rear floor repair panel on the nearside of the car, but in the event a full half floor was fitted. The author used the redundant repair panel to help position the spring hanger assembly.*

BELOW RIGHT *Plenty of self-tapping screws were used to pull the inner heelboard tight to the spring hanger front lips for plug welding, and the side joints for seam welding.*

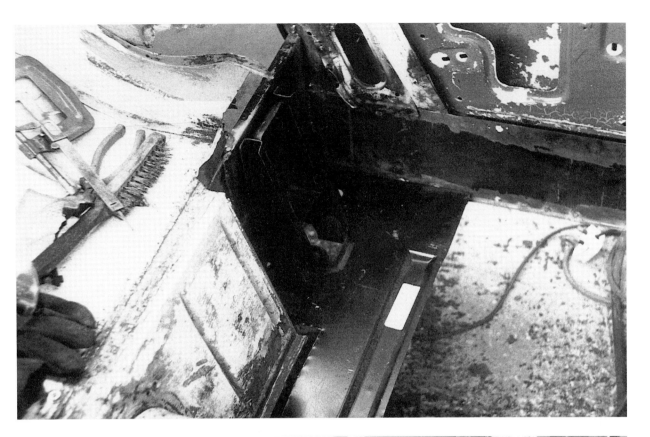

Instead of cutting out the entire panel, simply cut out either sufficient of the existing panel to allow the entire repair panel to be re-fitted, or cut back to sound metal and tailor the repair panel to match this. Working this way could allow you to leave the inboard sections of the panels intact including sometimes – the spring hanger box assemblies. The heelboard panels usually rot out along their outer edges where they come into contact with the rot-prone inner sill and wheelarch. It is not unusual to find these areas well rotted yet the damper brackets, spring hanger box sections etc. to be in good health.

The damper bracket and the heavy plate which connects it to the spring box assembly are both usually sound; if the damper bracket has to be replaced then be very careful to fully support the rear of the car so that it cannot sag, because the damper bracket provides rigidity.

Building up the heelboard assembly is very much the same as replacing the entire assembly, except that the transmission tunnel joints are unscathed, and either the repair panels or the existing panels should be joddled to allow a flush-fitting lapped joint (which in the case of the outer heelboard joint, can be seam welded both inside and outside), with optional plug welding. *Do not forget* to provide a captive nut for the fuel pump bracket. If the existing captive nut is unsound and the section which holds it is to be retained, then grind away the old nut then fit a nut and bolt through the hole, and tighten them so that the nut is held firmly in place against the bulkhead. It can be difficult to get a MIG gun to the nut, although one saving grace is that the nut is partially held behind the triangular strengthener lip, so that you need weld only the other (outer) side. Be careful not to get weld onto the bolt thread!

Remember to check that the spring hanger is in line and at 90 degrees to the centre line of the car (see preceding text). On the project car, the author used a redundant rear floor repair panel to line up the spring box hanger. This was achieved by bolting the hanger to the floor section, then offering the assembly into position and clamping the floor flanges. This highlighted that fact that the outer heelboard panel had warped during welding and consequently twisted the position of the spring hanger.

The inner heelboard repair panel was then welded into position, using plug welds to join it to the spring hangers and seam welds elsewhere.

CROSS MEMBER REPAIRS

The cross member is most liable to rot out at its ends where it adjoins the rot-prone inner sill. Repair and full replacement sections are available. It is possible to replace or repair the cross member with the floor in situ, although splitting the two is liable to result in such distortion to the floor that floor replacement becomes necessary. It is far better to deal with the cross member after the floor has been cut out. It would be a strange scenario, anyway, in which the sturdy cross member had rotted but the flimsy floor was still sound . . . Measure the repair section against the old member and make a cutting line, allowing a gap of .040″ for the butt weld. Fit the jacking point at this stage, then allow plenty of paint to run inside the whole section, to give protection against rust for many years to come. Clean the excess paint from the immediate vicinity of areas to be welded afterwards.

Because new sills will have been fitted before the cross member, locate the outer end using the jacking point and clamp it tightly into position. The Frost Intergrips make the next task far easier because they accurate align the old to the new, automatically give the correct gap for butt welding and hold the two sections tightly whilst the welding is undertaken. If you found yourself having to repair or replace the cross member on a car with a sound floor (if this had recently been replaced under a rotten cross member), then forget the Intergrips, because the locking pieces would be lost forever within the cross member!

FLOOR

A rotten floor can be dealt with in several ways. The most drastic and difficult is to cut out the entire pressing and replace it with the full floor panel which has recently become available from Heritage. These panels are available for cars from G AN 3 (Mark 2 Midget, Mark 3 Sprite) onwards. The Spridget differs from some rear wheel drive cars in having a single pressing for the floor, whereas many rear wheel drive cars have two separate floor pan sections which extend from the sills to the sides of the transmission tunnel. The Spridget floor pan passes right under the transmission tunnel, semi-enclosing it.

Fitting a complete floor pan is not for the inexperienced nor the feint of heart! Firstly, the car

Cutting out the old floor using the air chisel. Hearing protection is a must when using this incredibly noisy but invaluable tool. Forgiving or hard-of-hearing neighbours are also a necessity. Unusually, the author has chosen to wear gloves for this operation: a wise decision because those cut edges can be razor sharp, but to be honest it was because of the cold!

should be made sound in all areas except the floor, so that body distortion cannot occur. This entails rebuilding the footwell area, sill structure and heelboard assembly. At this stage it should be possible to cut out any remaining sections of the old floor using an air chisel and then to drill out the myriad spot welds which hold the floor edges to the transmission tunnel, cross member etc. The holes left by this will serve for later plug welding when the new floor pan is in position.

It is vital that the body shell is properly supported for floor pan replacement. Given that the rest of the panel work is sound and that the shell is as a result strong and not liable to distortion, the main support points will be the ladder chassis rails at the front of the car and the wheelarch reinforcers at the rear. These can be supplemented with sill supports. The main supports have to be spaced so far apart because any supports in the centre of the car will be in the way of the new floorpan. Alternatively, the car could be rolled up onto its side or right over onto its back. This option would be best left to professionals. The costs, however, of a professional body restoration on a car which was so badly rotted that full floor replacement was necessary would probably represent a large percentage of the cost of a new Heritage bodyshell, so if your car has a totally rotten floor then it may pay you to reconsider whether a reshell would be preferable to bodyshell restoration.

The second option is to fit a half floor repair panel. This will probably be the most popular solution to the problem of a rotten floor. The centre section of the original floor pan (which fits underneath the transmission tunnel) will not usually be rotted, because sundry oils and greases tend to find their way into the vicinity and these keep the dreaded rust at bay. On a car which had been left standing for many years, however, the centre floor section could have rotted, in which case the entire floor should be replaced as a unit.

Assuming that the centre floor section is sound, then half-floor replacement is within the capabilities of the DIY enthusiast. The first step is to make the car sound in the important areas of the sills, heelboards and footwell assemblies. There is little point in trying to fit a flimsy pressing like the floor if the only sound metal to which you can weld is the transmission tunnel! The actual procedure will vary according to whether the cross member and the heelboard assemblies have or are to be replaced. On the project car, the footwell outer side panel, A post and panel,

the sill and the wheelarch to B post pressing, plus the heelboard assembly had all received attention.

The rear section of the floor had already been cut out using an air chisel, and when the author attempted to repeat the exercise on the front half he found that ear protectors are essential because in order to see where he was cutting he had to lean forwards so that his head was inside the footwell. The din made by an air chisel in an enclosed space has to be heard to be believed, and is of a magnitude great enough to damage hearing.

With the bulk of the floor cut away, the author decided to remove the thin strip which runs under the cross member. It is possible to leave this in position and to weld the new floor underneath it to produce a three-layered join, but this course was decided against because the join will not be so strong as the correct two-layered join, nor will it enable the inside of the cross member to be cleaned up and rust-proofed. The thirty or so spot welds between the floor and the cross member were drilled out, then the joins were parted using the air chisel. The cross member lips were dressed as necessary, and the opportunity was taken to clean the inside of the cross member and to paint it with several layers of rust-resistant primer.

Whether you replace the full floor panel or fit a half floor repair panel, the removal of the old floor provides an excellent opportunity to clean up the exposed footwell panels. In fact, with the project car on its side, the author set aside a few days to clean away old underseal from the entire underside of the car, and to clean up all internal panel work which could be more easily accessed at this stage.

The floor repair panel chosen by the author was quite wide insofar as if fitted without modification, it would have extended some way underneath the transmission tunnel. It would also have extended underneath the forward part of the leg of the ladder chassis rail. The author chose to modify the panel before fitting it, so that the edge along the transmission tunnel could be joddled to sit flush and so that the section under the ladder chassis leg could remain undisturbed, and also be joddled. In both instances, the panel could be welded both inside the car (the stepped edge allowing the weld to join the new section to the actual transmission tunnel and ladder chassis leg rather than the remains of the old floor panel) and from underneath, to give a very strong joint.

Because the transmission tunnel slowly fills over the years with sundry oils and greases when the car

The reinforcing plate has to be lifted in order that the floor repair panel can be tucked underneath. Drill out the spot welds as best you can before bringing in the air chisel.

Take the opportunity to thoroughly clean the inside of the heelboard assembly, then treat it to several coats of BondaPrima or the like to prevent future rusting.

If fitted as supplied, the half floor section would come part-way across the section of the old floor under the transmission tunnel. It would also have covered part of the front chassis leg. The author opted to tailor it so that it followed the line of the transmission tunnel and, because the chassis leg bottom was in good condition, so

that it just overlapped the edge. From inside the car, a line was scribed on the floor repair panel to show the lines of the transmission tunnel and chassis leg, and a cutting line was established to allow the edge to be joddled.

Floor/transmission tunnel join

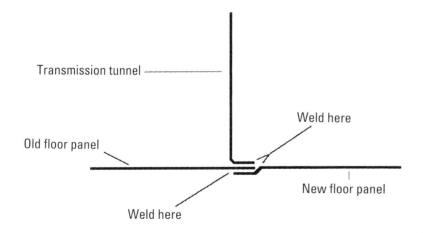

The floor to transmission tunnel join allowed the author to weld both top and bottom sides. In the event, he brought in a skilled welder to deal with much of the welding of the floor, and was advised that stitch welding was preferable to continuous seam welding. Apparently, in the event of a collision, continuous seam welds are prone to break open whereas stitch welds allow the metal to progressively distort and so absorb energy.

ABOVE *Cutting the new inside edge for the floor repair panel was arduous work. The author has since resolved to buy one of the powered 'nibbler' cutters. Aviation cutters seen here make a mess of the cut edge; the cut edge could make a mess of the author's hands because he is foolishly not wearing gloves!*

LEFT *This is where the home-made joddler really comes into its own, when there is a long edge to be stepped. Even using this progressive joddler makes the hands ache after a while, but it's a lot better than using some commercially available joddlers.*

Tuck the floor rear corner under the transmission tunnel rear reinforcer and then true up the reinforcer to grip the floor.

Use lots of self-tappers to pull the floor tight to the various edges to which it will be welded. Here the author is using a speed wrench fitted with the socket and bit from an impact wrench to quicken the process.

LEFT *Whilst the floor is removed, take the opportunity to clean up the inside of the car, especially the footwell area, while access is good. It is a real chore to have to clean this area with the floor fitted. The lip join between the transmission tunnel and the remains of the old floor panel was now very rough thanks to the air chisel, and this was trued up using a hammer and dolly. Also, the lip join was full of oils from the transmission tunnel, and these were burnt out using a blowtorch, because if they had been left they would have contaminated the weld.*

BELOW *The offside of the car. The inside of the crossmember has been cleaned and primed, and its lips will have to be trued up with a hammer and dolly. Clean and paint the toeboard assembly.*

is under way, some of these will undoubtedly have worked their way into the narrow gap between the transmission tunnel lip and the floor. If you attempted to weld with the gap full of oil, then the oil would mix with the weld and give a very weak contaminated join. Merely heating the lip using a blow torch will boil the oil and greases out of the gap – have a fire extinguisher handy before attempting this.

You will require a range of props and jacks to hold the floor panel in position prior to welding and it is worth using plenty of pop rivets or self tapping screws to draw the panels tightly together for the joins at the transmission tunnel, heelboard, cross member and footwell front panel. The author prefers to use seam welds throughout, with plug welds in addition where appropriate.

Because the heelboard assembly had been repaired and the sill replaced, the author decided that the bodyshell would be strong enough to be lifted onto its side to improve access (especially for the photography). The garage floor was heavily padded to prevent damage to the nearside rear wing, sill and door. Raising the car was accomplished single-handedly, although the author would recommend that two people are needed. Steel props were placed either side of the car to prevent it from falling on the author (although it was surprisingly stable) and the shell was checked for evidence of twisting with a spirit level. None was evident.

Having the bodyshell on its side makes the business of floor replacement far easier. It also enables work to proceed on the boot floor/side chassis rail areas, in addition to allowing you to attend to cleaning and repair work at the front of the car.

The third option is to fit a partial repair panel to deal with localised rot. This is not a choice which will appeal so much to the restorer, because if one area of the floor is rotten then other areas are liable to be substantially weakened. This option is more likely to appeal to those who merely wish to make a car roadworthy for a relatively short space of time, perhaps to keep the car on the road for a year or so until a full restoration or reshell can be undertaken. The exception to this is the outer edge repair panel.

The floor outer edge rots in concert with the inner sill which, as many people appreciate, can rot quite rapidly! Fitting a repair panel is not too difficult a task. Firstly, carry out any necessary repairs to the sill, the heelboard assembly and the footwell front panel. Offer the repair panel into position and mark a

cutting edge in the existing floor and allow an overlap for joddling before cutting into the floor. It is vital that you use a non-distorting cutting device, such as a Monodex, for this. A large, unsupported panel like the floor is easily distorted as it is cut.

The author recommends that the edge to be stepped sits underneath the existing floor edge, because the extra thickness of metal which will result from the joddled joint can easily be hidden using underseal. It is vital that the two panels are drawn tightly together and checked for distortion before they are welded. The author would favour seam welding them both inside and underneath for strength.

Rear Side Chassis Rail (Boot floor to wheelarch reinforcers)

These pressings are available as repair sections, although on the project car (as on many examples) the tops and sides were sound, and only the bottom of the pressing was rotten. The rotten metal can be cut out using a sharp chisel and hammer, or using an air chisel with the appropriate chisel attachment. The outer seam which joins the inner wing can be parted easily after the spot welds have been drilled out – the holes in the inner wing serving as plug welding holes later on. Fabricating a replacement panel is by no means easy. Begin by cutting a cardboard template which exactly fits the space, then transfer this shape onto sheet steel and add on extra width from which you can form the folded lips. A considerable amount of shaping is required to get the panel to fit. The author eventually succeeded using no more than a vice, a hammer and rubber mallet, and a wooden post which was used as an anvil. The repair section can be plug or seam welded.

With the advent of the Heritage bodyshell came the availability of complete rear sub-assemblies, consisting of the boot floor pressing, side chassis rails,

RIGHT *The author fabricated this panel (seen here clamped to a commercially made boot/rear wing repair panel) to repair the corroded boot edge. Clamped into position, it was also held with a number of screws plus three large bolts passed through the rear spring mounting plate, and eventually assumed the correct shape for welding. After making up two such panels (and welding them into position), the author thought better of this patch approach to boot floor repair and fitted a complete boot floor repair panel instead.*

damper brackets and inner wheel arches. Such major assemblies would usually only be fitted by professionals using jigs, although the DIY enthusiast could carry out the job satisfactorily if sufficient measurements were taken before any of the old metal was cut away. The same applies to the complete front end sub-assembly, also available from Heritage dealers. Your enthusiasm to try and fit one of these assemblies should be tempered with the thought that Heritage usc the same assemblies when they build complete bodyshells, but that Heritage find it necessary to use jigs in order to align them correctly.

Door re-skinning

Door bases rot, along with the lower section of the outer skin, and repair panels are available for both. Before spending good money on a new door skin and a base repair panel, remove the door from the shell and give the lower section a thorough examination. Compare the extent of the rot in the frame of the door with the sizes of available repair panels and, if the rot extends well beyond the repair panels, then simply get a new Heritage door.

The accepted method of removing an old door skin is to grind around the edge of the folded lip. On the project car, however, the metal of the fold was very thin, and much of it could easily be levered out, leaving only the top to be ground away. You will probably discover (depending on whether the door has been re-skinned before) several spot, MIG or gas welds along the seams, plus a few on the top fold (through which the quarterlight frame fits). Drill these out; try using a ⅛″ bit first, but if the resultant hole is not quite large enough to remove the weld, run a ³⁄₁₆″ or ¼″ bit through the holes.

The author did obtain base repair panels for the project car's doors, but decided against their use for a combination of reasons. Firstly, the sections were made of thinner gauge steel than the original door frame: secondly, the sections extended only as far as an area which was quite heavily rusted and which would have proven difficult to weld without burning through: thirdly, it would be far easier to patch repair the worst areas of rot. When the welding was complete, the affected areas were treated to a couple of costs of Bonda-Prima.

Skinning the door simply involves holding the frame in position and folding over the edge; special tools are available for this from companies such as

Frost, but the job can be accomplished by starting the fold using a small hammer, then finally tightening it using a wooden chase wedge – at all times, resting the new door skin on a protected surface. Before starting the fold, mark the area at the top of the frame to which you will be welding the top of the new skin, and clean both.

PAINTWORK

There is greater potential for things to go disastrously wrong when a car is being painted than at any other time during the restoration. Because of this and the not inconsiderable costs of primer, paint and thinners, it will often be better for the novice to have his car professionally sprayed than to do the work himself.

However, many DIY restorers will wish to learn to spray in order that they can carry out the whole restoration themselves, or to reduce costs. In fact, the cost of buying both paint and the necessary equipment can equal that of the highest quality professional respray. The most cost-effective route to top quality results is to carry out all preparation and perhaps to spray the primer at home, then to commission a paint shop to carry out the final stages.

It is recommended that the first-time paint sprayer firstly reads 'How to Restore Paintwork' by Miles Wilkins (Published by Osprey Automotive).

Paint types

Earlier cars would have originally been finished in a cellulose paint and, although more recent types of paint can be used to produce an equal or 'better' (under amateur conditions) finish more easily, they always look wrong – a little 'plastic' – on an older car.

Cellulose is an expensive paint to use because the wastage is very high. In its favour rates its rapid drying times, which reduce the chances of dust settling on wet paintwork, plus the fact that the thinners used will soften existing paintwork if a blow-in repair has to be carried out following future repairs, so blending the new paintwork with the old.

In addition to its expense, cellulose has other drawbacks. The preparation of the surface before painting must be of the highest standards, because cellulose shrinks after spraying and will show the

LEFT *The old door skin lower edge proved so rotten and weak that it could easily be levered off rather then ground away.*

BELOW *The author did purchase a door frame bottom repair section but, because it did not reach the good metal above this perforated area, he elected to patch as necessary instead. When you have folded the new door skin over, re-fit the door and manipulate it until it fits properly by pulling and pushing the corners (the skin and frame are still able to move relative to each other at this stage). Then and only then tack the frame and skin together.*

slightest marks and scratches from underneath. Cellulose must never be sprayed onto any existing synthetic paintwork, because the powerful thinners will lift the underlying paint.

The modern alternative to cellulose most likely to be used by the DIY restorer is synthetic paint. This has slower drying times, and so the premises must be kept dust-free for some time until the paint has air dried. This can often prove difficult in the typical workshop. Even with the concrete floor dampened down with water, dust, leaves and flying insects can often be blown in through gaps around doors.

Synthetic paints are entirely appropriate for later cars. They have a depth of body, however, that looks out of place on earlier examples.

Most professional paint shops today use two-pack synthetics, for the use of which the most stringent of safety precautions must be taken. The operator must not only wear a mask but also a protective airtight suit; the mask must be fully sealed and have a separate supply of fresh air because of the health hazards posed by the paint. Again, the finish is more appropriate to later cars.

Equipment

There are essentially three types of devices for spraying paint. The most common is a compressor allied to a paint gun. Alternatively, small 'airless' DIY units are available, but are better suited to small 'blow-in' repair work than complete car resprays as they invariably have a short 'duty-cycle' (ie. you will have to allow the machine to cool down frequently during work, which can result in visible dry edges when spraying cellulose). Finally, there is the new high-volume, low compression type of sprayer.

When choosing a compressor for spraying, you should always buy the largest and most powerful that you can afford, because smaller compressors have several drawbacks which can make achieving a good finish very difficult. Firstly, they lack sufficient tank volume and the air pump will consequently be working almost continuously in order to maintain sufficient air pressure. Often the gun will use air more quickly than the compressor can supply it, so that frequent stops have to be made while the compressor 'catches up', so to speak. This leads to a phenomenon

LEFT *Bonnet leading edge repair is not for the inexperienced. Here, the author is cutting away the old front end using a hacksaw to start the cut, which will be followed by a padsaw to cut through the centre section.*

RIGHT AND BELOW *The two bonnet repair sections. The author fitted the inner section with no problems but decided to leave the fitting of the outer panel until the wings and grille surround panel were back on the car, to ensure that the bonnet matched their lines. The rear edge of the outer panel comes ready stepped to fit under existing metal, but the edges will have to be tailored considerably because there is no room for a stepped edge between existing metal and the side runners.*

called the 'dry edge'. Basically, while you are waiting for the compressor to again build up pressure, the last paint band to be applied dries, giving a visible edge which can be difficult to hide.

Because a small compressor has to work continuously, the motor and pump become very hot. The heated air which consequently emits from the tank will help to cause the paint to dry in the air before it reaches the surface.

A 50 or preferably a 100 litre tank unit with a 3HP motor will be very suitable for spraying. Smaller units with only a 25 litre tank and a 1.5HP motor will be markedly less satisfactory.

In addition to the compressor and spray gun, you will require a rubber air hose and a oil filter/water trap. When air is compressed, water droplets form in the tank, often to be expelled along with the air. The water droplets can become contaminated with oil which leaks from the pump, the two combining into a sticky, oily liquid. Such contamination is apparent on the sprayed surface as tiny dark circles with lighter circles around them. The contaminated paint will be unable to adhere to anything and will eventually cause pin-holes in the top surface. This contamination is easily seen with grey primer paint – do not spray topcoat over contaminated primer, because it will lift. The author discovered (to his cost) that a single oil/water trap in line was insufficient to prevent oil contamination; two filters proved necessary.

When using a compressor it is advisable that the tank is drained at regular intervals, to permit water to escape; in damp weather a considerable quantity of water can build up in a short space of time. It is essential that the pump head bolts are checked for tightness at regular intervals; failure to do so can allow oil to escape into the tank.

The atmosphere must be kept dust and silicon-free during the spraying process, which in DIY terms usually entails sealing the spraying area. The air quickly fills with paint particles and it is vital that you use breathing apparatus. Simple dust masks are insufficient to protect against thinner fumes, and a proper spraying mask should be used. Eye protection is also needed.

Preparing to spray

All bare metal and areas of body filler must firstly be primed. When all repairs have been carried out,

flatting down may begin. Start using 400 grade wet n' dry progressing to 800 or even 1200 grade. The quality of the final finish will reflect the care taken during this lengthy stage, which can, if undertaken on an evenings-and-weekend basis, take weeks. The surface should be cleaned with a tack cloth to remove dust, then finally with a spirit wipe to remove grease and oil. All traces of oil, grease and any solvent or contaminent must be removed before the primer is sprayed on.

Firstly, stir then strain the primer. Even 'new' paint can contain impurities in the form of lumps. An old stocking will suffice for this. Then mix the primer with the appropriate thinner in the recommended quantity, and again stir well. Then stir again.

If using a compressor, set the pressure gauge to read 50–60psi when the gun is in use. Set both the paint and air controls to the fully open positions and make a rapid pass with the gun over a test surface. If large particles of paint are apparent, reduce the amount of paint until good atomisation is achieved. Then reduce both paint and air controls by equal amounts until the desired amount of paint emits from the gun. If the width of the spray pattern is too narrow, increase the pressure at the gauge by 5psi stages until a width of 6–8' is achieved with the gun 6–9' from the test piece.

Damp down the floor around the car to minimise the chances of dust being kicked into the air. Check that nothing is in the air such as seeds or insects. Take a deep breath and commit paint to metal.

It is advisable to 'spot' prime those areas which have been taken down to bare metal during the preparation, which have been repaired or which have been filled, in order to keep rust at bay and to keep moisture from newly-applied filler (which is porous) until the entire shell can be primed.

When the entire outer body is to be sprayed, begin with the bonnet and boot lid, then the doors, sides and wings and finally the valances.

If the entire shell is to be sprayed, then the engine bay and car interior/boot space can be sprayed separately before the exterior if desired. This will give a the novice a valuable opportunity to practice on slightly less important areas before tackling the unforgiving exterior.

When the shell is primered, it will almost certainly look as though the finish will be first-class, but do not be deceived; the matt finish of primer hides all manner of blemishes which the topcoats – particularly cellulose – will highlight. Carry out an inch by inch examination of the shell, looking for scratches and unevenness. These may be dealt with using very fine grade wet 'n dry and body stopper (cellulose putty).

The entire shell should then be flatted using the finest grade of wet 'n dry. If the topcoat is to be applied professionally, then it usually pays to ask the person doing the work to make sure that your preparation is acceptable before he starts spraying. The experienced eye of the professional can find blemishes which can escape your notice.

When spraying topcoat, it is advisable to firstly spray on a thin coat. This will 'key' strongly to the primer and also highlight flatting marks and other blemishes which can be dealt with before a lot of valuable paint is expended.

PROFESSIONAL RESTORATION

Few classic car owners actually carry out complete restorations themselves. Most engage the services of professionals for the majority of the body restoration, for engine and gearbox reconditioning, and for the paintwork.

Those who opt for professional engine and gearbox renovation usually simply obtain exchange units from MG/Spridget specialists, in which case they have the guarantee of the specialist's reputation. Few specialists in this relatively small field can afford to deal in poor quality units, because word of mouth between Spridget owners would quickly gain them an undesirable reputation if they did. Dealing directly with an engine restorer or with a company which is not an MG/Spridget specialist, however, can be more problematic. Tales abound of engines which were sold as 'reconditioned' but which were later found to merely be re-painted.

People restoring old cars usually develop a close working relationship with a specialist spares dealer, because there are so many components needing renewal or reconditioning on any old car that the spares business becomes in effect the restorer's second home! A company which had benefited from so much business from an individual would hardly be likely to sell them a poor reconditioned engine or gearbox. It is always best to buy from the specialist you know, even if a 'man down the road' offers apparently the same thing for a little less money.

Many of the people who restore old cars have

part or all of the body building work carried out by professionals, and there are many compelling reasons for doing so. Unless you are a competent welder and you have access to a good gas welding equipment and/or a MIG (and some previous experience of panel beating because many repair panels need a lot of attention before they will fit), you can quickly run into severe difficulties in attempting your own body rebuild. The consequences of poor welding might not be apparent until you try to negotiate a hump-back bridge at speed but, when they do become apparent, they can be quite horrific!

It is possible to engage professionals to carry out perhaps the actual welding, panel beating and so on, and to undertake simple but time-consuming and often back-breaking other work yourself. You can, for instance, strip the car to a bare shell and either clean off the old paint and underseal or (preferably) have it acid dipped before taking it along to the restorer. Following the body restoration, you then complete the mechanical re-build. Doing this can save a hefty 30% or more from the restoration bill.

Alternatively, you can strip the car as already described, then cut out the rot yourself and even tack repair and replacement panels into position before calling in a professional to do the actual welding. If the welder involved charges by the hour and gives you an estimate of the time needed to do the various jobs (few individual jobs will take the professional much more than an hour or two) the savings over a full professional job will be immense.

It can be difficult for the inexperienced to tell the difference between a good and a poor welder or restorer. In the case of the mobile welder, always follow personal recommendations, bearing in mind that a welder who usually works with agricultural vehicles and who might gain glowing references from farmers might not be very good when it comes to thin car body panels! If you cannot find anyone to recommend a welder then visit a few and ask to see examples of cars which they have previously worked on. If you see huge cover plates welded over rusted areas then do not deal with the welder involved. Remember that a good welded repair will usually be almost invisible, but do surreptitiously try the 'magnet test' on painted panels which are claimed to have been welded, to ensure that you are not being shown an example of the body filler's art!

Finding a good restorer for your car is not always easy, and there are many dubious outfits in business whose normal work entails smartening old cars up for quick sales to naive buyers and whose idea of a total body restoration is to tack heavy gauge plain steel panels over holes and use body filler to make the most atrocious mess look good! Steer well clear of general bodywork businesses at the lower end of the market.

There are some more reputable companies which carry out bodywork to all makes of car and which might, in a fleeting moment of madness, agree to restore a Spridget for you. The work will inevitably take far longer than the estimate suggests, because such people will not be familiar with the car and its little quirks; furthermore, there may be some unnecessary delays whilst the company tries to source body panels from a general panel dealership or from a Rover Group main dealer instead of going direct to an MG specialist spares business.

This type of business is not used to dealing with the huge quantities of rust and rot and the seized fittings typically found on old Spridgets. Their usual line will be straightening accident damaged fairly new cars. It is as well to leave them to what they do best.

Classic car restoration businesses have mushroomed with the growing popularity of classic cars. Many of these companies will deal with any and every type of classic and, as a result, they may lack specific model knowledge when compared to companies which specialise in a particular marque or even model. Go to such a business and you could discover craftsmen hand-making repair panels (at huge cost to you) which are readily available off the shelf at any reasonable spares stockist.

The best business to restore a Spridget is one which specialises in the car or in MGs or Austin Healeys, because they will (or should) have vast experience of the car which enables them to work in the quickest and most economical way. They should be familiar with the spares situation and be able to obtain any available spare quickly and without fuss (sometimes at trade prices, the benefit of which should be at least shared with the customer). The ideal restoration business will be linked to a spares supply operation, so that all necessary spares are bought in at trade prices and are always to hand.

Amongst Spridget/MG/Austin Healey restorers, there are good, mediocre and bad. Judging which category a particular business falls into is by no means easy.

The best guide to the excellence or otherwise of a restorer is to view cars which were restored by the business three or so years before. This is because almost all shoddy practices such as plating rusted panelwork which should really be replaced and using body filler to disguise poorly fitting panels will have become all-too- apparent during three years. Poorly applied paint will be starting to blister and lift, thick applications of bodyfiller will be working their way loose, ignored surface rust will be bubbling paintwork and so on.

A good restorer will be proud of the cars on which he has worked, whilst a poor restorer will claim to be too concerned with upsetting the owners of his cars by sending people to see them. In truth, few proud owners of well-restored cars can resist the opportunity to show them off at every opportunity to a fellow enthusiast such as yourself!

Probably the quickest way to find the 'right' restorer is to visit a classic car show, and preferably an MG or Austin Healey (even better – a Spridget) show. Do not look at the Concourse cars, because any business can restore a Spridget to Concourse condition – at a price. Look instead in the car park. Talk to owners of restored Spridgets and gain recommendations. If you cannot trace the owner of a car which is of particular interest then you could always leave a note under the windscreen wipers, giving your telephone number, praising the car and asking who the restorer was.

When you first visit a restoration business to appraise whether their standards and prices suit you, try to arrive well before the appointed time, so that you can see whether the workshop is being especially prepared for your benefit. This will also allow you to view the actual working practices of the business. If you can see a huge tub of body filler (which might have been hidden during the 'official' visit) then you can be sure that the business applies plenty of the stuff to each of the cars which it restores, because A. few business turn out restored cars at a fast rate and B. body filler has a finite shelf life.

Take a general view of the workshop; see whether the tools are stored neatly in some semblance of order or whether they are allowed to lie where they fall. In the latter case, much working time (for which you will be paying) will be wasted while lost tools are searched for. Look for 'traditional' tools such as hammers and dollys, lead loading supplies, even metal shrinkers and the like – all are good signs. Look at the hand tools used. If you see a socket set of dubious and mixed origins then the company buys cheap tools which do not last long and which will furthermore ruin many of the fittings of the cars they are used on.

Look at the work in progress. Are there no Spridgets (bad) or is there a predominance of Spridgets (good). Ask to see photographic records of previous Spridget restorations – all reputable restoration businesses now keep these. If you have read this far through the book then you ought to be able to spot poor workshop practices apparent on cars currently being restored, such as welding onto an improperly supported bodyshell or fitting a closing panel over bare metal.

You should be able to see a proper spray booth; if not, then ask where the cars are sprayed. If they are sprayed in the main workshop then move on to another restorer or tell this one that you wish the spraying to be carried out at a properly-equipped premises. The air at restoration premises is full of tiny particles of filler dust, of rust flakes and often of silicones – any of which can ruin the paint finish.

If the restorer suits your requirements, then and then only ask for an estimate for doing your own car. The estimate for a Spridget should be rather more accurate than for other classic sports cars such as the MGB, because, unlike the MGB, the Spridget has few body panels which are fully enclosed (in the case of the MGB and many other classics the amount of bodywork which is needed is not known until some external panels have been removed) and so the work involved can be far more accurately estimated.

The estimate should list all necessary components and consumables, and should give labour charges totalled in hours. Check the prices of the panels and compare these with those from Spridget spares specialists – if they appear unduly high or unduly low then treat the estimate with caution. Find the hourly labour rate by dividing the total labour charges by the number of hours, and compare this with the rates quoted by other restorers. Compare also the hours estimate between different restorers. Yes, you should always obtain at the very least two estimates and preferably more.

It is as well to carry out a thorough appraisal of the car before visiting a restorer, to allow you to list those jobs which you believe need doing. If the restorer misses out jobs which you consider important or if he lists jobs which do not really need doing, then you can draw your own conclusions!

Most restorers will be pleased to allow you to reduce your overall bill by carrying out certain repetitious and often back-breaking jobs yourself,

such as stripping the car to a shell and scraping off all the old underseal! This should save you a lot of money, because few restorers seem to employ low-paid personnel to carry out such work, and it has to be undertaken by an experienced craftsman at a high hourly rate of pay! Some companies might prefer to carry out all of the work themselves, and there is sense in this, because if the customer completes the rebuild on the restored shell and suddenly notices a scratch in the new paintwork, both he and the restorer will blame the other and the old business adage that the 'customer is always right' (even when you *know* he is wrong) will usually result in the company putting the matter to rights at their own expense in order to maintain customer relations.

When you visit a restorer, do not overstay your welcome. Restorers suffer more than most businesses with time-wasting 'dreamers' who visit the premises time after time and who ask endless questions, but never seem to get down to putting their hand in their pocket and commissioning a restoration.

When you agree to allow a restorer the privilege of working on your Spridget, you may be surprised to learn that he cannot make a start on it for several months. This is normal practice for a good (and therefore popular) restoration business, because the workshop will usually be booked up for months in advance. Occasionally, a cancelled job (from one of the dreaded dreamers) might allow a restorer to take in your car straight away, but normally this means that the business is not too popular with enthusiasts.

It is normal to pay a deposit (do not pay too high a deposit at this stage – 10% seems quite reasonable) on commissioning the restoration, which may or may not be refundable if for any reason you have to cancel the commission before it begins. Thereafter, you may be quite properly asked for part payments against the amount of work done, which might typically be a third of the balance at one and two thirds of the way through the job, with the remainder on completion. Try to deliver cheques for such payments in person, just to confirm that the restorer has really completed the amount he claims.

Professional restoration or re-shelling?

The advent of new Heritage Spridget bodyshells at attractive prices calls into question the wisdom of restoring a really rotten Spridget when the body restoration labour charges plus the costs of repair and replacement panels can represent a fairly large percentage of the price of a complete, new Heritage bodyshell. The Heritage shell also has the advantage that the thorough paint priming process allied to the fact that all of the panels involved are new should delay the onset of any rusting far longer than a typical restoration which only replaces a number of panels.

In order to 'compete' with the Heritage shell, some restorers have built body jigs which enable them to greatly speed up body restoration by negating the need to constantly take exhaustive measurements in order to ensure that panels are replaced in exactly the correct alignment. In fact, given the use of a good body jig, restoration work can proceed at almost production line speed to give high quality bodies at lower cost than that of the Heritage bodyshell.

The criteria for finding a good business to carry out a re-shell differ greatly from those for a general body restorer. Firstly, there will be no welding or other bodywork (unless especially commissioned) and so the work will break down into two parts. Firstly, the shell will have to be sprayed. There is no need whatever for it to be sprayed at this business, because it suits you better if they take it to a properly equipped paint shop. Secondly, there is mechanical work.

The ideal business to re-shell a car is one which has a full stock of necessary replacement and reconditioned parts – ie. a spares specialist with workshop facilities. This business will not have to wait for spares to be sourced because they will be sitting there on the shelf ready, and the business will be buying those spares at the lowest possible prices, some of the benefit of which should be passed on to the customer. In fact, the difference in price between re-shelling a Spridget yourself and paying full price for all spares, and having the work carried out professionally can represent a very small part of the total bill, especially because you will be tempting the proprietor with a huge chunk of business in one fell swoop! Do not be afraid to negotiate over price, because the proprietor will have some 'leeway' in the discount he gives on the prices of the spares.

As with restoration businesses, a company which offers a Heritage shell build-up service should be able to recommend previous satisfied customers who can vouch for the excellence of its work. If you don't possess a suitable donor car, then such a business will almost certainly be able to offer you one or obtain one on your behalf at the right price. Because the business will be very experienced in finding the best cars (and in obtaining them at the most attractive prices) this option is highly recommended.

Whether you wish to engage the services of professionals to re-shell a car, to carry out a complete or a partial restoration, you can do worse than beginning by joining a local MG, Austin Healey or Spridget club, and soliciting the views of members. They will be as eager to recommend a good business as they will to condemn a poor one.

6 · RE-SHELLING

The introduction of new Spridget bodyshells during 1991 promises to be as important a development for the car as the launch of MGB and GT bodyshells proved to be for the Spridget's 'big brothers'. When the MGB shell was introduced in 1989, the prices realised by bodily rotten MGBs began to rise as they became sought-after as donor cars for re-shelling. Cars which failed the MOT test and which might previously have been consigned to the breaker's yard were suddenly fetching almost as much as examples which could be used on the road. The same will almost certainly prove to be the case with the Spridget.

Perhaps more importantly, the introduction of the new bodyshells means that there is no reason why anyone would wish to scrap any example of the Spridget range for which the new bodyshell is available. The future of the car, like that of the MGB, seems assured.

Like the MGB, the Spridget is impressively served with an almost comprehensive supply of new spares, quite remarkably so for a car which ceased production way back in 1979. Components which cannot be obtained new can always be sourced in reconditioned (as good as new) form, so that it is possible for the DIY enthusiast to replace donor car components with new or reconditioned alternatives and so to build up a Heritage bodyshell into in effect a 'new' car. But there is always an outside chance that the Spridget could in reality become a new limited production car.

Like the MGB, there is a possibility that, at some time in the future, the Rover Group or a third-party company will find or manufacture alternatives for Spridget spares which cannot be obtained new, and build new cars along the lines of the new MGR V8.

A Spridget with improved suspension and a modern engine would almost certainly prove to be a great commercial success, judging by the sales levels of cars like the Mazda MX5.

In the first two years of production, Heritage turned out some 1500 MGB and GT bodyshells. Spridget bodyshell production could prove even faster due to the way in which the shells are assembled. Whereas the MGB and GT are built up onto a large jig, the Spridget shell consists of a number of sub-assemblies which are initially built up on separate small jigs and which eventually come together when assembled on a large jig. Each Spridget shell thus requires far less time on the major jig than an MGB shell.

The new bodyshells really call into question the wisdom of embarking on even a DIY body restoration of a car with advanced bodyrot when a complete new bodyshell can be obtained. The price for the fully panelled shell including doors, boot lid and bonnet, equates (at the time of writing) to roughly 115 hours of bodyshop time, at which, it must be considered an exceptional bargain.

A high quality professional body restoration on a typically rotten Spridget will usually take rather longer than the 115 hours' worth of workshop time which the cost of the Heritage shell represents, so that, depending on the extent of work required for a particularly car, a new bodyshell could prove cheaper than professional restoration costs.

The new bodyshell does not enjoy such a clear-cut economic advantage when compared to a DIY restoration, yet the repair and replacement body panels which will be needed even in amateur restorations will often add up to so high a percentage of the price of a new shell that it is worth starting any planned restoration by ascertaining the extent of rot and the costs of repair and replacement panels, then comparing this figure to the cost of a new bodyshell. Do remember to account for workshop consumables when attempting any such costing; items such as MIG wire and gas, sanding discs and primer paint are needed in bulk for a thorough restoration, and cost a substantial amount.

The 'average' Spridget in need of restoration might require a large number of repair and replacement body panels, the cost of which can easily approach 50% of the cost of the completed bodyshell. The difference between the costs of replacement panels and the Heritage shell is a very small price to pay for the privilege of possessing a brand new bodyshell rather than possessing a rotten old shell, a pile of replacement panels and the prospect of countless hours' cleaning and welding!

But there is more to this matter than pure economics. The new bodyshells are electrostatically paint primed, so that their rust resistance should exceed that of even the very best restoration which, after all, will only renew some body panels and almost certainly leave traces of surface rust or pitting on other panels or in various nooks and crannies. This rust will, sooner or later, begin to spread so that another restoration or a re-shell will become necessary at some point in the future and possibly within a few years.

There is also the question of build quality. The manner in which the Heritage bodyshells are manufactured (sub-assemblies on jigs) means that the original neat and strong spot welds cannot be replicated on a car which is being restored, due to restricted access in the various box sections such as (especially) the heelboard. The Heritage shell should be stronger than most restored bodies.

DONOR CARS

Many people will buy a new Heritage bodyshell in order to give a new lease of life to their own ageing and deteriorating Midget or Sprite. Others will wish to buy a 'donor' car specifically for re-shelling.

The choice of a suitable car for a re-shell project is no easier than the choice of an 'up-and-running' Spridget. The temptation may be to opt for a car which is in very poor bodily condition and hence very cheap, yet this can prove to be an expensive route to

take in the long run, because many of the mechanical and electrical components from such a car will prove to be unusable, and these will all have to be replaced at mounting cost. Even those components which are functional but which show signs of ageing will usually be replaced, because few people would wish to adorn a brand-new bodyshell with tired or tatty components!

It is best to avoid cars which have been off the road for any length of time, because mechanical and electrical components always seem to deteriorate more quickly if they are unused than if they are given normal use. Furthermore, on a car which has been left to rot out of doors, you can count on finding a predominance of seized fittings. Nuts and bolts which have seized will have to be drilled or ground away, a time-consuming process which carries the risk of your inadvertently damaging the components which you are trying to remove from the car.

The costs of re-shelling a Spridget are likely to mirror the pattern set by the MGB and GT. People who have re-shelled these cars have reported to the author that the actual bodyshell accounts for just a quarter or even a fifth of the total restoration costs. This is due to the fact that many components have to be replaced, and that many are replaced because they look dilapidated and would spoil the looks of the finished vehicle. In common with the MGB, the costs of mechanical, electrical and trim components for a Spridget can add up to a lot more than the cost of the Heritage shell. To prove this, take a current spares catalogue and add up the costs of obtaining the replacement or reconditioned mechanical and electrical units, new chromework and interior trim, etc., which might be needed in a re-shell. The total may frighten you.

This should be the greatest influence on your choice of a donor car. The best buy would be a car which the previous owner had kept in tip-top mechanical condition but which had a rotten body. Such cars are by no means rare, and usually come to the market after they fail the MOT test due to bodyrot. The cars are easy to locate; just look for advertisements which read along the lines of 'Spridget for sale. Much money spent. Some welding needed for MOT'. In the author's experience, an older car which fails the MOT test on bodywork grounds will usually (though not always) require extensive body restoration, although a large number are, of course, 'bodged' in order to scrape though the test. This gives them one extra year of road use whilst they deteriorate to the point at which the following MOT finally takes them off the road for good.

Unfortunately, many owners of MOT failure or generally rotten Spridgets have an inflated concept of their car's worth. Those who know that the Heritage shell is available will often ascribe 'donor' car value to their own vehicle and ask an inflated price. Others simply inflate their car's worth because it is a 'classic car'. Do not be drawn into spending too much money on a donor car, because in most instances they will yield comparatively few spares which can simply be transferred to the new shell. The price which you pay for the donor car should reflect the value of spares which it will furnish.

Probably the best donor car would be one which had extensive bodyrot but which was still road legal. You could actually use such a car on the road for a short while, in which time you could list those components which required attention. There would be no such easy way of checking drive components, for instance, on a non-runner, but any problems with the gearbox, propeller shaft etc will quickly manifest themselves during normal road use.

PROFESSIONAL RE-SHELLING

In the case of the MGB, it seems that quite a few people have had their cars re-shelled by professionals, and there is much to commend this approach. The time requirement for a DIY re-shell by a single person working alone will be many times greater than that for a team of experienced mechanics, so that the labour charges for the professional re-shelling will not be so great as might be imagined. Furthermore, some businesses combine spares supply with restoration and also mechanical repair facilities, and such companies not only have all necessary spares to hand (avoiding delays in the rebuild) but they also buy in those spares at the best quantity discount rates, and some of this saving can be passed on to the customer.

The difference in price between buying all of the new and exchange components likely to be needed for a re-shell at normal retail prices, and commissioning the whole job to be carried out by a combined restoration/spares supply company, should be surprisingly little. Again, using prior experience of professional re-shelling of the MGB, that extra labour charge has in the author's experience amounted to

around 15% to 20% of the total cost.

Those who do opt to have the re-shell carried out professionally and who do not possess a suitable donor car can often benefit from asking the company which will carry out the work to also source a donor car. Their experience should allow them to find the right car at the right price.

Before commissioning a professional shell build-up, do check the quality of previous work carried out by the company, and follow the general instructions about locating the right company to carry out the work, which are given in Chapter five of this book.

WORKING METHODS

There are two ways to go about re-shelling a Spridget. If the donor car is in excellent condition mechanically, then you can simply park it next to the new shell and transfer components from one to the other. The same applies if you live very close to a good spares supplier, because you can immediately replace any spare which proves to be unsuitable when removed from the donor car. If the car has many dubious components, you may be better advised to begin by stripping the donor car and attending to those parts. The great attraction of the former course of action is that you will know exactly where and how each component fits; if a component is shimmed then the shims will be transferred across along with the component instead of perhaps being set to one side, becoming separated from their component and later presenting you with the headache of having to guess where they fit!

However, few donor cars will be in such good condition mechanically that you can simply transfer over a predominance of components. Most donor cars will still leave you needing a lot of replacement or professionally reconditioned spares and, unless you happen to live next door to a major spares supplier,

OVERLEAF *This rear view of LSB 9, taken in the Frogeye Car Company workshop, shows the excellent finish and visual authenticity of the car, with the external seams and fillets re-created in rust-free GRP. This car currently lives in Belgium, is fitted with a limited slip differential and a five speed gearbox, and a 90 bhp engine. (Courtesy Frogeye Car Co. Ltd)*

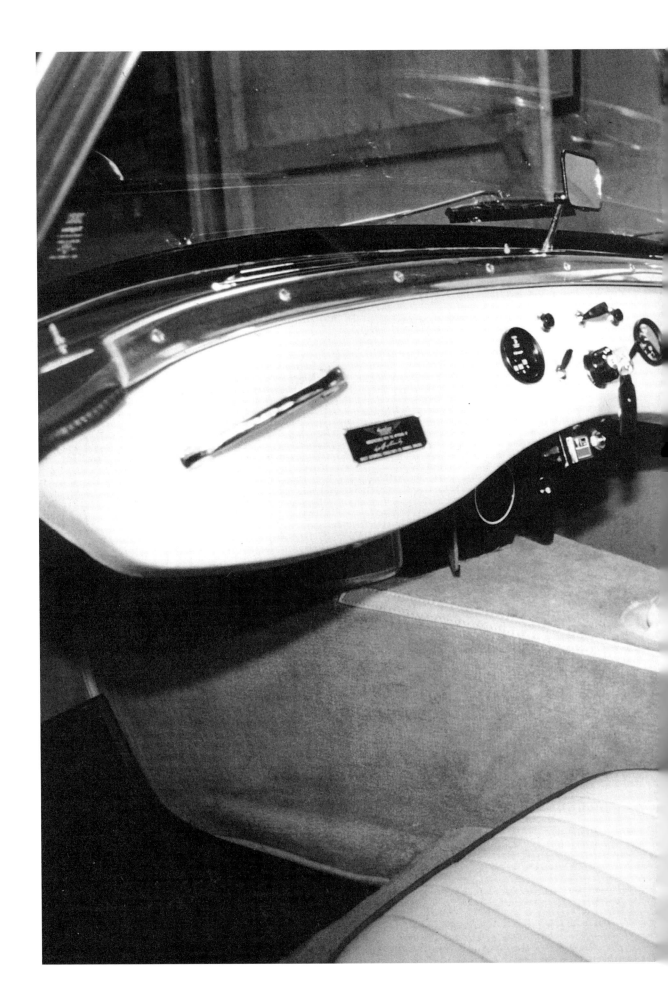

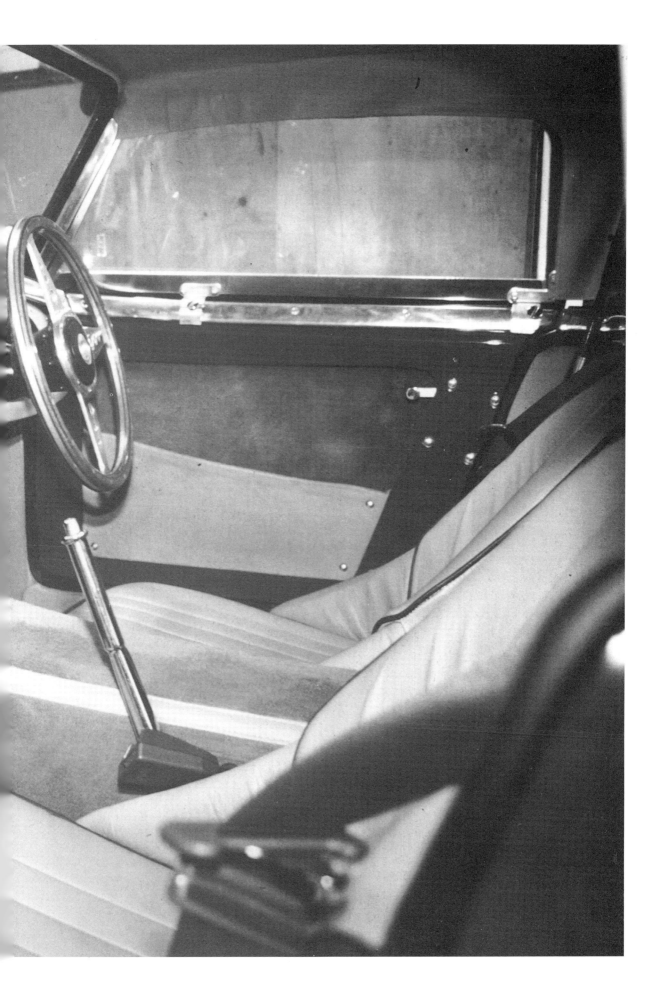

you will find yourself time and time again in the position of not being able to carry on working until some essential component has been acquired. In such instances, it can be preferable to begin by stripping the donor car and listing all components which will have to be reconditioned or replaced. This will usually prove to be a long list!

By creating a list of necessary components, the value of the order which you will be able to place with a spares supplier for new and reconditioned components should be high enough for you to be able to negotiate a substantial discount – especially if you order all the spares at once and the order includes the new bodyshell. Whilst you are waiting for the supplier to assemble your order, there will be plenty of work to keep you occupied, cleaning reusable components.

Whichever working method you opt for, do not dispose of the donor car shell until you have finally finished the reshell, because it will still prove an invaluable source of reference. When the new bodyshell arrives, examine it minutely and compare it to the old shell in order to ensure that all necessary holes have been drilled. Run taps through the threads of all captive nuts, because the electrostatic paint priming process will have attracted the primer into the threads.

Most people will probably opt to have their new bodyshell sprayed professionally, because they have paid out a lot of money for the shell (plus a substantial sum for the actual paint) and because there are a myriad of things which can go wrong if they attempt to carry out the spraying themselves. Having the spraying carried out professionally gives the option of going for a modern 2 pack paint and having it cured in a low bake oven. This will give a superb and long-lasting finish, although it will look out of character on an earlier car.

Alternatively, you might opt instead for the more authentic cellulose for a 1960s car. Whichever you choose, professional or DIY, 2 pack, synthetic or cellulose, leave it to harden for the advised period before you begin to carry out any work, and make your first task running taps through the threads of captive nuts. Cover surfaces such as the wings to prevent damage from occurring to them during the rebuild, and always avoid having sharp objects such as keys in your pocket when you work on the car – it is very easy to inadvertently scratch the new paint surface.

The Heritage bodyshell supplied with the front

wings already fitted begs the question of whether to remove the wings in order to apply extra paint protection to the enclosed area underneath. In the case of a DIY spray, the author would be inclined to remove the front wings, then spray the bodyshell and wings separately. This would not only give extra paint protection to the enclosed area behind the wings but would also leave the wing fixing nuts and their washers free of paint. It can be difficult to remove painted bolts without damaging the surrounding paint. Whether you prefer the look of unpainted or painted bolt heads is a matter for individual taste.

The next job is to fit the suspension and roadwheels, because this will allow the shell to be rolled around the workshop in order to improve access for the rest of the rebuild. Then, take advantage of the easy access within the engine bay and fit the wiring loom, the brake and fuel pipes. At this stage, you can actually stand inside the engine bay to work, so fit all components which are affixed to the engine bay sides (excepting those which will be in the way when you come to fit the engine/gearbox) plus the steering rack and column.

When fitting the engine/gearbox unit and throughout the rest of the rebuild, the primary rule must be – don't rush. Before fitting any component, stop and consider whether any areas of the new paintwork could get scratched, and apply plenty of padding to these before starting work. It would be as well to have two helpers when you come to fit the engine/gearbox unit, to help manoeuvre the heavy assembly into place without causing any damage to paintwork.

The effective and easy-to-work-on Healey Frogeye rear suspension will be improved greatly by the use of a telescopic damper and flexi-ride suspension unit. The splined end of the torsion bar allows adjustment of the ride heights. (Courtesy Frogeye Car Co. Ltd)

THE HEALEY FROGEYE

This is a very different animal from the Heritage bodyshell and, unlike the Heritage shell, you have the option of buying a Healey Frogeye complete and ready for the road. The DIY alternative is called the 'restoration assembly', and includes the bodyshell fitted to the chassis, with doors ready hung, bonnet fitted and a new rear suspension system in place. It costs considerably more than the Heritage shell, but then it includes rather more.

The Healey Frogeye can be built using any Sprite or Midget from the Mk.1 Sprite to the 1979 Midget as a 'donor' vehicle. Naturally, there will be many

LEFT *The son of Sprite designer Donald Healey CBE, Geoffrey, seen with a Healey Frogeye photographed en route to new owner Barbara Bellamy of Bellamy Engineering, in May 1990. This car is fitted with a standard 1275cc A series engine producing 65 bhp. Finished in jonquil/pale primrose, the trim is black with primrose piping. Two identical cars have been supplied to Japan, and another is on order. (Courtesy Frogeye Car Co. Ltd)*

components from later cars which will not fit or which would be inappropriate on a Frogeye, and the company supplies full details of where these can be sourced at the lowest cost.

The car is a faithful replica of the old Frogeye as far as looks go, but it offers important improvements in the suspension plus far more power courtesy of the recommended 1275cc engine. The rear suspension is a trailing arm system with telescopic dampers, and reportedly, a great improvement on the original.

Geoffrey Healey, the son of Sprite designer Donald Healey, nowadays runs a consultative business and is in fact a consultant to the Frogeye Car Company. The author has spoken with Geoffrey Healey about the Healey Frogeye, and his enthusiasm for the car was obvious. He listed the strengths of the Healey Frogeye as its longevity (due to the GRP bodywork and galvanised chassis), the fact that it drives more in the manner of the competition Frogeyes than the production car and that its handling is much improved.

The Healey Frogeye is the only production car currently approved to bear the Healey name – which must surely say more about the car than any testimonial.

7 · MODIFICATIONS

Spridget owners do not generally appear to be as enthusiastic about customising their cars as are owners of cars like the Volkswagen Beetle and Mini. In fact, it is comparatively rare to see a Spridget which is overtly customised. Some might say that it seems a shame to physically alter a classic car like the Spridget, because the car in standard trim does everything so well. It goes, it stops, it handles, it's comfortable – and it looks good. However, many people like to carry out minor cosmetic alterations which individualise their own cars; others like to make the car go faster or handle better, some like to perform drastic surgery on their Spridgets to turn them into real head-turners – and who is to lay down arbitrary rules governing what does and what does not constitute good taste? Possible modifications for the Spridget range from the fitting of simple performance-enhancing bolt-on goodies right through to engine and gearbox substitutions and major bodywork alterations. This chapter will concentrate on those performance-enhancing modifications which the average owner might choose, and will deal only briefly with more adventurous performance modifications and bodywork customisation.

ENGINE/TRANSMISSION

Probably the most common modification to the Spridget is to uprate the power of the engine, and this can be achieved in a number of ways. It is important to recognise before starting to look in depth at this subject that there is no virtue in trying to gain more power from the engine unless it is firstly properly set up, with ignition and mixture spot-on, and in good condition. Any deficiencies in the carburation or ignition, cylinders with poor compression, air induction and so on will negate the benefits of tuning and/or modifications.

There are a vast number of 'off the shelf' power-increasing goodies available for the A series engine, and the principles of getting more from the engine are widely understood, because the unit was also used in the Mini range. From the 1960s, a lot of effort has gone into making Minis faster, and the Spridget owner can happily take advantage of it. Fairly recent developments include an eight port crossflow (carbs on one side, exhaust on the other) cylinder head, giving – with other modifications around 120BHP with carburettors, and a potential 10–20BHP more with fuel injection! Although the Triumph 1500cc engine does not attract so many third-party developments, most if not all of the modifications described here for the A series engine can be applied to the Triumph. In either case, obtain expert advice before modifying your own engine.

Very mild increases in power may be obtained from simply allowing the engine to breathe more freely and hence pack more mixture into the available cylinder volume, by fitting better air filters and the right exhaust system. These are available both from Spridget spares suppliers and from specialist motorsports companies such as Ripspeed. The K&N pancake air filter is the usual choice and, coupled with a long centre branch (LCB) manifold and straight through exhaust, should give a small improvement in the order of perhaps 3–5 bhp. This will not turn your Spridget into a road-burner nor make much difference to the 0–60mph times of the car, but should give a little more 'grunt' to make overtaking easier. The usual next stage of modification is to swap the cylinder head, either for one from a larger A series engine or a specially modified version – the latter being the recommended choice. A modified cylinder head from a reputable company could add from 10 to 15 bhp at the rear wheels, which will make a very noticable difference to the speed of the car.

It is possible to further increase the power of your engine whilst keeping to the original cubic capacity, but there is a trade-off. The higher the state of tune, the more likely the engine is to tick over roughly (and it will probably have a much higher tick over speed) and to have a progressively narrower power band. It is reported that the 1992 MOT exhaust emission test is being failed by many engines in higher states of tune simply because they will not tick over at normal revolutions (at which they should be tested and for which the emission levels are calculated), so that even though their emissions are within the legal limit as a percentage of the total emission, they fail.

The narrower revolutions power band which comes with high states of tune means that the engine is less tractible; in order to maintain momentum, the revolutions must be kept high, which contrasts sharply with standard Spridget engine characteristics, which allow the driver to make gentle unhurried progress up hill and down dale. Town driving also becomes progressively less pleasant as the engine is further tuned.

To make matters worse, engines in high states of tune are quite likely to use far more fuel, out of all proportion to the performance gain.

There is an alternative to 'hotting up' the engine which retains all of the more desirable characteristics of the standard unit, and that is to either fit a larger capacity engine (sub-1275cc engines), or to have the cubic capacity of your own engine increased. This gives you a tractible unit which retains all of the virtues of the standard engine; it will pull evenly at low engine revolutions, and it has a wide power band so that you can keep gear changes down to a minimum.

Smaller engines are perhaps best simply swapped for one of the larger capacity units, so that a 948cc or 1098cc unit might be swapped for a 1275cc engine, which can be obtained easily and which will give a substantial increase in performance. The 1275cc engine can be taken out to larger capacities and, of course, fitted with larger pistons, and 1340cc appears to be the common choice. A 1340cc Spridget fitted

with the mildest of modifications would offer very good road performance.

Other engine modifications begin with a modified cylinder head, which will be 'gas flowed' or 'ported' – two terms with the same meaning; the inlet and exhaust ports are smoothed out, re-profiled and slightly enlarged to assist more mixture into the cylinders and more exhaust gas out. Larger valves also increase the engine's breathing rate, and exchange competition cylinder heads – usually called Stage One or Two, depending on whether larger valves are fitted and/or the compression ratio is increased – are available for both the A series and Triumph engines. Alternatively, many rally preparation businesses will carry out the work on the existing cylinder head.

Don't try to gas flow your own cylinder head, because the job requires lots of experience if you are to avoid grinding right through the wall and ruining the head! Furthermore, unless the work is accurately carried out, some cylinders will receive or emit more gasses than others, and the engine will never run satisfactorily. The best option is either to obtain an exchange modified head from a Spridget spares business, or to take the head to an engine preparation specialists and let them carry out the job. Do be sure to get new valves and guides fitted at the same time.

A performance camshaft is a popular modification, but there are pitfalls for the unwary. The idea behind a performance cam is to allow the valves to let in more mixture and let out more burnt exhaust gasses, and this could be achieved by making the valve lift higher, making the valve stay open for longer or in common practice by a combination of these. The recommendation is to opt for a camshaft – sometimes referred to as a 'modern technology' camshaft – which increases lift but which does not increase the duration of the opening to any appreciable extent.

The carburettors can be swapped, usually for a pair of larger bore SUs; HS1s are swapped for HS2s, HS2s for HS4s, and so on, with, of course, larger inlet manifolds. Going further down the performance road (and paying more money), it is possible to obtain non-SU carburettors and manifolds for Spridgets for even more power.

The list of performance 'goodies' which you can bolt onto and into your engine seems endless, as does the bill you receive at the end of it! Generally, only those who wish to campaign their cars on the track will seriously consider going to such lengths to wring the last ounce of performance from the A series engine, because every extra bhp means a little less tractibility, less miles per gallon. A full race engine with all the trimmings in a road-going car is not really practical.

To retain the characteristics of the standard A series and Triumph engines but with rather more performance than is possible from a 1340cc mildly tuned lump, there is always the option of fitting an entirely different engine. Toyota engines (with, it must be added, their delightful 5 speed gearboxes) have been fitted into Spridgets, as have other engine/gearbox combinations. The mighty Rover V8 has found its way under the Spridgets (modified) bonnet, and even big American V8s have been fitted – these more extreme transplants usually intended for use off the public highway, where their bonnet bulges, necessarily wide wheels and general demeanour would probably attract unwelcome attention from the constabulary.

BRAKES/SUSPENSION

Having lots of power on tap certainly makes the Spridget go, but the question has to be raised of just how well it can stop from higher speeds. At the very least, the braking system should be in first class order, the discs and drums clean and free from marks, the pads and shoes replaced regularly. Considering that there are so many available modifications to make Spridgets go faster (many of them probably spin-offs from Mini developments), there appear surprisingly few modified braking system components available. Competition shoes and pads are well worth considering if you envisage much fast road work. A brake servo might be worth considering. This uses the vacuum from the inlet manifold to decrease the amount of brake pedal pressure needed for a certain braking effort – in other words, it saves the driver from having to 'stand' on the brake pedal in order to achieve maximum braking effort. Unfortunately, such a modification is well beyond the scope of this book, and specialist advice should be sought by anyone comtemplating it.

As far as steering and suspension are concerned, the Spridget suspension is quite firm enough for most people without stiffening it up even more; however, uprated front and rear springs are available, and stiffer dampers might be preferred by a few

(masochists). The light and responsive steering needs no alteration.

There is plenty of scope to modify the axle area. The standard differential could be swapped to lower engine revolutions at speed and make the car more pleasant for touring, or for one which raised revolutions for a car with a modified engine to give faster acceleration.

More usefully, anti-tramp bars are available and help combat the axle's propensity to twist against the force of the leaf springs as power is applied. A rear anti-roll bar helps reduce the amount of body roll on hard cornering, but whether this is necessarily a good thing is by no means assured. A Spridget pushed really hard on a corner responds with understeer as the outside tyre scrubs, and it is difficult to get the rear end to actually break away. If body roll is reduced, the way in which the rear tyres share grip is altered and the characteristics could change for the worse unless the whole suspension (including the dampers and the front springs) was balanced to act properly as a whole. Before fitting individual suspension modifications, it is probably as well to consult a company which has set up Spridgets for (successful) track use, and to model a complete (but possibly softened) suspension system on their more successful cars – not forgetting that a competition car will be uncomfortable on the roads.

BODYWORK

A car which is a 'looker' (a title for which the Spridget certainly qualifies) appears to be rarely heavily modified as far as bodywork goes, unlike the everyday saloons for which a daunting range of tack-on wings, skirts and spoilers seem to be widely available.

Commercially available modifications for the Spridget have included the Lenham GT conversion, which turned the Spridget into a copy of the famous 60s Le Mans racing Spridgets. In concept, it is very akin to the 1965 Berlinetta conversion for the MGB, which pipped the actual MGB GT to the post but which was probably unable to find a market after the factory GT hit the showrooms. In both cars, the rear ends are cut away and a glassfibre GT fastback hard top is bonded into place. Both cars looked and still look magnificent.

Staying with GRP rear ends, at least one Spridget owner has fitted a GRP Frogeye back end onto an

The Arkley SS conversion kit is suitable for all Spridgets.

1960s Spridget to create a replica Mk.1 ½ Spridget. This car attracted a lot of media attention when it was unveiled, so look out for it at any large shows you attend in the UK.

The Arkley SS is a kit car (possibly the only remaining example to be based upon the Spridget) which replaces the front and rear wings, plus bonnet and boot lid, to create an easy to build and very attractive special based on the standard Spridget floorpan and running gear.

The front end of the Arkley is a one-piece GRP moulding, which hinges at the front to allow access to the engine in the same manner as the Frogeye. Fitting the front end appears simplicity itself, entailing merely cutting away the inner wings, resiting the windscreen wiper motor and horn on later cars, then bolting the new front end into place. This is without doubt far easier than butt-welding repair sections onto an old bonnet and front wings!

The rear end is a little more involved. Firstly, the old rear end must be cut back to leave the boot floor and rear chassis rails, then the one-piece rear moulding bonded into position using glassfibre tape and resin. The car is then re-sprayed, lowered, and preferably has wider wheels fitted prior to the final fitting up.

The current vendors of the Arkley SS, Peter May engineering, state that the conversion is simple and that the costs amount to half those for the equivalent new Spridget body panels. They are always willing to undertake some or all of the work on behalf of the customer, or to give advice if problems are encountered. The kit is suitable for all Spridgets (although it is difficult to imagine anyone cutting up a valuable Frogeye at today's prices), including rubber bumper models – the only differences between the various versions being connected with the rear hood/tonneau fixings.

The Arkley SS kit replaces rusted front and rear

Peter May Engineering, the home of Arkley Sportscars, works on competition machinery like this, but also fettles standard road cars.

wings, bonnet and inner front wings, but it should not be used on a car with rot in the scuttle/A post assembly, sills or heelboard/rear chassis rails, until those sections have been replaced.

For more details and for a copy of the brochure (which gives further details of the conversion), contact Peter May engineering (address at the end of the book).

Frontline Developments of Bath have a range of

exciting modifications for Spridgets, chief amongst which is their Toyota 5 speed gearbox conversion. The conversion kit comprises a gearbox with 12 months' warranty, a clutch kit, new engine back plate, exchange propellor shaft, exchange speedometer and cable, a new chassis crossmember and easy-bleed clutch slave cylinder and pipes.

The advantages of the conversion can be summarised as offering better ratios to make more of the engine's power and give relaxed high-speed touring, a stronger, slicker and quieter gearbox, and a better clutch. Unlike the majority of performance modifications listed in this chapter, the Toyota gearbox conversion aims to make the most of whatever power the engine develops, and Frontline's

Tim Fenna explains that one customer has fitted the conversion kit to a Spridget with an engine developing 173BHP with no problems posed by that power. The conversion can be fitted to Sprites Mk 1-4, and Midgets Mk 1-3.

The same company also offers and is developing some fairly radical suspension modifications. At the front, the lever arm damper is replaced by a steel top arm and a Spax adjustable telescopic damper. At the rear, available modifications include a modified Watts linkage and inverted 'A' bracket to provide positive axle location.

Engine modification is not overlooked by the company, and as this is written a turbo and other mods are under development.

APPENDICES

Recommended Lubricants and fluids

Engine oil SAE 20W/50 Multigrade;

6.5 pints (3.7 litres) 1098/1275cc; 8 pints (4.5 litres) 1500cc

Gearbox oil SAE 20W/50 Multigrade (all except 1500cc)

EP80W hypoid gear oil (1500cc)

2.25 pints (1.3 litres) 1098/1275cc; 1.5 pints (.85 litres) 1500cc

Axle oil EP90 hypoid gear oil;

1.75 pints (1 litre) 1098/1275/1500cc

Carburettor dashpots SAE 20W/50 Multigrade Steering rack EP90 hypoid gear oil (not 1500cc)

Steering rack Multipurpose lithium-based grease 1500cc

All grease nipples; Multipurpose lithium-based grease.

Cooling system

10.5 pints (6 litres) 1098cc; 6 pints (3.7 litres) 1275cc; 7.5 pints (4.25 litres) 1500cc

Anti-freeze solution. To −13 degrees C 25%. To −19 degrees C 33%. To −36 degrees C 50%.

Petrol tank capacity 6 gallons (6.5 gallons 1500cc)

Fuel 97RON (4 star).

TORQUE WRENCH SETTINGS

948/1098/1275cc engines

Cylinder head nuts

948cc; 40ftl.lb. (5.5 kg.m)

1098/1275cc; 42 ft.lb. (5.8 kg.m) – Plain studs.

50 ft.lb. (6.9 kg.m) – Studs stamped '22' or with drill point.

Rocker shaft nuts 25 ft.lb. (3.4 kg.m)

Rocker box cover 4 ft.lb. (.6 kg.m)

Manifold/cylinder head 15 ft.lb. (2.1 kg.m)

Timing cover

¼" bolts 6 ft.lb. (.8 kg.m)

⁵⁄₁₆" bolts 14 ft.lb. (1.9 kg.m)

Main bearing caps 60 ft.lb (8.3 kg.m)

Connecting rod caps

948cc, 1098cc 35 ft.lb. (4.8 kg.m)

1275cc 45 ft.lb. (6.2 kg.m)

Nyloc nuts 32–34 ft.lb. (4.4–4.7 kg.m)

Flywheel bolts 40 ft.lb. (5.5 kg.m)

Crankshaft pulley nut 70 ft.lb. (9.6 kg.m)

Water pump 17 ft.lb. (2.3 kg.m)

Water outlet elbow 8 ft.lb. (1.1 kg.m)

Oil pump 9 ft.lb. (1.2 kg.m)

1500cc engine

Cylinder head nuts 50 ft.lb. (6.9 kg.m)

Rocker shaft nuts 32 ft.lb. (4.4 kg.m)

Rocker box cover 2 ft.lb. (.3 kg.m)

Spark plugs 20 ft.lb. (2.8 kg.m)

Main bearing caps 65 ft.lb. (9 kg.m)

Crankshaft rear oil seal housing 20 ft.lb. (2.8 kg.m)

Sealing block attachment 14 ft.lb. (1.9 kg.m)

Sealing block/engine plate 20 ft.lb (2.8 kg.m)

Flywheel bolts;

Cadmium 40ftl.lb. (5.5 kg.m)

Phosphated 45 ft.lb. (6.2 kg.m)

Camshaft sprocket 24 ft.lb. (3.3 kg.m)

Timing cover:

Small bolts 10 ft.lb. (1.4 kg.m)
Large bolts 20 ft.lb. (2.8 kg.m)

Crankshaft pulley nut 150 ft.lb. (20.7 kg.m)

Engine rear plate 14 ft.lb. (1.9 kg.m)

Sump drain plug 25 ft.lb. (3.4 kg.m)

Sump 20 ft.lb. (2.8 kg.m)

Water pump housing/cylinder head 20 ft.lb. (2.8 kg.m)

Water pump/housing 14 ft.lb. (1.9 kg.m)

Water pump housing/outlet 20 ft.lb. (2.8 kg.m)

Fuel pump/block 14 ft.lb. (1.9 kg.m)

Manifold/cylinder head 25 ft.lb. (3.4 kg.m)

Starter motor 34 ft.lb. (4.7 kg.m)

Alternator bolts 20 ft.lb. (2.8 kg.m)

Clutch to flywheel 22 ft.lb. (3 kg.m)

Rear damper bolts 25–30 ft.lb. (3.4–4.1 kg.m)

Axle pinion flange nut 140 ft.lb. (19.3 kg.m)

Brake caliper 45–50 ft.lb. (6.2–7 kg.m)

Bleed screws 4–6 ft.lb. (.5–.8 kg.m)

Steering rack clamp bolts 20–22 ft.lb. (2.8–3 kg.m)

Steering rack mounting bracket bolts 17–18 ft.lb. (2.35–2.4 kg.m)

Track rod end ball joint nut 28–32 ft.lb. (3.9–4.4 kg.m)

Steering column pinch bolt 9–12 ft.lb. (1.3–1.6 kg.m)

Steering wheel nut 37 ft.lb (5.1 kg.m)

Front damper bolts 25–30 ft.lb. (3.4–4.1 kg.m)

Hub nut 46 ft.lb. (6.9 kg.m)

Brake disc to hub 43 ft.lb. (6 kg.m)

Swivel pin top nut 40 ft.lb. (5.5 kg.m)

Steering arm/swivel housing 40 ft.lb. (5.5 kg.m)

Road wheel nuts 44–46 ft.lb. (6–6.3 kg.m)

Tracking 0 to 0.125″ toe-in.

Dynamo belt tension .5″ deflection on longest run

Alternator belt tension .75″ deflection on longest run

Tyre pressures

Crossply 18psi front; 20psi rear.

Radial 22psi front; 24psi rear.

ENGINE DATA

Firing order 1–3-4–2 (No. 1 cylinder nearest radiator).

Compression 165psi 1098cc; 120psi 1275cc

Valve/rocker clearance (engine cold)

.012″ 1098/1275cc; .01″ 1500cc

Ignition timing:

Static; 5 degrees BTDC 1098cc;
7 degrees BTDC 1275cc

Dynamic; 8 degrees BTDC at 600rpm 1098; 13 degrees BTDC at 1000 rpm 1275cc with 25D4 distributor; 16 degrees BTDC at 1000 rpm 1275cc with 23D4 distributor; 10 degrees BTDC at 680 rpm 1500cc

Idle speed 1000rpm 1098cc; 700rpm 1275cc; 650–680rpm 1500cc.

Spark plug Champion N5 (1098); N9Y (1275/1500); gap .025″

Contact breaker gap .014″–.016″

Dwell angle 60 degrees + or − 3 degrees 1098/1275cc

51 degrees + or − 5 degrees 1500cc

SPECIALISTS' ADDRESSES

Bromsgrove MG Centre
(Proprietor Graham Sawyer)
Unit 10, Sugarbrook Road,
Aston Fields Industrial Estate,
Bromsgrove B61 3DW
Telephone 0527 79909 *Fax.* 0527 575385
Bromsgrove MG Centre stock a comprehensive range of spares for the Spridget. Graham and his staff are very knowledgeable and always very helpful. The company has a well-staffed workshop and will undertake any work on the Spridget, from servicing to complete restoration work and re-shelling. The company has achieved 5-Star ratings with the MG Owner's Club as a spares supplier and for its workshop.

Ron Hopkinson MG Centre
(Proprietor Ron Hopkinson)
850 London Road, Derby DE2 8WA
Telephone 0332 756056 *Fax.* 0332 572332
Ron Hopkinson MG Centre is a long-established and large MGB spares supplier which has taken over the well-known company, Spridgebits, and now specialise in the supply of Spridget spares. The company possess facilities for engine and gearbox rebuilding. The staff have always proved helpful and knowledgeable. The company publishes a mail order spares catalogue.

Brown & Gammons Ltd.
(Proprietor Ron Gammons)
18 High Street, Baldock, Herts SG7 6AS
Telephone 0462 893914 & 894212
Fax. 0462 896167
Ron Gammons has enjoyed immense success in Historic rallying, with MG cars prepared by his own company taking 2nd, 3rd and 4th places in the 1990 Pirelli Classic (plus 1st place in 1992). The company thus supplements its comprehensive range of spares

with a selection of performance engine, gearbox and suspension components which in many cases have been proven in the most testing of competition work. The company publishes a mail order spares catalogue.

The Frogeye Car Co.
Simeon Motor Works,
Simeon Street, Ryde,
Isle of Wight PA33 1JQ
Telephone 0983 616616
Manufacturers of the Healey Frogeye. Contact the company for full details of both the restoration kit, completed cars, plus the new Ford CH engine version.

Pete Harper Restorations
Sugarbrook Industrial Estate, Aston Fields,
Bromsgrove B61 3DW
Telephone 0527 579700
Pete Harper's premises are usefully situated right next door to the Bromsgrove MG Centre. Pete undertakes body repair work and all work from respraying to a complete Spridget restoration.

SIP (Holdings) Ltd.
Gelders Hall Road, Shepshed,
Leicestershire LE12 9HN
SIP supply an excellent range of compressors and accessories, MIG and arc welding equipment, for the home restorer. The author used a SIP Handymig gasless MIG welder during the compilation of this book and was impressed with its ease of use and the very good results which were achieved with it. The author's SIP Airmate Tornado 21025 compressor has proven to be one of the most useful tools in the workshop.

Hickman-Peaveley Racing Services. (RATS)
Unit 10/11 Maylight Trading Estate, Berrow Green
Road, Martley,
Worcestershire WR6 6PQ
Telephone 0886 888789
HPRS specialise in the preparation of rally and race
vehicles, but also offer their services to the owners of
road-going Spridgets. The company will handle any
performance modification work to the A series
engines and to the 1500cc unit. Whether you merely
want the carburation sorted out or whether you
want the engine, suspension and braking prepared
for competition, this company is highly
recommended.

MG Owner's Club
2–4, Station Road, Swavesey, Cambridgeshire
Telephone 0954 31125
The MG Owner's Club is reportedly the largest single-
make car club in the world, with branches in all
major export market countries. The club organises a
huge range of events, publishes a monthly magazine,
runs an insurance scheme and publishes a list of
approved spares suppliers and restorers/workshops.

MG Car Club
Kimber House, PO BOX 251,
Abingdon, Oxford OX14 1FF
Telephone 0235 555552
The MG Car Club has 65 centres outside the UK and
over 100 within the UK. The club specialises in
organising competitive events, including track, rally,
hill climb and sprint events. Other club benefits
include a magazine, insurance and social/concours
events.

Midget and Sprite Club
Terry Horler
Telephone 0454 312659
Although the smallest of the three main UK clubs
which deal with Spridgets, the Midget and Sprite Club
is exclusively for owners of Austin Healey Sprites and
MG Midgets. Organised by a highly enthusiastic and
energetic team, the club offers a monthly magazine,
car valuations and all the other usual club benefits,
and has many regional branches in the UK.

Austin Healey Club
4, Saxby Street, Leicester LE2 0ND
The club caters for all Healey, Austin Healey and
Jensen Healey cars.

British Motor Heritage Ltd.
Unipart House, Cowley, Oxford OX4 2PG
Telephone 0865 713510
We must all thank the British Motor Heritage
company for the vast range of spares available for our
Spridgets today. The company supplies (to their own
Heritage-approved trade outlets only) body shells for
the Spridget, plus a wealth of spares.

British Motor Industry Heritage Trust
Archive Department, Castle Road, Studley,
Warwickshire
Telephone 0527 85 4015
The BMIHT offers a service which allows Spridget
owners to ascertain the original specifications of their
own car when manufactured, as mentioned in Chapter
2. *Phone* to find the current charge for this service.

Bristol MG Centre
Telephone 0272 570752
Bristol MG Centre carries a full range of Spridget
spares, and offers servicing, mechanical repair work,
engine rebuilds and tuning.

Country Lane Classics
The Barn, Macclesfield, Cheshire SK10 1QS
Telephone 0625 860149
This company has 5 years' experience in restoration
of the Mk1 Frogeye Sprite. In addition to carrying out
restorations for customers, they supply spares, sell
restored and unrestored cars, offer an exchange
service on bodyshells and all other major components,
and are an excellent source of specialist advice.

Econosports
Telephone 091 232 2913
Econosports sell the 'Rotstopper' guards for the
triangular chassis apertures.

MG International
Telephone 051 647 4752
MG International is a large spares supplier offering a
fast mail order spares service for all Spridgets. The
range includes special tuning equipment. The
company publishes a mail order spares catalogue.

Bristol Sprite & Midget Centre
Telephone 0272 428333
The company specialise in the Spridget, retail spares,
offer a mail order service, car servicing, repairs and
restorations.

233

Frontline Developments
23, Crandale Road, Oldfield, Bath BA2 3HX
Telephone 0225 481069
Tim Fenna's company offers a conversion to fit a Toyota 5 speed gearbox to the Spridget, and (at the time of writing) is also working on other exciting developments. These include a turbo modification and re-designed suspension.

Peter May Engineering
92, Windmill Hill, Halesowen West Midlands
Telephone 0384 635691
Vendors of the well-known Arkley SS Spridget-based kit car, Peter May Engineering are also a specialist Spridget performance centre, with rolling road and engineering facilities. The company works on competition and road cars.

SPRIDGET SPARES SPECIALISTS
Abbey Clasics
1–18 Lea Road, Waltham Abbey, Essex EN9 1AD
Telephone 0992 650000
Spares supplier with workshop facilities for mechanical and body restoration.

A&C MG Spares
473 Blackfen Road, Sidcup, Kent
Telephone 081 301 5239
Spares retail counter, mail order, workshop facilities including bodyshop.

Aldon Automotive Ltd.
Telephone 038478508
Performance modifications work and components.

Ballenger Auto Services
8 Twyford Business Centre, London Road, Bishops Stortford, Herts CM23 3YT
Telephone 0279 508686
Spares, mechanical repair and body restoration.

Beech Hill Garage
Beech Hill, Nr. Reading, Berkshire RG7 2AU
Telephone 0734 884774
Spares (including Frogeye), mechanical repair, body restoration.

Brandon MG Centre
Brandon Lane, Brandon, Co Durham CH7 8SU
Telephone 091 378 0592
Spares, mail order service.

Brighouse Cars
Birds Royd Lane, Brighouse, West Yorkshire
Telephone 0484 715192
All servicing, repair and restoration work, plus specialised engines.

Britbits
Unit 2, Wheelgate Farm, Church Lane, Saxilby, Lincoln LN1 2PE
Telephone 0522 704128
Spares, mechanical repair, body restorations.

AJ Buckle Sportscars
40 The Drive, Caldecote, Nuneaton CV10 0TW
Telephone 0203 325293
Car sales, spares, servicing, mechanical repair, body restoration.

Car Craft
Ransome Park, Ipswich IP3 9RR
Telephone 0473 723991
Spares, all mechanical repair and body restoration work.

Composite Automotive Technology Ltd.
Unit 6, Audnam Trading Estate, High Street, Audnam, Stourbridge
DY8 4AH
Telephone 0384 442203
CAT supply Spridget spares both over the counter and mail order, in addition to carrying out all mechanical repair and restoration work.

Paul Depper MGs
Unit 2, Landywood Lane, Cheslyn Hay, Nr. Walsall, West Midlands
Telephone 0922 413623
Spares. Mechanical repair, body restoration. Used spares specialist.

Euro MG Centre
32 Bellbrook Industrial Estate, Uckfield, East Sussex.
Telephone 0825 763051
Car sales, spares, servicing, mechanical repair and body restoration.

G&H Motor Services
Leamington Spa
Telephone 0926 881887
Spares, servicing, mechanical repair and body restoration.

Gloucester MG Centre
Unit A, Ryeford Industrial Estate, Stonehouse, Gloucestershire GL10 2LA
Telephone 0453 825164
The company supplies all new and second-hand spares both over the counter and mail order, in addition to offering restoration and all mechanical services.

Jacob Engineering
Grove Court, Upton St. Leonards, Gloucester GL4 8DA
Telephone 0452 612006
Jacob engineering possess a jig on which your original Spridget bodyshell can be accurately rebuilt to 'as new' condition no matter how rotten it is. The company uses only genuine panels, and the use of a jig enables them to accurately fit entire assemblies if necessary.

John Hill MG Centre
Arthur Street, Redditch, Worcestershire B98 8JY
Telephone 0527 20730
Spares, mail order.

Leacy MG
102 Tame Road, Witton, Birmingham B6 7EZ
Telephone 021 328 3735
Car sales, spares, mechanical repair and restoration.

LV Engineering
11, West Hampstead Mews, London NW6 3BB
Telephone 071 328 3653
Servicing, mechanical repair, body restoration.

Meonstoke Garage
Alton Road, Corhampton, Hants
Telephone 0489 877823
Car sales, spares, servicing mechanical repair and body restoration.

Mercury Motors
Ludlin Links, Leven, Fife KY8 6DJ
Telephone 0333 320096
Car sales, servicing, mechanical repair and body restoration.

MG Bits
Guildford, Surrey GU23 6EL.
Telephone 0483 223830
Spares, mechanical repair.

MG Car Clinic
St Stephens Pathway, North Lane, Canterbury, Kent
Telephone 0227 453471
Spares, servicing, mechanical repair and body restoration.

MG Services
34 Fulmer Drive, Gerrards Cross, Bucks
Telephone 0753 880267
Spares, mail order, servicing, mechanical repair and body restoration.

MG Sprite & Midget, B, C & V8 Centre
991 Wolverhampton Road, Oldbury, West Mids B69 4RT
Telephone 021 544 4444
Spares.

MG Sprite & Midget B, C, V8 Centre
22–28 Manor Road, Richmond, Surrey TW9 1YB
Telephone 081 948 6464
Spares.

Midget Motorsport
42 Albert Drive, Morley, West Yorkshire LS27 8SF
Telephone 0532 529112
Mail order performance parts specialist.

MJS Sportscars
(Mike Satur)
Derwent Way Industrial Estate, Wath on Dearne, Rotherham SG3 6EX
Telephone 0226 750147
Car sales, spares, mechanical repair and body restoration.

Moss Darlington
15 Allington Way, Yarm Road Industrial Estate, Darlington, Co. Durham DL1 4QB
Telephone 0325 281343
Huge spares business with eight UK retail showrooms (mail order address above) plus others in the USA. Special tuning equipment, free quarterley magazine to customers. The company publishes a mail order spares catalogue.

Moto-Build
328 Bath Road, Hounslow, Middlesex
Telephone 081 572 8733
All body panels, mechanical spares, interior fittings etc. for all Spridgets. Special tuning equipment. Frogeye Sprite specialist. Mail order catalogue.

MS Classic MG Parts
Unit 3, Lyons Farm Estate, Lyons Road,
Slinfold, Horsham, West Sussex.
Telephone 0403 791190
Spares.

NE MG Services
Unit 34C Ellesmere Court,
Leechmere Industrial Estate, Sunderland.
Telephone 091 523 8124
Spares, mechanical repair and body restoration.

Nottingham MG Centre
Unit 13, Colwick Business Park, Private Road No. 2,
Colwick, Nottingham NG4 2JR
Telephone 0602 615283
Spares, servicing, mechanical repair and restoration.

PJM Motors
Unit 1a, Bert Smith Way, Adderley Road,
Market Drayton, Shropshire TF9 3SN
Telephone 0630 652873
Spares, servicing, mechanical repair, plus upholstery.

RK Autos
Unit 3, Swift Lane, Bagshot, Surrey
Telephone 0276 52569
Spares, servicing, mechanical repair and body restoration.

Romney Shields MG Spares
25 Rutherford Close, (off Progress Road), Eastwood,
Leigh-on-Sea, Essex SS9 5LQ
Telephone 0702 529070
Spares. Fast mail order service.

Rugby MG Centre
122 Oxford Street, Rugby
Telephone 0788 571896
Car sales, spares, mechanical repair, body restorations.

Rusper MG Services
Wayside Garage, High Street, Rusper, West Sussex
Telephone 0293 871218
Spares, servicing, mechanical repair, body restoration.

Sprite & Midget, B, C, V8 Centre
93, Newfoundland Road, Bristol BS2 9LU
Telephone 0272 232523
Spares.

Steve McKie MG Services
Albert Street North, Whittington Moor,
Chesterfield S41 8NP
Telephone 0246 453681
Spares, servicing. Crypton tuning, mechanical repair and body restoration.

Sussex MG Parts
Unit 19 Huffwood Trading Estate,
Partridge Green, Nr. Horsham,
West Sussex RH13 8AU
Telephone 0403 711551
Spares. Mail order catalogue.

Sutton MG Centre
51–53 Newhall Street, Sutton-Coldfield B72 1RU
Telephone 021 354 7611
Spares, servicing, mechanical repair and body restoration.

Tamar Valley MG Centre
Harrowbarrow, Callington, Cornwall PL17 8JQ
Telephone 0579 50542
Spares, servicing, mechanical repair and body restoration.

Welsh MG Centre
Pen-y-Bryn, Wrexham, Clwyd, North Wales
Telephone 0978 263445
Spares, servicing, mechanical repair, body restoration and MOT testing.

York Midget Spares
Monk Bar Garage, Lord Mayor's Walk,
York YO3 7HB
Telephone 0904 647260
Spares.

Adrian Wadley
(Worcestershire)
Telephone 08865 673
If you encounter difficulties when restoring a bodyshell and are fortunate enough to live in Worcestershire, then Adrian is a highly-recommended welder (and panel beater) who can get you out of trouble.

Trevor Hudson
(Worcester)
Telephone 0905 420407
Trevor is a restorer of classic cars, specialising in MGs.